THE MULTINATIONAL FIRM

The Multinational Firm

Organizing Across Institutional and National Divides

Edited by

GLENN MORGAN,
PEER HULL KRISTENSEN
and
RICHARD WHITLEY

OXFORD
UNIVERSITY PRESS

OXFORD

UNIVERSITY PRESS

Great Clarendon Street, Oxford OX2 6DP

Oxford University Press is a department of the University of Oxford.
It furthers the University's objective of excellence in research, scholarship,
and education by publishing worldwide in

Oxford New York

Athens Auckland Bangkok Bogotá Buenos Aires Cape Town
Chennai Dar es Salaam Delhi Florence Hong Kong Istanbul Karachi
Kolkata Kuala Lumpur Madrid Melbourne Mexico City Mumbai Nairobi
Paris São Paulo Shanghai Singapore Taipei Tokyo Toronto Warsaw

with associated companies in Berlin Ibadan

Oxford is a registered trade mark of Oxford University Press
in the UK and in certain other countries

Published in the United States
by Oxford University Press Inc., New York

© The Several Contributors, 2001

The moral rights of the authors have been asserted
Database right Oxford University Press (maker)

First published 2001

British Library Cataloguing in Publication Data

Data available

Library of Congress Cataloging in Publication Data
The multinational firm: organizing across institutional and national divides/edited by Glenn
Morgan, Peer Hull Kristensen, and Richard Whitley.
p.cm.
Includes bibliographical references.
1. International business enterprises—Management. I. Morgan, Glenn.
II. Kristensen, Peer Hull. III. Whitley, Richard.
HD62.4. M8427 2001   658.049—dc21   2001033951

ISBN 0–19–924755–2

1 3 5 7 9 10 8 6 4 2

Typeset by Florence Production Ltd, Stoodleigh, Devon
Printed in Great Britain
on acid-free paper by
Biddles Ltd., Guildford & King's Lynn

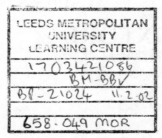

Preface and Acknowledgements

This is an edited volume of the revised papers that were originally presented in the sessions of the Standing Working Group on Comparative Study of Economic Organizations at the 15th EGOS (European Group on Organization Studies) Colloquium at the University of Warwick in July 1999. Revised versions of the papers were then presented at the Research Workshop of the European Summer Research Institutes for the Study of Comparative Economic Organization (known as ESRI) held in Gillelje, Denmark in September 1999.

This particular volume represents the latest in a series of edited books arising out of collective and collaborative discussions beginning in the early 1990s. First, within the framework of the European Science Foundation's Programme on European Management and Organizations in Transition (known as EMOT) and, more recently, within the ambit of ESRI, a series of workshops has been convened which has enabled a sustained analysis of comparative economic organizations. The editors and authors owe a number of debts of gratitude arising from this, particularly in relation to the current piece of work. First, the funds made available for ESRI participants by the European Science Foundation, the Danish Research Council, and the Copenhagen Business School have been extremely important. They were also supplemented by the provision of travel grants for non-European scholars attending ESRI by the Transnational Communities Programme of the UK Economic and Social Research Council. Secondly, the administrative coordination of the ESRI workshop, including the provision of papers on a website, was undertaken by Marianne Risberg from the Copenhagen Business School; without Marianne's help, the workshop would not have been the success it was. Thirdly, there were many more participants at the ESRI workshop than those represented in this volume; their contributions both before and after the ESRI workshop are gratefully acknowledged: Lucio Biggiero, John Brown, Christophe Dorrenbacher, Gary Gereffi, Anne-Wil Harzing, Chris Hendry, Marko Jaklic, Ray Loveridge, Joao Peixoto, Sigrid Quack, Martin Rademakers, Junko Sakai, and Arndt Sorge.

Warwick, Copenhagen, and Manchester
Glenn Morgan
Peer Hull Kristensen
Richard Whitley

Contents

viii   *Contents*

List of figures

List of tables

List of contributors

JABRIL BENSEDRINE, University of Marne-la-Vallée, France

MARIE-LAURE DJELIC, ESSEC, Paris, France

HENRIK GLIMSTEDT, Stockholm School of Economics, Sweden

MIKA HUOLMAN, LTT-Research Ltd and Helsinki School of Economics, Finland

PEER HULL KRISTENSEN, Copenhagen Business School, Denmark

CHRISTEL LANE, Faculty of Social and Political Sciences, University of Cambridge, UK

KARI LILJA, Helsinki School of Economics, Finland

ELI MOEN, University of Oslo, Norway

GLENN MORGAN, Warwick Business School, University of Warwick, UK

DIETER PLEHWE, Wissenschaftszentrum, Berlin, Germany

MATTI PULKKINEN, LTT-Research Ltd and Helsinki School of Economics, Finland

DIANA ROSEMARY SHARPE, Warwick Business School, University of Warwick, UK

RISTO TAINIO, Helsinki School of Economics, Finland

RICHARD WHITLEY, Manchester Business School, UK

JONATHAN ZEITLIN, University of Wisconsin-Madison, USA

1

The Multinational Firm: Organizing Across Institutional and National Divides

GLENN MORGAN

1.1. Introduction

This book develops a distinctive approach to understanding the internationalization of firms and markets in the global economy. In contrast to economic and managerialist perspectives that treat them as cohesive, goal-directed rational actors, the contributors to this volume draw on traditions of comparative organizational analysis to understand multinationals as organizations with complex internal processes of contradiction and conflict that are distinctive from those present in non-international firms. In different ways, the contributors share the following presumptions. First, multinational firms are social constructions; in particular, they are built out of specific national institutional contexts that shape how they internationalize. All the authors have been active in the debate about 'national business systems' and 'divergent capitalisms' (see, e.g., previous edited collections Quack, Morgan, and Whitley 2000; Whitley 1992; Whitley and Kristensen 1996; Whitley and Kristensen 1997). They share an interest in understanding how national institutional contexts shape the strategies and structures of firms. In this book, they take that interest a stage further by asking what happens when a firm organizes across institutional and national divides. The working assumption is that the result will not be convergence towards a single model of the 'global firm', as predicted by some commentators (e.g. Ohmae 1990), but rather continued diversity and divergence between firms from different institutional contexts. However, the authors recognize that internationalizing the firm involves more than the simple reproduction of existing structures and practices. Organizing across institutional and national divides can set challenges to existing routines. The chapters seek to identify what these challenges are and how they differ across distinctive institutional contexts and then to examine how firms from different national contexts and with different competences adapt to these challenges. A central concern of these chapters, then, is the diversity of forms of multinational companies (MNCs). This is reflected in Part I of the book, which is entitled 'Convergences and Divergences in the Visible Hand of International Management'.

Secondly, multinationals are not homogeneous social actors; on the contrary, they are sites within which multiple actors will play a role. In national contexts, as the 'divergent capitalisms' literature has revealed, there are certain patterned ways of behaving which most actors understand and abide by. Thus even social conflict, e.g. between employers and employees, is channelled through institutionalized structures and rules. However, once firms become international in their scope, they incorporate within their organizational space new social actors. Depending on the nature and extent of internationalization, one can identify a range of new social actors whose presence within the firm will make the reproduction of old routines problematic. For example, firms may internationalize their shareholding base, bringing in new types of investors with distinctive expectations about issues such as performance and transparency. Firms with overseas production facilities will bring in host country nationals. Host country managers may have their own distinct views on 'how to manage' as well as their own interests in career progression and development. Technical and supervisory staff will have their own views on their distinctive package of skills and how these should be used, as will shop-floor employees, who will also have a view on appropriate systems of collective representation. How do firms maintain order across these institutional and national divides? The authors all share an interest in a detailed understanding of different institutional contexts and, from this position, management in multinational firms faces huge challenges. The chapters in Part II of the book particularly examine this, under the title of 'Constructing and Deconstructing the Visible Hand'.

Thirdly, the authors recognize that this is not simply an issue for the managers of multinationals. It is also the concern of all those in governments and international bodies seeking to establish cross-border forms of economic regulation that ease the problems of organizing across institutional and national divides. Just as multinational firms cannot be understood separately from the *national* contexts in which they are embedded, so they have to be seen as an integral part of the creation of an emerging web of *international* institutional contexts. International regulation is another form of social space with which the firm's problems of organizing across institutional and national divides intersect. On the one hand, firms have an interest in creating a 'level playing field' which reduces transaction costs associated with different national regulations and practices and potentially increases economies of scale in production and distribution. On the other hand, in a world of 'divergent capitalisms', it is always going to be the case that the international regulatory regimes and standards approximate to some existing national systems more than others. Firms, governments, and international agencies will interact in ways that mean that regulatory attempts to ease the problems of organizing across institutional and national divides will be highly diverse, conflictual, and complex, varying greatly in their speed and scope. In the final section of the book, we consider this under the heading of 'Changing National and International Economic Orders: Constructing and Reconstructing Systems of Economic Organization and Regulation'.

1.2. **Dominant Approaches to the Study of Internationalization and Multinational Firms**

A huge amount of literature and research in the area of international business and multinationals already exists. It can be broadly characterized in terms of three major concerns that are interconnected and tend to share a certain set of assumptions. The first views firms as rational actors balancing the costs and benefits of different forms of serving foreign markets. It is a development of transaction cost economics in that the internalization of activities in cross-national settings is determined by features such as bounded rationality, asset specificity, opportunism, and small numbers. Thus, internalization (i.e. the development of foreign direct investment and foreign production facilities, rather than just exporting, licensing, and franchising) is an outcome of specific features of the markets in which firms operate and the transaction costs that are incurred. The second concern focuses on the process of internationalization itself and how firms prepare themselves for more extensive involvements outside their home base. This relates to the idea of sequences in the

internationalization process. The third focus considers the managerial issues arising from different types of foreign involvement.

The first concern focuses on how firms make choices about how to
expand their operations, both at home and overseas. For example,
Buckley and Ghauri state that 'the growth of the firm is the background to internationalization and to some degree the distinction
between internationalization and growth is false. The crossing of
national boundaries of growth may be argued to be a meaningless
threshold' (Buckley and Ghauri 1999: ix). Although they go on to
acknowledge that 'there are significant degrees of difference between
growth at home and internationalization' (ibid.), it is not accidental
that they begin with such a strong statement about the continuity of
firms' operations at home and abroad. This is because the basic model
supposes that firms have certain specific competencies and skills
(ownership assets) which are reflected in their goods and services and
determine their potential for overseas investment. If firms want to
extend their markets overseas, they have to consider whether to
do so through agents, franchises, joint ventures, licensing agreements, or the development of production facilities in foreign markets.
Locational decisions are affected by the costs and qualities of
resources in different settings—land, labour, and capital. All of these
issues are just as important inside the home base as in the overseas
context. The differences are matters of degree not substance.
Summarizing Buckley's work with Casson, Buckley and Ghauri state
that within the internalization approach, 'the direction of internationalization can be predicted by predicting changes in cost and
market conditions. These factors are classified as industry specific,
region specific, firm specific and nation specific' (ibid. xi) (see also
Dunning's (1998) eclectic theory of internationalization).

This view of the firm construes it as a rational economic actor with
the ability to calculate the costs and benefits of various types of move
towards internationalization. The approach is not insensitive to arguments concerning the limits of rationality. It allows 'bounded rationality' and incremental decision-making to enter the equation. It
accepts the existence of various forms of information uncertainty that
make such decisions problematic and lead to the creation of mechanisms to protect against or compensate for risk arising from infor-
mational uncertainty (Casson 1997). Out of this, the approach can
generate a range of possible outcomes in the internationalization
process. The diversity and variety of types of multinational activity
(including joint venture and licensing activities), their trajectory over

time, and their impact within different sectors and contexts can be examined through empirical research. Nevertheless, the underlying determining mechanism is based on transaction costs and firms having to act in accordance with these calculations in order to survive in competitive markets. As Williamson states, 'transaction cost economics . . . maintains that later, if not sooner, inefficiency in the commercial sector invites its own demise'. Everything else is described by Williamson as 'tosh', 'a source of interesting variety' that 'adds spice to life' but does not get to the essentials of economic ordering (Williamson 1994: 87, 97–8).

The second main strand of research builds on this approach but examines more explicitly the notion of stages of internationalization. This is associated with three issues. First, there is the question of whether there is a fixed sequence of stages which firms have to go through in order to move from an export orientation to foreign markets to a system of local production facilities in different countries. Can firms jump stages? Can they move back and forth along the sequence?

Secondly, there is the influence of what Swedish researchers term 'psychic distance' (Johanson and Wiedersheim-Paul 1975). Is it the case that firms' locational and marketing strategies are determined by the degree of 'psychic distance' between their own culture and that of the foreign market into which it is entering? The 'psychic distance' model also leads to a debate on sequences—do firms have to go through experiences in countries with low psychic distance before they move into more distant cultural contexts?

Thirdly, there is the idea that internationalization is partly a networking process; firms do not necessarily proceed singly but, rather, in chains of interrelated groupings (Axelsson and Johansen 1992; Forsgren et al. 1995). This is a further elaboration of the sequencing model. Lead firms drag their local home-based suppliers or distributors into new contexts as their preferred way of managing certain risks. Thus networks become more extended as some members of the network lead on to new contexts (with higher 'psychic distance'). These firms act as innovators and experimenters, providing a safe shelter under which more cautious members of the network can be protected as they make similar moves.

This research is also underpinned by a view of the world in which firms are goal-directed, unified rational actors embedded in market contexts where competitiveness determines survival. Managers rationally calculate the costs and benefits of different sorts of internationalization within their own product markets and sectors;

they build into these calculations their perceptions of how they can move from one stage of development to another. The result is a further set of empirical questions about how multinational firms develop, the sequences which they go through, how these vary across markets and sectors, and the role which network relationships play in this process.

The third main strand of research applies these insights to the issue of how multinational firms are managed. The dominant trend is to assume that the structures of MNCs can be explained as contingent upon the requirements of globalization. Thus competitive tendencies within sectors select firms which have not properly resolved issues of transaction costs and staging. Therefore, managers need to understand the relationship between these processes and build the appropriate organization structure and management system. This places the research orientation firmly within a classical contingency approach to organizations. In other words, the environment is taken as a given—a given which comes from the operation of market forces as determined by transaction costs. The goal of managers is to 'fit' the structure to the environment.

Early models, such as that developed by Egelhoff, theorized this analysis in terms of information requirements. For example, he stated that 'there is a good fit between structure and strategy when the information-processing requirements of a firm's strategy are satisfied by the information-processing capacities of its structure' (1982: 436). On this basis, Egelhoff analyses the 'fit' between certain types of structure for multinationals (functional structures, international divisions, geographical regions, and product divisions) and certain patterns of information requirements (depending on whether the strategy is export-oriented or based on the establishment of foreign manufacturing plants). In later papers, he also added in the matrix structure and sought to explain its existence in similar terms (1993).

It was the idea of the matrix model that lay at the basis of conceptual developments in this field in the 1980s, as authors began to explore the interrelationship between global integration and local responsiveness as a key issue in the management of multinationals. Prahalad and Doz argued that:

The Integration-Responsiveness (IR) grid provides us with a way of capturing the pressures on a given business—pressures that make strategic coordination and global integration of activities critical, as well as the pressures that make being sensitive to the diverse demands of various national markets and achieving local responsiveness critical. (1987: 18)

Bartlett and Ghoshal (1989) later developed the link between these strategic tensions and the issues of organization structure and management. Observing the increasing complexity of international operations in their case companies, they argued that it was the requirement of balancing the needs of local markets versus the needs to maximize the efficiencies of global operations through economies of scale and scope that was the crucial issue facing MNCs. Firms had to decide how far the sectors in which they operated required local responsiveness versus global integration. Global integration was linked to the creation of global brands and globally coordinated systems of production, both of which reduced costs and therefore made firms highly competitive on price. However, because national tastes, cultures, and regulations continued to differ, it was important that the local context was taken into account when developing and marketing products. The balance differed across sectors. In some sectors, global products could sell across the world; in other sectors, distinctive local tastes meant there was a need for strong local identity in production and distribution.

From this argument, Bartlett and Ghoshal developed a typology of four types of firms. *Multinationals* were decentralized firms, highly sensitive to local conditions but with subsidiaries weakly linked together across nations and divisions. *Global* companies were firms insensitive to local conditions and dependent on centrally determined plans and processes to produce global products, that could be produced and sold with minor variations in any country. *International* companies possess core competencies which are generated and renewed centrally but are transferred/adapted to local contexts. *Transnational* companies in their model were described as 'dispersed, interdependent and specialized' with 'differentiated contributions by national units to integrated worldwide operations' and 'knowledge developed jointly and shared worldwide' (1989: 65).

In a later development of this approach, Nohria and Ghoshal have renamed the transnational company a 'differentiated network'. The differentiated network is 'composed of distributed resources linked through different types of relations: (1) the "local" linkages within each national subsidiary; (2) the linkages between headquarters and the subsidiaries; and (3) the linkages between subsidiaries themselves' (1997: 4). This complex and multifaceted pattern of relationships is seen as providing the company with the means to innovate rapidly for national, regional, and global markets, as well as to maximize the efficiency of its operations by locating production, R&D and marketing/sales efforts wherever is most appropriate.

This approach, in turn, has led to two further developments. First, there is the concern with subsidiary operations and how these are linked to headquarters' strategic goals. Birkinshaw and Hood have identified three strands in this research; first, the concern with head-quarters–subsidiary relationships, leading to ideas such as Hedlund's notion of the multinational as a 'heterarchy' (Hedlund 1986, 1993), i.e. possessing multiple centres; secondly, and associated with this, the idea that subsidiaries take on different roles allocated to them by head offices; thirdly, the idea that subsidiaries can develop these roles entrepreneurially and are not simply the passive recipients of head office decisions (Birkinshaw 2000; Birkinshaw and Hood 1998: 5–8).

Secondly, there is the concern with the conditions underpinning organizational learning in differentiated multinational networks or 'heterarchies'. This links into the general debate on organizational learning but focuses specifically on multinationals (e.g. Bresman et al. 1999; Gupta and Govindarajan 2000; Kogut 2000: Nobel and Birkinshaw 1998; O'Donnell 2000).

These three concerns in the international business literature provide a powerful template for examining the development of multinationals. They are bound together by a certain underlying set of assumptions that define an economic view of the world (and multi-nationals in the world). First, there is an underlying assumption about academic knowledge, social reality, and models of the world. From the economists' point of view, analysis begins with models of a market system in which actors pursue their interests on the basis of calculations of costs and the 'hidden hand' provides the mechanism for allocating resources. Scaling these processes up to the level of firms is a process of transfer of the basic model, even if the condi-tions under which rationality and markets operate become more complex. The construction is therefore primarily an example of model-building that can become increasingly complex as new vari-ables are placed into it. Its underlying presuppositions are powerful yet simple, generating models of how markets operate.

Secondly, the connection to empirical data operates at a secondary level, in the sense that it is useful to confirm the model or to stimu-late its further development and refinement. Empirical research cannot, however, have any impact on the underlying presuppositions about rationality, goal-directed action, and the determinant nature of market processes. Thirdly, at the level of management action, there-fore, the goal is to identify structures and processes that can fit, match, and maximize the opportunities arising from markets. The approach to multinationals is an extension of these underlying logics. What are the conditions under which firms should engage in internationalization? How should these developments be staged and how should they be managed? Underlying these questions is a view of economic life as a rational process in which self-interested actors make decisions on the basis of costs about the form of activities that they wish to undertake. Failure to make appropriate decisions is punished by the process of market competition that selects out the inefficient and rewards the efficient.

Model-building and the development of theory from these presuppositions have little to say about the social embeddedness of rationality and the contingent and precarious nature of organizational order. It is therefore unable to address systematically the social determinants of organizational structures, the political nature of decision-making, the irrationality of organizations, and the social construction of markets. It leaves as either unexamined or unproblematic a huge part of the social life of firms and multinationals in favour of model-building based on assumptions of rationality and efficient market mechanisms. It is in this area that this volume seeks to make a contribution, building on an extensive range of theorizing and empirical research.

1.3. **Multinationals and Social Embeddedness**

The social embeddedness of rationality implies that there is no essence of rationality that is context-independent. Rationality is socially constituted such that the nature of rational action varies between institutional contexts. These frameworks are not exogenous variables that can simply be fed into the model to explain deviance. The construction of markets is a social process that is institutionally constituted. This means that different sorts of market and different sorts of firm emerge as a result of distinctive historical trajectories that societies have taken. Therefore, the sociological understanding of firms and markets is driven by sensitivity to history and place, variation and difference. It seeks to explain 'actually existing' differences in firms and markets by understanding differences in social institutions and practices.

The notion of contextual rationality provides a crucial link to the internal functioning of the firm. In sociological accounts of the firm, it is perceived as a structured set of relations between a range of actors with their own powers and interests. Decision processes are characterized by political bargaining and negotiation. The outcomes of decision processes do not reflect an underlying economic rationality but the ability of different sorts of actors (endowed with differential powers by the social contextual shaping of organizational structures) to make their interests count in the various arenas of negotiation that exist within and across firms. The issue of coordination and control within firms is not a technical question; it is imbued with political significance. Rather than assuming that firms are rational, unified actors, this approach asks how 'organization' is achieved and how 'disorganization' is avoided.

In complex organizations such as multinationals with multiple sites of production, different sorts of managers and workers, and economic processes that need coordinating from across the world, it is probably more appropriate to admit a sense of wonder that organization is accomplished rather than to start with this expectation. Thus, from this point of view, we can open up the multinational as a set of social processes of coordination and control, disorganization and resistance. Again, the important questions are concerned with how these processes are managed in different multinationals; what are the sources of variation, difference and convergence between multinationals and how are these affected by changing institutional contexts in local, national, regional, and global processes. The focus is invariably historical and comparative in order to build up ways of understanding difference and disorder.

One approach to encapsulating these dynamics is to consider multinationals not as rational goal-directed economic actors but as specific forms of transnational communities. This terminology is drawn from the interface of ethnic studies, labour migration, economic globalization, and cultural identities. Underlying it is the sense that forms of social action and identity are increasingly coordinated across national boundaries and it is therefore important to understand the modes of social organization, mobility, and communication that enable these processes to hang together. In terms of multinationals, the argument is that they constitute a form of transnational social space. Inside this space, a huge diversity of activities takes place. Clearly, the space would not exist were it not for the existence of economic goals. The multinational firm is created as a means to achieve certain economic goals, and senior managers will construct forms of coordination and control that attempt to ensure that these goals are met.

However, the interactions that occur alongside this and around it generate other patterns of cooperation and conflict. As the transnational space by definition incorporates distinct institutional settings, it sets up potential interactions across national boundaries. Over time, these boundaries are subject to renegotiation and change as new sites of production and distribution are brought into the multinational and old sites are discarded, sold, or rationalized out of existence. Creating order with such a transnational social space, either synchronously or diachronically, is a precarious practice. It depends on the 'space' (social as well as geographical) which is being encompassed and how far practices, routines, norms, and values from within these spaces are different, transferable, adaptable, or resistant to change. To reduce this to rational models of hierarchy, control, and coordination is therefore to miss a huge amount of the dynamism, conflict, and change that occurs inside multinationals.

The notion of multinationals as transnational communities, exhibiting the dynamics of complex social systems not *sui generis* but as an outcome of the specific process of internationalizing, offers an alternative starting point to that provided in the traditional international business literature. It breaks with the notion of firms as unified rational social actors and instead considers them as spaces of social relationships that are internally structured in complex ways. How the boundaries of these transnational communities are structured, managed, redefined, and negotiated is a central focus of this approach. The goal is to produce systematic explanations of how social relationships within these spaces differ. This can be achieved by drawing on our understanding of, first, how social institutions penetrate organizational relationships; secondly, how institutions structure different actors and their interests in organizational contexts; and, thirdly, how stretching firms over national boundaries leads to new structures, actors, and possibilities of action.

Such an approach does not have to leave the economic dimension out. Rather, it reconstructs it by considering markets as specific types of social phenomena with their own rules of action. What is essential is therefore to understand how markets (and in particular international markets) are socially constructed and managed, what are the organizations that construct these markets, how they manage their workings, and how this is reflected in different patterns of firms and organizations. Therefore, this perspective draws research towards very concrete issues to do with the social processes that occur in order to create multinational firms and international markets. It opens up a range of theoretical and empirical problems that can draw on existing traditions within organizational analysis to build a powerful agenda for research into multinationals. This research will be based on the importance of comparative and historical study of social institutions, markets, and organizations. This book is an attempt to show the potential contribution that can be made to the understanding of multinationals and international organizations by taking this approach and applying it in a systematic and rigorous fashion.

1.4. Transnational Space and Multinationals

There are three aspects of the transnational space of the multinational corporation which are considered in this volume. First, there is the level of corporate governance and in particular the extent of 'financial internationalization' of this system. Secondly, we consider the internal management system of the firm; here we look at the internal organizational structure, the systems of monitoring and accountability, and, finally, the roles that expatriate and local managers take. Thirdly, we consider the level of work systems in multinationals and how these are coordinated. In all these contexts, we emphasize the need to consider the social basis of multinationals and the precarious and conflictual nature of the social order that develops within them.

1.4.1. *Financial internationalization*

How far have MNCs internationalized their financial and governance structures and what impact has this had on their functioning? How does it change the social space within the firm when financial internationalization occurs? With regard to financial internationalization, there are, as Hassel et al. (1999) suggest, a number of dimensions to be considered, each of which can vary independently of the other and can therefore have distinctive consequences. First, there is the degree of foreign ownership. Our concern is not with foreign ownership per se but with foreign ownership of the shares of major multinationals within an economy. It is also important to consider the source of the foreign ownership and the objectives that it brings to the ownership role. Overseas portfolio investment is usually managed by institutional fund-owners, mostly based in the USA and the UK and mostly operating with a 'shareholder value' driven set of goals for their investments (Williams 2000; Lazonick and O'Sullivan 2000). In

Chapter 6, Tainio and his colleagues explore this theme in relation to the Finnish experience, where the recent opening up of the society to foreign ownership has led to rapid changes. Foreign institutional investors have become increasingly active in the Finnish context and they have brought with them a shareholder value orientation that contrasts with the previous Finnish model of corporate governance. Finnish companies are having to readjust both their structure (to fit in with the more focused-firm model which is the current favourite of institutional investors) and their management practices (to be more 'flexible' in their use of labour). Gaining access to capital from overseas may be necessary for Finnish companies but it has considerable consequences for the ways these companies are run (an argument also developed by Moen and Lilja in Chapter 4, which compares the evolution of forest sector firms in Norway and Finland).

On the other hand, in Chapter 7, Kristensen and Zeitlin show how financial internationalization of this sort actually has quite complex effects on the transnational social space that the multinational constitutes. The organization that they describe is a multinational headquartered in London. Its head office is closely integrated into the City of London and spends much time meeting with its institutional investors and managing their expectations about shareholder value. In Kristensen and Zeitlin's analysis, this MNC is a form of coordinating the relationship between what was traditionally termed finance capital and industrial capital. As stock markets (particularly in the USA and the UK) demand greater returns from firms, head offices become increasingly concerned with and skilled at meeting these demands through the purchase, sale, and financial management of sites of industrial production. Where these authors extend the traditional concern with the impact of financial internationalization and the role of institutional investors is by linking it to the question of the role of local subsidiaries. These sites of industrial production, they argue, can also play their own games of survival and expansion within a context where production entities are regularly bought and sold, integrated into, and then disposed of by these MNCs. The local sites can in some circumstances envisage and construct a future for themselves outside of the current MNC structure in which they are located. There is no corporate culture that binds all the sites together. Indeed, given that the collection of any such set of sites at one time is likely to be temporary, it is impossible to imagine how a common corporate culture could be formed across such diverse and relatively independent entities (see also Solvell and

Zander 1998). As Anglo-American capital markets force MNCs to reorganize in order to meet expected rates of return (leading to variable impacts on particular local sites of production), these local sites may also look for and find room for manoeuvre.

For example, they may, in a sense, seek to 'capture' a new owner for themselves—a move that may or may not be either acknowledged or supported by the financial controllers in head office. Whether they do this or not is fundamentally affected by the nature of the social embeddedness of the local production facility within particular national contexts and how this affects their particular expertise, reputation, and capacity to establish new linkages. It is easier to find such a new owner if the site has a broader reputation that goes beyond the existing owner. Kristensen and Zeitlin argue that this is exactly the case in their example, where engineers from the local production sites are actually highly mobile, travelling widely to meet customers, suppliers, and competitors, and thereby building their own reputational networks internationally. By contrast, they note the relatively low levels of mobility of head office financial staff whose key networks are within the City of London and who therefore tend not to move much beyond this.

Secondly, it is important to consider the number of stock market quotations that a company has. This is most relevant for companies from outside the USA and the UK seeking access to these capital markets, for which listings on the London and New York Stock Exchanges are helpful. In most cases, therefore, multiple listings will be about accessing the most developed capital markets in which there are the strongest requirements for disclosure and for shareholder rights. This is related to Hassel et al.'s (1999) third aspect of financial internationalization—the degree to which company accounts are presented purely according to home country requirements or in some other way (designed to appeal to international investors, e.g. through the use of international accounting standards and quarterly reporting; on these points see also Sassen 1996), a point which I explore in detail in Chapter 9 in this book, and which is a crucial site of intersection between the actions of firms and those of national and international regulators developing forms of managing across institutional and organizational divides.

Firms can prepare themselves either to achieve multiple listings on different national exchanges or to attract foreign investors by shifting towards more transparent and internationally recognized accounting standards even where their local markets do not demand the same level of transparency. An essential part of this process is a systematic compartmentalization of the firm in accounting terms in order that investors can 'read' which areas are the most profitable. This has profound implications on how firms operate. In particular, highly aggregated financial data enable managers to conceal areas which are either failing in profit terms or are being built up for some long-term goal. In other words, it leaves a high level of discretion in the hands of the managers to determine the internal allocation of funds. Active institutional investors, on the other hand, are increasingly inclined to make those decisions for themselves. This leads to a series of changes.

First, firms are pressurized to break their activities down into more clearly demarcated divisions that produce their own profit and loss figures. Secondly, firms are pressurized towards achieving a common level of return on assets across divisions. Failure to achieve the expected level of return is seen as leading to a restructuring or a divestment of parts or the whole of the division (see Froud et al. 2000; Lazonick and O'Sullivan 2000). Thirdly, firms have to justify their range of businesses in terms of focused activities that link systematically together. Institutional investors want to manage their portfolio of different types of activity themselves and not to leave managers in diversified conglomerates to do this.

Therefore, the more powerful institutional investors have become and the more they have enforced shareholder value-driven norms on companies, the more they are insisting on 'focus' and acting to force diversified firms to split into separate units (a point discussed by Tainio and his colleagues in Chapter 6). Lane's discussion of Germany in Chapter 3 provides an important empirical contribution to the interrelationship between forms of financial internationalization and the transnational space of the multinational corporation. Through examining some of the largest and most international of German companies, she shows that the pace and impact of these changes in ownership can vary within national contexts, a point reinforced in Jurgens' study of shareholder value, institutional investors, and their impact on the German system (Jurgens et al. 2000). Finally, in Chapter 5 Glimstedt provides a useful historical corrective to these discussions. He demonstrates how large firms can coordinate their international activities through the use of cartel agreements. Thus, they are able to guarantee financial returns to their owners through managing and controlling international markets by virtue of their combined power.

In conclusion, financial internationalization is strongly related to opening the firm up to the influence of shareholder value-driven institutional investors. This has profound implications for how the multinational is structured and how it develops strategies and carries these through. Particularly at the interface between investors and senior management, this process is changing the shape of the multinational with implications for other groups inside the organization. This occurs because in some cases firms may now be owned by shareholders with very different perspectives and senior managers are therefore faced with the task of balancing the requirements of these different groups because different national traditions of corporate governance still exercise an influence.

1.4.2. *The internal management system of the firm*

As firms internationalize, they have to adapt their existing systems of managerial coordination. In particular, they have to adapt, first, the range of activities which they undertake; secondly, the range of systems for monitoring and controlling these activities; and, thirdly, the roles that expatriate and local managers play in coordinating and controlling the firm's activities. These adaptations are partly to different national contexts but, as I reveal in Chapter 9 in my discussion of regulatory issues, a significant part of this is increasingly concerned with adaptation to various forms of cross-national regulatory standards. To compete internationally, firms have to abide by certain standards as to their governance structure and their modes of action. This in turn requires that they 'stretch' or incorporate within their own practices new norms (see also Djelic and Bensedrine's discussion in Chapter 10).

However, as Whitley demonstrates in a systematic manner in Chapter 2, these adaptations build on existing firm competences; as these differ across countries, the mode of adaptation, the problems faced, and the consequences for the multinational will vary (a process graphically illustrated by Moen and Lilja's comparison, in Chapter 4, of the development of firms in the forest sector in Finland and Norway). Whitley argues that the range of activities undertaken by the MNC is a function of its strategy that, in turn, is influenced by the competences derived from its home base and the expectations of its key stakeholders. Multinationals from different countries tend to share the features of other large firms in their local context.

Thus, Japanese firms in general tend to be the least diversified; they concentrate on a particular range of skills and competences around specific technologies and markets. As markets and technologies evolve, Japanese firms develop new but related products, learning incrementally to adapt their existing skills (see, in particular, Fruin 1992, 1997). As multinationals, Japanese firms tend to build on their existing expertise and transfer its main elements to overseas contexts with limited adaptation. Their organizational structure is built on high levels of integration between the Japanese head office and the subsidiaries (see the discussions in Beechler and Bird 1999; Campbell and Burton 1994). Overseas expansion may occur through new start-ups, joint ventures, or takeovers but, whichever is the case, the overseas operation will be considered not on its own merits (as a profit-making entity) but in terms of its contribution to the integrated strategy of the company. Japanese companies base their internationalization strategies on extending their existing technological expertise to new markets. Therefore, there remains a tight integration between the technological competences based in Japan and those transferred to overseas contexts; however, as Sharpe reveals in Chapter 8, these processes cannot be guaranteed, and there is substantial negotiation and conflict over the transfer of specific practices and their acceptance or otherwise by local employees.

The contrast with British and American multinationals concerns the nature of the integration between the parts of the organization. US and British multinationals have been forced to become more 'focused' by their institutional investors. This move has seen a reduction in the number of diversified conglomerates that were previously relatively common in these two contexts, and a move towards a more integrated firm structure. Unlike the Japanese context, however, this integration is less likely to be based on a limited set of technological competences. Integration is a matter of linking together a range of productive units that have some commonalities in terms of markets or products. Subsidiaries and units within the multinational are then more likely to be assessed in terms of their own specific financial performance rather than in terms of their overall strategic contribution (with consequent effects for organizational integration, as described by Kristensen and Zeitlin in Chapter 7). The way in which units are combined into divisions is driven by the search for shareholder value and the opportunities that exist for both divestment and acquisition. Thus the selection of overseas opportunities will be driven primarily by the degree to which firms can hope to achieve shareholder value returns commensurate with the expectations of their investors, whilst integrating the operation with its existing structure of operations, units, and divisions.

The pattern in German firms appears to be more complex. In their home base, German firms tend, like Japanese firms, to focus on a limited range of skills and competences. As Lane argues in Chapter 3, their patterns of internationalization appear rather more diverse. On the one hand, there are some examples of international activities that reflect the traditional preoccupation concerning access to markets and utilizing home-specific advantages. On the other, there is an increasing number of international activities that appear to concern developing the firm in new ways. The degree to which these are really radical changes in the nature of the firm will vary.

For example, BMW's purchase of Rover (in 1995) aimed to extend the range of their cars but it was built primarily on the notion that BMW would upgrade Rover. How this would occur appears in retrospect to have been ill thought-out. An initial stage of basically hands-off management by BMW failed to achieve the expected improvements and led to a crisis-management approach to Rover, culminating in its disposal and the failure of the BMW strategy for internationalization, leaving it vulnerable to takeover itself. Plehwe's discussion in Chapter 11 of transport and logistics in Europe includes the interesting case of the state-owned Deutsche Post, hardly a likely candidate for internationalization, yet, as he reveals, this company has been very active in acquiring overseas firms in order to extend its internationalization.

In Chapter 3, Lane also emphasizes that there is a range of responses in German firms to the internationalization process. Some firms are more radical than others in their internationalizing processes, seeking to develop both new competences in different contexts (such as Hoechst, now part of Aventis, in pharmaceuticals) and a new approach to production, location, and design, drawing on different competences outside Germany (such as Volkswagen). Thus, there is evidence that, in certain cases, internationalization is being used as a strategy to change the firm in fundamental ways and enable it to learn from new environments, though, as Whitley points out in Chapter 2, environments offer different potential for learning. Finally, it is important to emphasize that these features arise out of the interaction between local managers, expatriate managers, and systems of control and coordination operated through the head office. Kristensen and Zeitlin are very clear that this is not a cohesive and coherent hierarchical structure, but one in which groups have different interests which lead them into conflicting and distinctive patterns of alliance, cooperation, and conflict with others (both inside and outside the multinational itself).

1.4.3. *The work system in multinationals*

The issue of adaptation and hybridization of work systems has been most thoroughly examined in relation to Japanese multinationals and the so-called 'Japanization' debate (for overviews, see the contributions in Elger and Smith 1994, Smith and Elger 1997 and also the special issue of *Employee Relations* on 'Post-Japanization in UK manufacturing', vol. 20, no. 3, 1998). In Chapter 8 Sharpe considers this issue in relation to a detailed case study of work relations in a Japanese subsidiary in the UK. She illustrates how the relationships between Japanese managers, local managers, and local employees in the context of different socio-technical systems led to distinctive forms of adaptation. Referring back to Whitley's discussion in Chapter 2, she argues that it is the structure and systems of the Japanese multinational as developed in its home base that provide the framework for the sort of transnational social space which opens up in these contexts. Because the Japanese firms are highly centralized and concentrate on particular forms of production, adaptation at the local level is quite limited. In comparison, Whitley suggests that the more decentralized character of UK and US firms may lead to more local adaptation, experimentation, and, in some cases, learning.

In Chapter 3, Lane develops similar points to Whitley in trying to account for changes in work practices in German firms as they internationalize. One obvious trend which she notes is that firms move production to outside Germany in order to overcome all the legal regulations about work and non-work employment conditions which exist within the German system. This strategy may be accompanied by the use of 'coercive comparisons' by, for example, trying to force German trade unions to negotiate concessions on the grounds that, otherwise, jobs may be lost to overseas workers. However, as Dicken notes, there is a 'high-tech' flavour about German foreign direct investments (FDI), which is dominated by the chemicals sector (34 per cent of the total) and motor vehicles (18 per cent) (1998: 55). Transfer of work systems overseas, therefore, seems to have two elements to it in the German case.

On the one hand, there is the argument that German multinationals use overseas subsidiaries to 'taylorize' aspects of their production system, away from the coercive power of the German regulatory system and the institutions of collective bargaining. Ferner and Quintanilla refer to these processes as 'Anglo-Saxonization but in the German manner' (1998: 724; see also Ferner 1997). On the other hand,

Lane's argument is that, in internationalizing, German multinationals are seeking to experiment with new forms of work organization in different environments. The result may be that the German firm is left with a variety of competing sites and the possibility of fissure between sites in the German base and those outside—a situation that is unlikely to occur to any degree in the Japanese case. Coexisting work systems within a single governance structure of the German type may lead to clear cross-national conflict which can only be minimally resolved through cross-country trade-union cooperation in European Works Councils (see, e.g., the discussions of the Rover/BMW situation in Whittall 2000 and Whittall and Tuckman 2000). As Kristensen and Zeitlin demonstrate in Chapter 7, managing these tensions is achieved within the US/UK multinational enterprise through the use of financial controls and the ability to acquire or divest local sites of production with relative ease (and sometimes even the support of the local managers and workers, who may see a brighter future for themselves under the protective umbrella of a different owner).

1.5. **The Structure of the Book**

The book reflects these themes by focusing specifically on the following points. The chapters in Part I concentrate on analysing how multinationals are socially embedded in specific settings but that, as they internationalize, they face new questions and issues. They seek to adapt their routines and practices to these new contexts, but in doing so they may set up patterns of learning and change. How wide is the impact of these patterns? What is their impact on existing competences and routines and on the home base? Part I, 'Convergences and Divergences in the Visible Hand of International Management', considers the importance of understanding the national contexts of firms and how this affects processes of internationalizing.

Part II, 'Constructing and Deconstructing the Visible Hand', considers this more from a processual perspective. What sorts of social relationship emerge from these formal structures and how do they impact on internationalization? Part III, 'Changing National and International Economic Orders: Constructing and Reconstructing Systems of Economic Organization and Regulation', examines the space within which the multinational is located, and the interrelationship between changing regulatory contexts and firms.

Overall, the book offers a rich variety of theoretical, conceptual, and empirical chapters, which challenge existing orthodoxy in the field of multinationals and international economic activity. They offer the potential for an exciting new definition of the field, bringing together organization theory, institutionalist approaches, and historical and contemporary empirical research in order to study the social embeddedness of multinationals and international economic activity. The book is by no means a definitive statement of an alternative approach. It is also important to acknowledge that there are differences of emphasis in the approaches taken by the various authors. The goal is not to try to create a new orthodoxy but rather to suggest a range of lines of enquiry for future consideration. One line of enquiry concerns developing a more theoretical approach to the nature of transnationalism and, in particular, the role of multinational corporations as transnational social spaces, a theme that is developed more strongly in some chapters than others. This would be associated with a more systematic cross-national and extended historical account of the emergence and development of different types of multinationals, distinguishing sectoral, national, and regional effects on these processes. In turn, this needs to be embedded more strongly in the sort of 'deep ethnography' represented by Kristensen and Zeitlin's chapter and discussed in Burawoy 2000. Finally, it is important to connect these issues with the ongoing formation of international structures, as discussed by me in Chapter 9 as these are crucial mechanisms setting the frameworks for how managers can bridge institutional and national divides. This in turn means engaging with the substantial literature in disciplines outside business and management, which have made substantial progress in understanding this sphere of activity (see, for example, Braithwaite and Drahos 2000; Rosenau 1997).

We present this book, therefore, as much in the spirit of a proposal for future research as a finished and final statement on the nature of the multinational firm. In this respect, also, what is proposed is not to be seen as a negation of current international business literature but rather an attempt to open out this field to new forms of theorizing and research. If the study of multinationals and international business can be opened out to allow a greater dialogue with competing views of the firm drawn from a sociological perspective, it is likely that there will be huge gains on both sides.

22 *Glenn Morgan*

REFERENCES

Axelsson, B. and Johanson, J. (1992), 'Foreign Market Entry—The Textbook vs. the Network View', in B. Axelsson and G. Easton (eds.), *Industrial Networks: A New View of Reality*. London: Routledge, 218–34.

Bartlett, C. A. and Ghoshal, S. (1989), *Managing Across Borders: The Transnational Solution*. London: Century Business.

Beechler, S. L. and Bird, A. (eds.) (1999), *Japanese Multinationals Abroad: Individual and Organizational Learning*. New York: Oxford University Press.

Birkinshaw, J. (2000), *Entrepreneurship in the Global Firm*. London: Sage.

Birkinshaw, J. and Hood, N. (eds.) (1998), *Multinational Corporate Evolution and Subsidiary Development*. London: Macmillan.

Braithwaite, J. and Drahos, P. (2000), *Global Business Regulation*. Cambridge: Cambridge University Press.

Bresman, H., Birkinshaw, J. and Nobel, R. (1999), 'Knowledge Transfer in International Acquisitions', *Journal of International Business Studies*, 30(3): 439–62.

Buckley, P. J. and Ghauri, P. N. (eds.) (1999), *The Internationalization of the Firm: A Reader* (2nd edn) London: International Thomson Business Press.

Burawoy, M. (ed.) (2000), *Global Ethnography*. Berkeley: University of California Press.

Campbell, N. and Burton, F. (eds.) (1994), *Japanese Multinationals*. London: Routledge.

Casson, M. (1997), *Information and Organisation: A New Perspective on the Theory of the Firm*. Oxford: Clarendon Press.

Dicken, P. (1998), *Global Shift* (3rd edn) London: Paul Chapman Publishing.

Dunning, J. (1998), 'Reappraising the Eclectic Paradigm in an Age of Alliance Capitalism', in M. Colombo (ed.), *The Changing Boundaries of the Firm*, London: Routledge, 29–59.

Egelhoff, W. G. (1982), 'Strategy and Structure in Multinational Corporations: An Information Processing Approach', *Administrative Science Quarterly*, 27: 435–58.

—— (1993), 'Information-Processing Theory and the Multinational Corporation', in S. Ghoshal and D. E. Westney (eds.), *Organization Theory and the Multinational*. London: Macmillan, 182–210.

Elger, T. and Smith, C. (eds.) (1994), *Global Japanization? The Transnational Transformation of the Labour Process*. London: Routledge.

Ferner, A. (1997), 'Country of Origin Effects and HRM in Multinational Companies', *Human Resource Management Journal* 7(1): 19–37.

Ferner, A. and Quintanilla, J. (1998), 'Multinationals, National Business Systems and HRM: The Enduring Influence of National Identity or a Process of "Anglo-Saxonization"', *International Journal of Human Resource Management*, 9(4): 710–31.

Forsgren, M., Holm, U. and Johanson, J. (1995), 'Division Headquarters Go

Abroad: A Step in the Internationalization of the Multinational Corporation', *Journal of Management Studies*, 32(4): 475–91.

Froud, J., Haslam, C., Johal, S. and Williams, K. (2000), 'Restructuring for Shareholder Value and Its Implications for Labour', *Cambridge Journal of Economics*, 24: 771–97.

Fruin, M. (1992), *The Japanese Enterprise System*. Oxford: Clarendon Press.

—— (1997), *Knowledge Works*. New York: Oxford University Press.

Gupta, A. K. and Govindarajan, V. (2000), 'Knowledge Flows Within Multinational Corporations', *Strategic Management Journal*, 21: 473–96.

Hassel, A., Hoepner, M., Kurdelbusch, A., Rehder, B. and Zugehoer, R. (1999), *Two Dimensions of the Internationalization of Firms*, Working Paper: Max Planck Institute for the Study of Societies, Cologne.

Hedlund, G. (1986), 'The Hypermodern MNC—A Heterarchy?', *Human Resource Management* 25(1): 9–35.

—— (1993), 'Assumptions of Hierarchy and Heterarchy with Applications to the Management of the Multinational Corporation', in S. Ghoshal and D. E. Westney, *Organization Theory and the Multinational*. London: Macmillan, 211–36.

Johanson, J. and Wiedersheim-Paul, F. (1975), 'The Internationalization of the Firm—Four Swedish Cases', *Journal of Management Studies*, 12: 305–22.

Jurgens, U., Naumann, K. and Rupp, J. (2000), 'Shareholder Value in an Adverse Environment: The German Case', *Economy and Society*, 29(1): 54–79.

Kogut, B. (2000), 'The Network as Knowledge: Generative Rules and the Emergence of Structure', *Strategic Management Journal*, 21: 405–25.

Lazonick, W. and O'Sullivan, M. (2000), 'Maximizing Shareholder Value: A New Ideology for Corporate Governance', *Economy and Society*, 29(1): 13–35.

Nobel, R. and Birkinshaw, J. (1998), 'Innovation in Multinational Corporations: Control and Communications in International R&D Operations', *Strategic Management Journal*, 19: 479–96.

Nohria, N. and Ghoshal, S. (1997), *The Differentiated Network: Organizing Multinational Corporations for Value Creation*. San Francisco: Jossey-Bass.

O'Donnell, S. W. (2000), 'Managing Foreign Subsidiaries: Agents of Headquarters or an Independent Network?', *Strategic Management Journal* 21: 525–48.

Ohmae, K. (1990), *The Borderless World*. London: Collins.

Prahalad, C. K. and Doz, Y. (1987), *The Multinational Mission: Balancing Local Demands and Global Vision*. New York: Free Press.

Quack, S., Morgan, G. and Whitley, R. (eds.) (2000), *National Capitalisms, Global Competition and Economic Performance*. Amsterdam: John Benjamins Publishing.

Rosenau, J. N. (1997), *Along the Domestic-Foreign Frontier: Exploring Governance in a Turbulent World*. Cambridge: Cambridge University Press.

Sassen, S. (1996), *Losing Control?—Sovereignty in an Age of Globalization*. New York: Columbia University Press.

Smith, C. and Elger, T. (1997), 'International Competition, Inward Investment and the Restructuring of European Work and Industrial Relations', *European Journal of Industrial Relations*, 3(3): 279–304.

Solvell, O. and Zander, I. (1998), 'International Diffusion of Knowledge: Isolating Mechanisms and the Role of the MNE', in A. D. Chandler, O. Solvell, and P. Hagstrom (eds.), *The Dynamic Firm: The Role of Technology, Strategy, Organization and Regions*. Oxford: Oxford University Press, 402–17.

Whitley, R. (ed.) (1992), *European Business Systems*. London: Sage.

Whitley, R. and Kristensen, P. H. (eds.) (1996), *The Changing European Firm*. London: Routledge.

—— (eds.) (1997), *Governance at Work*. Oxford: Oxford University Press.

Whittall, M. (2000), 'The BMW Works Council: A Cause for European Industrial Relations Optimism?', *European Journal of Industrial Relations*, 6(1): 61–84.

Whittall, M. and Tuckman, A. (2000), 'The Influence of European Works Councils on British Industrial Relations: The Case of Rover', *18th Annual International Labour Process Conference*, University of Strathclyde, Scotland.

Williams, K. (2000), 'From Shareholder Value to Present-Day Capitalism', *Economy and Society*, 29(1): 1–12.

Williamson, O. (1994), 'Transaction Cost Economics and Organization Theory', in N. J. Smelser and R. Swedberg (eds.), *The Handbook of Economic Sociology*. Princeton, NJ: Princeton University Press, 77–107.

PART I

CONVERGENCES AND DIVERGENCES IN THE VISIBLE HAND OF INTERNATIONAL MANAGEMENT

2

How and Why are International Firms Different? The Consequences of Cross-Border Managerial Coordination for Firm Characteristics and Behaviour

RICHARD WHITLEY

2.1. Introduction

The growth of foreign direct investment (FDI) and related forms of organizational coordination of economic activities across national boundaries have been seen as central features of the increasing economic globalization taking place at the end of the twentieth century. Indeed, globalization is often understood as a process of increasing integration of national and regional economies, such that decisions, activities, and competitive strategies in one part of the world are closely linked to those in other parts. In some variants of the 'strong' globalization thesis, this integration is seen as leading to the institutionalization of a distinct global level of economic coordination and control (see, for example, the discussions of contrasting views of globalization in Held et al. 1999; Hirst and Thompson 1996; Ruigrok and van Tulder 1995).

Multinational companies (MNCs) are central agents of such integration since they coordinate and control operations in many different parts of the world through unified authority and ownership structures. They therefore represent the extension of the visible hand of managerial hierarchies from national economies to supranational regional and worldwide ones. In theory, this managerial integration permits the establishment of competitive and cooperative relations across borders such that firms' strategies in one market are interdependent with those in others, and firm-specific advantages developed in the domestic economy can be extended to others. Such firms thus facilitate the transfer of competences and practices from one business environment to others and organizationally integrate economic activities across diverse contexts.

The expansion of MNCs in the last two or three decades of the twentieth century is often viewed as particularly significant for international economic coordination, because many are more organizationally integrated and dynamic than earlier international firms (Bartlett and Ghoshal 1989; Hedlund and Ridderstrale 1998). They also focus more on integrating activities across the developed industrial world than on coordinating those in developing economies, and increasingly develop distinctive organizational capabilities that are 'transnational' rather than being extensions of those generated domestically (see, e.g., Bartlett and Ghoshal 1989; Ghoshal and Westney 1993).

Regardless of the empirical accuracy of many claims of this globalization thesis (questioned for example, by Hirst and Thompson 1996; Kenworthy 1997; Koechlin 1995; Ruigrok and van Tulder 1995), they emphasize the distinctive nature of the MNC as an organization because of its management of significant operations in many and diverse national territories. Whether such firms are really 'global corporations' (Doremus et al. 1998)—however that is understood—is less significant than the possibility that growing managerial coordination across borders could generate novel forms of organization and competitive capabilities distinct from more nationally focused companies.

From this point of view, late twentieth-century MNCs have been crucial agents in the development of a more global and supranational system of capitalism in so far as they become different kinds of organization as a result of operating across markets and societies. Where they remain largely national firms with international operations (Hu 1992), as perhaps has been the case throughout most of the twentieth century, they are unlikely to change radically established patterns of economic organization or to lead to the establishment of a new, global business system. If, on the other hand, it could be demonstrated that new organizational properties and capabilities are being developed by such firms as a direct consequence of their authoritative coordination of economic activities across territorial boundaries and societies, then the increasing number and significance of MNCs in the world economy could indeed represent a qualitative shift in the organization of economic activities throughout the world (Dicken 1998; Dicken et al. 1994; Whitley 1998).

In this chapter I consider the ways in which cross-national managerial coordination in itself could change key characteristics of firms
to the extent that they significantly affect established patterns of economic organization. In particular, I examine the kinds of internationalization of economic activities that can be expected to generate
novel organizations as well as outlining the contrasting logics that
firms from different types of business system are likely to follow in
their international expansion. Initially, I discuss the specific features
of MNCs that make them particularly important as agents of organizational change across national boundaries in a weakly institutionalized international business environment. Following this, I consider
the major ways in which different kinds of MNC vary as integrating
agents and their consequences for organizational change. These variations in patterns of internationalization are linked to the nature of
firms in domestic business systems as well as to the characteristics of
the environments they invest in. The extent to which MNCs 'learn'
from FDI, and how they do so, differ between types of firm, as do the
consequent effects of such learning upon their domestic business
system.

2.2. The International Business Environment and Modes of Internationalization

The generally limited scope and regulatory power of institutional
arrangements governing economic transactions and relationships
across national borders mean that the international business environment is less organized and predictable than many national and
regional ones. Although varying over time, between sectors, and
across regions, the institutionalization of (1) procedures regulating
business practices,(2) norms governing market boundaries and identities, and, (3) dispute resolution mechanisms remains much lower
for business activities that cross national borders than for those
within them.

This greater uncertainty concerning the governance norms regulating international transactions is, of course, reinforced by the
common disjunction and contrast between established business practices and norms in different countries. Even within Europe, for
instance, significant differences in the meanings and uses of formal
contracts, and in the expectations of contracting partners, remain
institutionalized in national legal systems (Lane 1997; Lane and

Bachmann 1996; Teubner, 2001). These are much greater between Europe, North America, and Asia, such that relying on domestic written procedures to ensure compliance with agreements and pre-dictable behaviour abroad could lead to major errors.

Additionally, the very variety of business practices and institutionalized governance mechanisms across the world capitalist system means that the prevalent ways in which transactions between firms from any two business systems are managed will only rarely be appropriate for exchanges between different kinds of firm from contrasting contexts. More often, those characteristic of dominant political economies are extended to like societies and/or those susceptible to economic-cum-political pressure, as Braithwaite and Drahos (2000) suggest has happened with intellectual property rights in the WTO (World Trade Organization). As a result, the degree of standardization of coordination processes and forms of economic organization across national boundaries tends to be less than that within them, given the greater institutionalization of governance mechanisms and regulatory norms within most industrialized states. This is why distinctive national business systems are more common than international ones. Even within the broad category of 'Anglo-Saxon', or liberal, market economies, for instance, there remain significant differences in the ways that the legal and financial systems operate between, say, Britain and the USA (see, e.g., Teubner 2001; Tylecote and Conesa 1999).

This weakly institutionalized international context of economic activities means that developing stable and wide-ranging partnerships and long-term commitments across borders is difficult, albeit feasible in capital-intensive industries with high technological entry barriers, as Glimstedt illustrates in Chapter 5. To some extent, family ties and, more broadly, ethnicity and other ascriptive bases of trust may encourage such collaboration across national boundaries, as in the case of many Chinese businesses in Pacific Asia. However, these factors often prove rather fragile in practice and typically limit cooperation to fairly specific, low-commitment and fixed-term relationships (Redding 1990). Relying solely on common ethnicity to ensure continuing commitment and 'goodwill' trust (Sako 1992) between business partners from different territories in a generally adversarial and anomic environment seems rather risky. Rather, family ties and reputation may help to overcome some of the barriers to international trade and joint ventures—as they do in 'particularistic' business environments more generally (Whitley 1999: ch. 2)—but are unlikely to prove strong enough to outweigh market power and opportunistic strategies in the medium term.

More common is the extension of alliances and partnerships from domestic economies to foreign ones. Here, collaborating firms share the risks and resources of investing abroad with established business partners, often in current or former colonies (Jones 1996), and rely on domestically institutionalized regimes to reproduce cooperation in novel environments. Authority-sharing across borders in such cases is not likely to generate major changes in firm type or behaviour, since domestic institutions and arrangements remain critical to its feasibility and effectiveness. In contrast, establishing authoritative integration and collaboration between economic actors from different business systems on a continuing basis is much more difficult, given the absence of strongly institutionalized environments that encourage lock-in between business partners across countries.

Together with the limited range and effectiveness of formal institutions for managing disputes and ensuring compliance between business partners from different territories, this means that most international transactions tend to be short term, with limited commitments to any particular relationship, and resemble classical contracting much more than obligational contractual relations. Market power and mutual self-interest, rather than authority, play the dominant role in ensuring compliance, and common adherence to joint objectives and norms is correspondingly difficult to establish on a continuing basis. In Lazonick's (1991; Lazonick and West 1998) terms, the degree of international organizational integration of economic activities remains relatively low. This also applies to the international cartels and market-sharing agreements between firms from different countries that characterized so much of the interwar period, such as that described by Glimstedt in Chapter 5. These arrangements institutionalized the separation of markets rather than their integration, and were unlikely to lead to significant changes in coordination and control systems.

Where ownership rights have become more institutionalized in different business environments, so that foreign investors can be confident that their interests will be respected, ownership integration of economic activities across national boundaries is more feasible. In the relatively anomic international business environment the integration of activities across national boundaries is more likely to be achieved through single-firm hierarchies than through long-term alliances and partnerships, as long as authority derived from private property rights is recognized and reproduced in different societies. Together with market power, often linked to relatively large size, direct ownership control of foreign operations is more likely than authority-sharing between ownership entities once substantial commitment to such operations has been made. Overall, then, the risks of operating in diverse institutional contexts with weak international regulatory institutions encourage ownership-based economic coordination rather than alliance-based authority-sharing.

However, the combination of varied business systems with the lack of strongly institutionalized global governance norms that could standardize modes of economic coordination and control does, of course, mean that the kinds of ownership integration developed by firms from different systems vary considerably. Just as the ways that firms manage diversification strategies within their domestic economies reflect their idiosyncratic organizational competences, so too do their approaches to internationalization extend prevalent organizing principles across borders (Kogut 1993). The kinds of investment they make, where and when they make them, and how they subsequently manage and develop them, depend on the sorts of governance structures and capabilities they have developed in their home business systems, as I shall discuss in the next section. The relatively limited institutionalization of worldwide governance regimes means that MNCs differ more in their patterns of development than do more domestic firms in cohesive and integrated business systems. They also vary greatly in the extent to which they are likely to change as distinctive kinds of firms as a result of internationalization.

Before considering the differences in how firms from contrasting domestic business systems internationalize and, consequently, may alter key characteristics, though, it is necessary to discuss how variations in the form and organization of FDI are likely to affect the nature of MNCs. A particularly important factor here is the coordination of economic activities in a variety of business environments with different kinds of business partners. MNCs, that is, are of interest as distinctive organizational entities in so far as they authoritatively integrate economic resources and activities in quite different locations that involve managing contrasting kinds of employees and competing and cooperating with varied sorts of firms in differently organized markets. It is the coordination of major activities across significantly different institutional contexts through organizational routines that potentially makes MNCs distinctive kinds of organizations. The greater complexity of the environments, markets, and personnel they have to manage within firms' boundaries suggests that they become more complex organizations than more domestically focused firms and may develop distinctive routines and capabilities as a result.

The extent to which they do indeed develop greater complexity and distinctive organizational routines depends on the following three factors. First, the degree of managerial commitment to different kinds of market economy; secondly, how much MNCs innovate organizationally in different business units as the result of such commitments; and, thirdly, the extent to which they then institutionalize new ways of doing things throughout the organization. In general terms, MNCs are more likely to become distinctive kinds of organization when they locate major proportions of key assets and activities in quite different kinds of business system, allow foreign subsidiaries to adapt to local conventions, and 'learn' from these novel developments by adapting and integrating them through organization-wide routines and procedures. It is the combination of diversity of markets, employees, business partners, and institutions with organizational integration within ownership-based boundaries that makes MNCs potentially significant different kinds of economic organization.

It follows from this characterization of MNCs as distinctive organizations that only some types of them have innovative consequences for economic coordination and control systems (Whitley 1998). In particular, where (1) the commitment of economic resources and activities to different kinds of business environments is limited, (2) subsidiary autonomy is low, and/or (3) foreign subsidiaries are managed at arm's length, so that any organizational innovations in host economies are limited to those units, the firm as a whole is unlikely to change its basic nature. It is only when they integrate major operations located in quite distinctive and strongly isomorphic business systems through organization-wide routines and procedures that MNCs are likely to develop novel and distinctive characteristics as a result of internationalization (Westney 1999).

The organizational implications of the managerial integration of economic activities across national borders can, then, be contrasted in terms of two orthogonal dimensions. First, the variety of business systems and different kinds of institutional contexts in which significant economic assets and activities are located, and, secondly, the degree to which new organizational routines developed as a result of such varied business locations are integrated throughout the parent firm. The first dimension can be described as the *variety of different kinds of business environment* the MNC is committed to. This implies both a high level of resource commitment to these different locations —and, one moreover, that involves core capabilities rather than peripheral activities—and strong institutions in these host economies that exercise significant isomorphic influences on business behaviour (Westney 1993, 1999).

For high contextual variety to be significant in affecting the nature and behaviour of MNCs, then, they have to invest major assets in different kinds of business system and be strongly influenced by dominant institutions in these societies. Examples of such institutions are the German education and labour systems (Lane 1989, 1992) and the British and US capital markets. Variety, in other words, is only meaningful for organizational change when it implies considerable pressure to do things differently for an important part of the business. It is not just a matter of geographical dispersion (Porter 1986).

The second dimension can be summarized as the *extent of organizational integration* of routines. This implies that where MNCs adapt to different ways of doing business in contrasting host economies— and as a result develop organizational innovations—these affect practices and procedures elsewhere so that innovations become generalized beyond individual subsidiaries. Where such integration is low, as in the traditional multi-domestic MNC structure, each major subsidiary in different countries or regions can adapt to its particular environment and develop routines that are idiosyncratic relative to the rest of the firm, without these impinging much on other subsidiaries or head office. As long as agreed targets are met and broad guidelines followed, subunits can evolve quite varied practices and so the firm as a whole becomes more differentiated between business environments without significantly changing its core characteristics, which remain similar to those of its domestic business system. In the case of the British firm described by Kristensen and Zeitlin in Chapter 7, this differentiation—encouraged by acquisition-based growth strategies—is also vertical, between head office and all subsidiaries, including domestic ones.

Highly integrated MNCs, on the other hand, have much more standardized routines throughout the organization, and innovations in one subsidiary, once established, can have much more impact on practices and procedures in others. This does, though, depend on how much top managers wish to learn from foreign operations and alter established ways of doing things in their domestic organization. In practice, of course, the degree of integration can vary considerably between functional areas. Often, personnel policies and marketing strategies are more idiosyncratic to major subsidiaries than production, engineering, and financial control routines. Many Japanese MNCs seem quite willing to adapt some practices to local labour market conventions in different business environments, while standardizing production systems and other routines across all subsidiaries, as Sharpe discusses in Chapter 8. Such localized innovations are rarely transferred back to the dominant units in their domestic operations.

It should be noted here that this dimension differs somewhat from the notion of global integration as discussed by Bartlett and Ghoshal (1989) and others (for example, Dicken et al. 1994). While these writers, and indeed much of the international business literature, focus on the degree of central direction and control of overseas subsidiaries, I am here more concerned with the organizational integration of operations and subunits across borders. This may be combined with varying degrees of centralization in terms of which unit decides on the standardization of procedures and routines, but the important aspect of this dimension is the extent of their commonality across units. Thus, both 'globalized' and 'transnational' MNCs as described by Bartlett and Ghoshal exhibit high levels of organizational integration in my terms, while multi-domestic ones are typically weakly integrated.

However, it is also important to recognize that learning in the sense being discussed here arises from subsidiaries adapting to host economy conventions and practices. This requires them to have sufficient autonomy to develop novel routines without being sanctioned by head office, and so will not take place in highly globally integrated firms, or highly coordinated ones in Porter's terms (1986: 23–7). For highly varied business environments to affect organizational characteristics and behaviour, MNCs have to delegate some powers to their foreign units without fragmenting the organization so much that there are few standardized routines throughout it. The problems that some German banks have had in managing their investment banking subsidiaries in the UK and the USA illustrate some of the difficulties involved in coordinating different kinds of activity in very different environments.

Combining and dichotomizing these two dimensions of variety and integration enable us to identify four contrasting ideal types of internationalization: *similar multi-domestic, fragmented, similar integrated*, and *hybrid*, as shown in Table 2.1. The first of these has the

Table 2.1 *Modes of internationalization*

		Variety of institutional contexts	
		Low	High
Organizational integration	**Low**	Similar multi-domestic	Fragmented
	High	Similar integrated	Hybrid

least impact on the home organization because it operates the bulk of its key assets and activities in business systems that are similar to its domestic one and manages them in a highly decentralized manner. Pressures to innovate as a result of such internationalization are correspondingly weak and when innovation does occur, it is highly localized.

Fragmented MNCs also operate their foreign subsidiaries at arm's length, but are much more committed to markets and locations in very different kinds of business system. Here, we would expect more of the firm's key activities to adapt to strong isomorphic pressures in host economies, and so develop novel organizational routines in local subsidiaries, but these would have little impact on domestic operations or on those in other subsidiaries. Such MNCs become highly differentiated organizations, more so than their domestic counterparts, but do not greatly alter their core capabilities and priorities or institutionalize new routines throughout the whole organization. 'Learning' takes place in each distinctive business system the firm operates in, without being extended elsewhere. Firms that grow through foreign acquisitions often develop such differentiated structures, as illustrated by the company described by Kristensen and Zeitlin in Chapter 7.

More integrated MNCs operating in similar foreign business environments, and/or those with relatively weak institutional arrangements, are unlikely to change very much as a result of FDI. Their strongly institutionalized routines and procedures, which constitute the distinctive character of the firm and express its core capabilities, permeate all subsidiaries. Since these—or at least those with major assets—operate in similar kinds of business system to the firms' domestic one, and are not subjected to strong isomorphic pressures from host economy institutions that diverge greatly from home economy ones, they are unlikely to change these routines significantly. Rather, most foreign units will extend domestic patterns of behaviour to their new locations. Many Japanese firms in the Association of South-East Asian Nations (ASEAN) economies have been able to do this, except perhaps in some areas of personnel management.

Hybrid MNCs, on the other hand, invest major resources and carry out key activities in much more varied contexts with strong institutions at the same time as integrating these systematically on a 'global' basis. By locating core capabilities and processes in quite different kinds of business system that are interdependent with cohesive and integrated societal institutions, these firms have to modify their routines and innovate at the local level, in a similar way to fragmented MNCs. However, their equally strong concern to integrate operations and business units on a worldwide basis through establishing common routines and procedures throughout the entire organization means that they have to change their domestic operations as well as further modifying subsidiaries' routines to adapt to innovations being developed elsewhere in the network.

Hybrid MNCs thus exhibit continuing organizational change as they expand into diverse business systems and integrate new ways of doing things from different locations into the established organization. In principle, then, not only are they the most likely MNCs to change their core capabilities and routines as the result of internationalization, but they are also likely to continue to change these as they diversify key operations across different kinds of market economy. To some extent, the large German firms discussed by Lane in Chapter 3 followed this pattern in the 1990s, but it is not clear that they actually integrated their foreign innovations into the parent organization. Rather, they probably became less integrated and more differentiated as a result of investing in the Americas and Asia.

These four combinations of low and high variety of business systems and of organizational integration are, of course, abstract types of internationalization that are rarely exemplified by empirical MNCs. Most firms do not locate central assets and activities in quite different kinds of business systems (Dicken et al. 1994; Doremus et al. 1998; Ruigrok and van Tulder 1995), nor do they fragment organizational routines completely or totally standardize them across units operating in diverse environments. Even the most integrated and cohesive enterprises adapt some aspects of their managerial procedures to novel circumstances, as the extensive literature on 'Japanization' illustrates (see, for example, Elger and Smith 1998), while all firms establish some coordination and control routines over all foreign units despite adapting considerably to local pressures.

In general, though, MNCs vary considerably in the extent to which they invest key resources in contrasting business systems and integrate foreign operations with each other and with their domestic core activities. They therefore differ greatly in the level of organizational innovation and change they undergo as the result of internationalization, and in their development of novel and distinctive characteristics. These variations stem from both the nature of the firms concerned, which in turn are connected to their domestic business system characteristics and institutional pressures, and the nature of the business systems to which they commit significant resources. To explore how and why different kinds of firm are likely to internationalize their activities in different ways—and so to vary in the extent of their consequent change —I shall now discuss the key differences between three idealized types of firm that develop interdependently with particular institutions and social structures in contrasting business environments.

2.3. Three Ideal Types of Business Environment and Firm

Given the variety of firms in different business systems, the nature of the international business environment, and the variety of business systems in which companies invest significant resources, both the nature of internationalization strategies and their consequences for MNC characteristics vary considerably between firms (Doremus et al. 1998; Ruigrok and van Tulder 1995; Sally 1994). Rather, then, than seeking to identify how internationalization, per se, affects the nature of firms in general, we need to consider how different firms from contrasting business systems are likely to invest in varied kinds of market economies with different results in terms of organizational change.

To highlight the significance of these differences, I shall focus on three types of enterprise that develop in distinctive kinds of business environment. These environments are dominated by different institutional arrangements controlling access to capital and skills that encourage different ways of coordinating and controlling economic activities, and hence lead to contrasting strategic priorities, forms of owner control and authority-sharing, and varied collective competences. Firms' management of risks, perceptions of dominant interests, and competitive strategies all differ as a result and affect their predilection for, and management of, internationalization.

Three types of business environment, in particular, encourage quite different sorts of firm to develop and dominate them. *Particularistic* environments are notable for the lack of institutions encouraging cooperation and trust, whether between owners and managers, employers and employees, or buyers and sellers. They combine a weak and/or predatory state—in terms of its mobilizing and coordinating capacity—with weak collective intermediaries and norms governing economic transactions, and predominantly paternalist authority relationships (Whitley 1999: ch. 2). In general, formal institutions are unreliable and too weak to structure the behaviour of economic agents in these kinds of society.

Collaborative business environments, on the other hand, have a number of important institutions that together lock key actors into each others' destinies and so encourage cooperative behaviour by restricting exit opportunities. In some collaborative business environments, such as that of postwar Japan, the state plays an important coordinating and developmental role, guiding investment strategies with business associations. In others, such as that of postwar Germany, it is less involved in directly coordinating economic development activities, but encourages private associations to coordinate a range of activities, and supports a strong public training system in collaboration with employees and unions.

Arm's length business environments, in contrast, provide highly flexible entry and exit arrangements for economic actors, but do so within a strongly institutionalized formal system of rules and procedures that facilitate delegation and trust. In these societies, the state acts more as regulator than coordinator, finance flows through competitive capital markets rather than banks, and training is more a matter for individual investment than for coordinated collaboration between state agencies, employers, and unions. Both of these last two sets of institutional arrangements produce more predictable environments for firms, managers, and owners so that they can make strategic decisions about the competitive environment in a relatively rational manner, whereas particularistic ones do not. Each of these environments generates a characteristic type of firm: *opportunistic, cooperative hierarchy,* and *isolated hierarchy,* respectively. Their main characteristics are summarized in Table 2.2 and will now be discussed.

Opportunistic firms are essentially products of adversarial, unpredictable, and highly uncertain business environments, in which the state is typically poorly integrated and controlled by private

Table 2.2 *Distinctive characteristics of three kinds of firm*

Distinctive characteristics	Firm type		
	Opportunistic	Cooperative hierarchy	Isolated hierarchy
Owner control type	Direct	Alliance	Market
Significance of employee interests	Low	Considerable	Low
Significance of business partners	Low	Considerable	Low
Development of distinctive organizational capabilities	Low	Considerable	Considerable
Extent to which competitive competences are ownership-specific	High	Limited	High
Competitive focus on continuing improvement and innovation	Low	High	Low
Competitive focus on rapid responses to customer changes	High	Some	Low
Typical business environment	Particularistic	Collaborative	Arm's length

rent-seeking elites. Here, dominant institutional arrangements are either antagonistic to private wealth accumulation or else too weak to provide the basis for predictable outcomes from strategic investments. Thus, making large-scale commitments on a rational basis that involves calculating long-term returns, anticipating the responses of key competitors, etc. is difficult in these kinds of environment. Strategic decision-making in general in such societies typically involves gaining political or related forms of support, which are highly particularistic and subject to radical change at short notice. Similar points apply to employer–employee relations, including owner-manager connections, such that trust and commitment between most groups are difficult to establish, except on a highly personal basis such as family membership or family-like relationships.

Consequently, these kinds of firm rarely develop complex and stable organizational capabilities and routines for managing activities and resources across geographical and temporal boundaries. Rather, authority and coordination are highly personal and non-routinized. Owner control is typically direct and personal, with little account being taken of employee and business partner interests, and family wealth accumulation is often the dominant objective of owners. Flexibility and responsiveness are key competitive strategies, as these firms have to be adept at adjusting to unpredictable environmental changes and typically limit commitments to any one technology, product, or industry. This kind of firm shares many characteristics with the Chinese family business (Gates 1996; Hamilton 1997; Redding 1990).

Cooperative and isolated hierarchies develop in more institutionalized business environments that permit strategic decisions to be made with a reasonable expectation that the outcomes of major investments can be rationally calculated. The established rules of the competitive game are here sufficiently institutionalized and stable for owners to delegate some authority to salaried managers and enter into long-term commitments with business partners on a continuing basis. Firms therefore are able to develop complex organizations through authority relationships derived from private property rights without requiring direct owner supervision and high levels of personal trust. Thus, distinctive organizational competences develop in these business environments and firms take on many attributes of Penrosian administrative structures (Penrose 1959).

They differ, however, in respect of their ability and willingness to collaborate with employees and business partners. While the overall degree of organizational integration and coordination of economic activities is much greater in these business environments than in particularistic ones, it varies considerably between collaborative and arm's length ones (Lazonick 1991; Lazonick and West 1998; Soskice 1999).

Owners and managers share authority much more with employees and partners in the former institutional contexts than in the latter ones. Skilled manual workers are typically integrated into the organization as core 'members' in cooperative hierarchies, but rarely so in isolated ones, and suppliers, customers, and competitors are more used to cooperation, and information and risk-sharing in collaborative environments than in arm's length ones, often through strong industry and trade associations. This is largely because the state, financial, and labour systems in 'collaborative' societies encourage considerable interdependence between the providers and users of capital and labour power as well as the institutionalization of strong intermediary associations between the family, the firm, and the state. In these business environments, lock-in effects between banks, employers, employees, and business partners in general are quite strong, so that interests are shared rather than adversarial.

Arm's length environments, in contrast, are characterized by a high degree of pluralism and separation of major institutional arenas and regulatory conventions, perhaps symbolized most strongly by the separation of powers in the US Constitution. Interdependence between collective actors is low here, and formal procedures are the prevalent mode of governing interrelationships. Few organizations and groups are locked in to the fates of others and market contracting between relatively unconnected business partners dominates. Owners tend to be remote from managers and capital is typically managed in investment portfolios with financial claims traded on highly liquid markets. Interest groups in general are neither especially encouraged nor discouraged by the state—which in any case is rarely cohesive and capable of acting consistently as a coordinating agency over the medium term—but left to compete in a predominantly market-like manner for legitimacy and resources.

Firms are more units of financial control than broadly encompassing systems of organizational integration in such environments, and are reluctant to share authority with either non-managerial employees or with business partners. They operate as isolated islands of order in a sea of market disorder. As such, their distinctive organizational competences and competitive capabilities are highly firm specific and not developed or shared with customers and suppliers, unlike those of cooperative hierarchies. This means that the 'firm' as an organization consists largely of the managerial and administrative apparatus, excluding most technical and manual employees who are not integrated into it.

Given that the international business environment is less regulated by dominant institutions on a worldwide basis than most national ones in the industrialized capitalist world, it can be characterized as particularistic rather than collaborative or arm's length, except that there is no predatory state capable of seizing economic surpluses and expropriating wealth-holders. As discussed above, uncertainty about business partners and transactions across many borders tends to be quite high, encouraging spot market behaviour and limiting commitments in a similar manner to weakly institutionalized environments in general.

However, this low degree of institutionalization of regulatory norms also means that established domestic patterns of economic coordination dominate international ones, so that attempts to institutionalize the sorts of standards discussed by Morgan in Chapter 9 typically follow the domestic norms of the dominant economy, at least initially. Equally, many firms extend domestic patterns of business unit control to their foreign subsidiaries at first. The weak standardization of international coordination forms, in other words, encourages a plurality of integration patterns of foreign subsidiaries such that different kinds of firm will follow quite contrasting internationalization styles, once they go beyond simple one-off transactions.

2.4. **Internationalization Strategies of Different Kinds of Firms**

These contrasting patterns of internationalization can be compared on a considerable number of dimensions, as the extensive literature on FDI management illustrates (see, for example, Bartlett et al. 1990; Doremus et al. 1998; Dicken et al. 1994; Lane 1998; Sally 1995). Most of these focus on the significance of FDI as a proportion of total investment, the reasons for FDI, parent–subsidiary relationships, and patterns of subsidiary development. Since I am here concerned with how FDI might generate significantly different kinds of organization, I shall concentrate on three major aspects of internationalization. First, its strategic significance, rationale, and location. Secondly, how firms manage the risks associated with FDI and their foreign subsidiaries. Thirdly, the nature of subsidiaries' adaptation to, and integration with, local host economies. These can be divided into seven more specific characteristics of internationalization patterns that vary considerably between the three types of firm just outlined.

Considering first the extent to which firms commit major resources to foreign locations that are quite different in key respects from their domestic business system and its associated institutions, this continues to vary between, say, British, German, and Japanese companies (Lane 1998 and Chapter 3 in this volume; see also Doremus et al. 1998; Heiduk and Hodges 1992; Hirst and Thompson 1996; Ruigrok and van Tulder 1995). A major contrast here is between firms that have preferred to export to foreign markets initially, before undertaking FDI at a later stage, and those that have invested directly in those markets. Secondly, the importance of firm-specific competitive advantages that can be transferred to foreign subsidiaries varies considerably between firms making foreign investments. While much US internationalization in the 1960s and 1970s, and Japanese manufacturing FDI in the 1980s and 1990s, were seen as gaining market share through exporting distinctive organizational capabilities that were superior to their host economy rivals, more recent FDI has been focused on gaining access to foreign technologies and innovative capacities, especially that in the USA.

Thirdly, the considerable risks involved in FDI in the relatively weakly institutionalized international business environment can be managed in a number of different ways that reflect firms' experience of risk management in their domestic business systems. This is linked to, fourthly, the extent of parental control over major foreign subsidiaries, as well as, fifthly, the dominant mode through which this control is exercised. Sixthly, foreign subsidiaries vary greatly in their integration into local host economies with regard to technology and product development/modification, components and materials supplies, distribution and marketing. Allied to this is, seventhly, their adaptation to local business conventions and practices that lead to major foreign units developing distinctive organizational capabilities. The ways that opportunistic firms, cooperative hierarchies, and isolated hierarchies can be expected to vary on these dimensions are summarized in Table 2.3 and will now be further discussed.

There are two key characteristics of these kinds of firm that affect these seven dimensions of their internationalization. First, the extent and nature of their organizational capabilities, and their organization-specific competitive advantages based on such competences, greatly influence both their ability to coordinate operations across borders and how they do so. Secondly, the prevalent mode of owner control and authority-sharing affects how firms manage foreign subsidiaries and deal with uncertainty in different business environments.

Considering, first, opportunistic firms, these have few organization-specific competitive advantages based on standardized routines and procedures that coordinate complex activities and skills. Accordingly, these kinds of enterprise will gain relatively little from extending their organizational coordination of economic activities to overseas locations. Additionally, since owner control tends to be direct and personal in such companies, FDI will be limited to those operations that can be controlled by top management. In general, this concern with direct owner control in opportunistic firms is likely to restrict the amount and significance of their FDI since such investment increases the already considerable level of uncertainty and distrust between business partners by locating major commitments in new and relatively unknown contexts.

This uncertainty may be mitigated to some extent by such firms locating FDI in geographically or culturally proximate territories,

Table 2.3 *Firm type and patterns of internationalization*

Patterns of internationalization	Firm type		
	Opportunistic	Cooperative hierarchy	Isolated hierarchy
Willingness to transfer/invest major resources in different kinds of business system	Limited	Limited	Considerable
Transferability of firm-specific competitive advantages to foreign subsidiaries	Limited	Limited	High
Prevalent risk management strategies	Flexibility and personal obligation networks	Transfer domestic alliances and market power	Market power and firm-specific advantages
Central control of subsidiaries and integration with parent operations	High	Considerable	Variable
Prevalent control mode	Direct supervision	Access to strategic resources	Financial
Integration of subsidiaries into local economies	Variable and ad hoc	Limited	Considerable
Subsidiary development of distinct organizational capabilities	Low	Limited	Considerable
Dominant mode of internationalization	Similar, integrated	Variable, integrated	Diverse, limited integration

where owner-managers are able to maintain close supervision and/or rely on common sets of expectation and convention that permit the use of domestic routines and control practices to govern behaviour in foreign subsidiaries. This is arguably what has happened in much Taiwanese investment in China and Malaysia. Thus, we would not expect opportunistic firms to transfer major resources and key value-added activities away from their domestic economies, and, when significant amounts of FDI did occur, this would probably be located in similar sorts of environment and be restricted to relatively easily controlled, routinized activities, using cheap, semi-skilled labour (Yeung and Olds 2000).

As in their domestic contexts, such firms are likely to limit commitments to employees, business partners, and markets in foreign locations, and to emphasize flexibility over the long-term development of organizational capabilities in and between subsidiaries. These foreign units would, then, be subject to tight central control. Any integration of such subsidiaries into host economies is, consequently, likely to be short term and ad hoc, such that they will not readily adopt local conventions and routines, or develop distinctive organizational capabilities. Overall, then, opportunistic firms are likely to limit major amounts of FDI to business environments where they feel able to control activities through similar routines to those used domestically and/or through market power, and will strongly integrate foreign subsidiaries' operations with domestic ones.

Both cooperative and isolated hierarchies, on the other hand, do have some firm-specific competitive advantages that could, in principle, be transferred to foreign subsidiaries. However, as emphasized above, they differ in the extent to which these depend on, and are shared with, employees and business partners. The boundaries of the firm with such advantages are much broader in cooperative hierarchies than they are in isolated ones. While the former typically include their core skilled workforce, first-tier suppliers, lead banks, and so on, isolated hierarchies are largely constituted as distinct organizations by the routines and knowledge of the managerial hierarchy and key professional experts. Their competitive advantages are therefore the property of a more limited and more authoritatively integrated set of people and groups than are those of cooperative hierarchies. As a result, their willingness and ability to invest major resources across borders vary considerably, as does the predominant manner in which they do so.

Cooperative hierarchies develop much of their organizational capabilities and competitive advantage through cooperation with banks, suppliers, customers, and competitors. Because they are strongly embedded in a network of mutual obligations and commitments, their ability to implement radical strategic decisions that would dramatically change the nature of their business and key resources is quite limited in the short term. Change in these firms tends to be incremental, continuous, and interdependent with major business partners. As a result, they find it difficult to shift key activities and significant resources rapidly to foreign locations, and, moreover, are unlikely to see the need for such investment as long as their domestic location and commitments are viewed as providing major advantages. FDI by cooperative hierarchies, then, is likely to take place incrementally, be subsequent to exporting and establishing sales offices, and will not typically involve transferring central activities that are closely linked to domestic partners and agencies.

Furthermore, since these kinds of firm have had limited experience of managing major facilities in adversarial, weakly institutionalized environments, they will find it difficult and time-consuming to develop new ways of operating in the relatively anomic international business environment. This will reinforce their reluctance to commit large-scale resources to radically different foreign environments without substantial previous experience of them, through, for example, distribution and product modification units. The growth of German investment in the USA towards the end of the twentieth century, discussed by Lane in Chapter 3, occurred after considerable experience of operating sales and marketing subsidiaries in North American markets, and when the advantages of operating in the domestic environment appeared less overwhelming. This was especially so for firms in sectors, such as pharmaceuticals, where radical innovations became critical to competitive success.

One way of managing the risks and difficulties faced by cooperative hierarchies investing abroad, especially those from highly coordinated business systems, is to persuade suppliers and other business partners to move as well. This has been a common pattern among large Japanese firms in the postwar period, and also occurred among some European groups before the First World War (Jones 1996: 33–40). Indeed, an important motive for many service companies, such as banks, to establish foreign subsidiaries has been to maintain their close connections with major customers who have undertaken significant FDI. This pattern replicates many key characteristics of the domestic business system in foreign locations and typically reinforces the strong and detailed central control of subsidiaries that these kinds of firm tend to exercise when establishing units in unfamiliar and sometimes threatening business environments.

Because their organizational capabilities are so embedded in particular relationships and contexts, managing major subsidiaries in different locations where partners, employees and institutions are new requires these kinds of firm to develop new competences—and that takes time. At least initially, then, most foreign subsidiaries of any significance will tend to be quite closely supervised and integrated into the parent activities of cooperative hierarchies, as Lane (1998) suggests has largely been the case for major German companies for many decades since the end of World War II. This close supervision of key functions, together with the highly domestically embedded nature of these kinds of firm and their competitive competences, limit the integration of foreign subsidiaries into host economies and their development of distinctive organizational capabilities (Doremus et al. 1998), at least until they gain considerable experience and understanding of novel environments.

In summary, then, cooperative hierarchies are likely to limit the size and centrality of their initial FDI, and confine it to locations that are already familiar and easy to control, as many Continental European firms have done in the twentieth century by concentrating their major foreign investments within Europe (Hirst and Thompson 1996; Jones 1996; Ruigrok and van Tulder 1995; Sally 1995). Foreign subsidiaries of these kinds of firm are typically quite closely integrated with parent company operations and will often be linked to host economy units of their domestic business partners. Where the export of such relationships and risk-sharing arrangements to foreign locations is feasible, as in, for instance, pluralist, arm's length environments, cooperative hierarchies may well be more willing to invest in these different kinds of business system, as many Japanese firms have done in the UK and the USA. In other words, the reluctance of these kinds of firms in general to commit major resources to quite contrasting economic coordination and control systems can be mitigated, if not completely overcome, by sharing the risks involved with domestic partners and limiting subsidiary autonomy.

In contrast, isolated hierarchy types of firm develop their organizational capabilities and advantages without much authority-sharing with the bulk of their labour force and business partners. Competences are here more firm-specific and exclusive to individual managerial hierarchies, rarely depending on alliances or cooperation between firms in trade associations and similar groupings, at least over the medium term, or involving non-managerial staff. Units of financial control are coterminous with units of authoritative integration such that authority and ownership are combined in relatively self-contained and discrete entities. As a result, these kinds of firm are much more able to move resources and subunits across borders without being greatly constrained by obligational ties to business partners, including employees. Since their competitive advantages over foreign firms are also more self-contained and less dependent on links with domestic partners, they will be more willing and able to invest major resources abroad. Such investments will not typically be associated with suppliers and customers also moving to foreign locations.

Another difference between cooperative and isolated hierarchies results from the contrasting ways in which they manage risk and uncertainty in their domestic economies. While the former firms share some of their investment and market risks with business partners and typically engage in relatively long-term commitments to particular business areas and capabilities, isolated ones manage such risks more on their own. Because of this, and the greater constraints on radical changes in business activities and skills imposed by such obligational linkages, cooperative hierarchies are less likely to make major discontinuous moves into different kinds of technologies and markets as a way of hedging against changes in their core industry.

Isolated hierarchies, on the other hand, are more able to undertake major switches of financial and other resources into novel sectors that are unrelated to their core technologies and markets. They also have more need to do so since they cannot rely on business partners to manage sector risks on a joint, cooperative basis. In general, then, we would expect isolated firms to control more widely varied and unconnected activities and resources than cooperative ones, and be more prone to move assets and business units between sectors discontinuously. As a result, they gain more experience and knowledge of managing activities in different kinds of industy and business conditions than do more sector-focused firms. This encourages their managers to believe that they can manage operations in foreign locations with different business environments effectively, and so is additionally likely to lead to higher rates of overseas investment by isolated hierarchies than equivalent cooperative hierarchies.

Furthermore, this greater experience of managing diverse activities and undertaking radical restructuring is likely to encourage managers of isolated hierarchies to delegate more operational control to foreign subsidiaries. Because the more diversified range of activities, technologies, and markets in such firms means that top managers have less detailed knowledge of particular industries and markets than in those that are less diversified, they tend to develop, and rely more on, financial measures of performance and planning. As a result, these firms have more techniques and procedures for managing diverse businesses in varied contexts that required substantial operational delegation than do managers of cooperative hierarchies, and so are likely to extend such decentralization to foreign subsidiaries. This tendency of many UK and US multinational firms to rely on financial performance and control systems is exemplified by the British company described by Kristensen and Zeitlin in Chapter 7.

This experience of, and confidence in, formal control systems mean that isolated hierarchies are, on the whole, more likely to manage 'at a distance' from most of their foreign units and not insist on them following domestic routines. Provided the formal procedures and targets are followed, subsidiaries will be quite able to adapt detailed practices to prevailing norms in different business environments, and will not be as fully integrated into their parents' operations as those of cooperative hierarchies, especially those taken over rather than being developed on a 'greenfield' basis. This means that they may well become quite integrated into their host economies with considerable local sourcing and product adaptation to local market conditions, as many subsidiaries of US firms seem to have done (Doremus et al. 1998). As a result, we would expect the foreign subsidiaries of isolated hierarchies to develop distinctive organizational capabilities at a faster rate than those of cooperative ones. FDI of these kinds of firm, then, is more likely to be located in relatively diverse environments and be limited in its integration, relative to that of cooperative hierarchies.

2.5. **Internationalization and Organizational Change**

This comparison of the internationalization patterns of three different kinds of firms suggests that cooperative hierarchies are less able to extend their prevalent ways of managing activities to subsidiaries in different kinds of business environment than are opportunistic and isolated hierarchies, unless they can transfer key features of their domestic business system. This implies that they will internationalize major activities more slowly and incrementally than isolated hierarchies, and initially replicate many of their domestic routines in foreign subsidiaries which will be quite integrated with domestic operations, especially those in similar kinds of business environments.

When they do invest substantial resources in quite different institutional settings, partly to innovate and learn from those environments as the German firms discussed by Lane in Chapter 3 have been doing in the 1990s, their overall degree of organizational integration has declined. With the possible exception of Hoechst—though exactly how its merger into Aventis will turn out remains to be seen—these companies seem to be quite differentiated between their 'collabora-tive' core in Germany and similar European countries, and their more varied non-European subsidiaries. Whether, and how, they will inte-grate these units into a new kind of enterprise remain unclear, but the above analysis suggests that this is unlikely to be achieved in the medium term, as long as the dominant institutions constituting their varied business environments remain stable and cohesive.

Additionally, the extent to which, and likely ways in which, these three types of firm do change as a result of investing major resources in foreign locations are also affected by the sorts of business envir-onment in which they establish subsidiaries. How firms from con-trasting business systems are likely to manage their FDI in particularistic, collaborative, and arm's length foreign economies is summarized in Table 2.4 and will now be discussed. Their main fea-tures can be analysed along similar lines to the patterns of interna-tionalization discussed above, beginning with the extent of FDI, the management of risks and control modes, then dealing with sub-sidiary characteristics and the extent of organizational learning that is likely to take place.

Considering, first, investment in particularistic environments, it seems unlikely that any of these kinds of firm will commit a large proportion of their key resources to countries where uncertainty over property rights and the reliability of formal institutions remains high. As one Japanese top manager put it when asked about investment in China in the early 1990s: 'we rent space there', rather than making irreversible commitments to such an environment. It might be thought that opportunistic firms would find it easier to manage sub-sidiaries in these kinds of society because they are more used to dealing with highly uncertain and unpredictable contexts and their domestic routines may be generalizable to similar kinds of culture and political economy. However, their general unwillingness to make irreversible commitments of substantial resources makes it unlikely that they would invest in large-scale facilities on a long-term basis abroad any more than they do at home.

When FDI in such locations does take place, typically because of the large potential market and/or major cost reductions, oppor-tunistic firms seem likely to follow the same strategy for managing risks as they do at home, i.e. maximizing flexibility, minimizing com-mitment, and developing close personal connections to those in power. This seems to be the dominant pattern reported by many authors in Yeung and Olds's *Globalization of Chinese Business Firms*

Table 2.4 *Firm type, foreign business environments, and management of FDI*

Management of FDI by different firm types	Types of foreign business environments		
	Particularistic	Collaborative	Arms' length
Significance of FDI			
Opportunistic firms	Low	Low	Low
Cooperative hierarchies	Low	Limited	Some
Isolated hierarchies	Low	Variable	Considerable
Prevalent risk management strategies			
Opportunistic firms	Flexibility, personal networks	Personal networks	Personal networks
Cooperative hierarchies	Market power	Market power and incremental alliances	Transfer domestic alliances and market power
Isolated hierarchies	Market power	Market power and short-term alliances	Market power and firm-specific advantages
Extent and mode of parent control of major subsidiaries			
Opportunistic firms	High, direct, personal	High, personal	High, personal
Cooperative hierarchies	High, direct, resource access	Considerable, resource access	Considerable, resource access
Isolated hierarchies	High, resource control and targets	Limited, formal targets	Limited, formal targets
Extent of subsidiary integration into local economy			
Opportunistic firms	Limited, ad hoc and short term	Limited and ad hoc	Limited and ad hoc
Cooperative hierarchies	Limited and ad hoc	Limited and incremental	Limited
Isolated hierarchies	Some, but short term	Considerable	Considerable
Subsidiary development of distinctive capabilities			
Opportunistic firms	Low	Low	Low
Cooperative hierarchies	Low	Limited	Limited
Isolated hierarchies	Low	Considerable	Considerable where host economy differs significantly
Extent of organizational learning and change from FDI			
Opportunistic firms	Low	Limited	Limited
Cooperative hierarchies	Low	Limited, but more complex	Limited, but more complex
Isolated hierarchies	Low	Limited, but more complex	Some, increased complexity

(2000). Cooperative and isolated hierarchies, on the other hand, are likely to be much larger and be able to exert market power over local business partners and the state. Since institutional regulation of economic relationships is weak in these environments, relying primarily on economic dominance and straightforward short-term advantages seems more probable than developing long-term collaborations or formal structures.

Similarly, the high level of uncertainty encourages strong parental control of subsidiaries in such economies. This will be exercised differently by the different kinds of firm, as outlined above. As a result, their adaptation to local norms and practices will be limited to the minimum necessary to ensure efficient operations in a similar manner to that practised in the home country. The combination of limited commitment, strong central control, and considerable technology and product dependence on the parent company limits the likelihood that subsidiaries in particularistic environments will develop distinctive organizational competences or become highly integrated into local economies. Equally, few MNCs are likely to change their organizational routines much as a result of investing in such societies.

Collaborative business environments, on the other hand, are more predictable and consist of coordinated social systems that encourage longer-term commitments and cooperation. They are, therefore, less risky sites for FDI than particularistic ones. However, foreign firms may find it difficult to gain access to the established networks and alliances that dominate such economies, at least initially. They also have to adapt to prevailing norms and practices that are quite strongly institutionalized in these societies. Since dominant business practices typically involve considerable authority-sharing and mutual commitments, opportunistic firms seem unlikely to make major investments in them.

Cooperative hierarchies, in contrast, are used to these sorts of arrangement, but of course are embedded in different alliances in their home economies. They will therefore limit their commitments to new partnerships initially and proceed incrementally. Given the coordinated nature of these host economies, and the strength of institutional arrangements, the likelihood that cooperative firms could extend their domestic network to such foreign locations is low. As a result, when they do invest in such environments these kinds of company are likely to integrate their subsidiaries quite strongly into their parent firm's operations and only slowly develop local linkages.

Isolated hierarchies have less close links with domestic business partners and institutions, but are also less familiar with the benefits that cooperation can bring and less willing to invest in the development of long-term linkages. It seems probable, then, that their commitments to collaborative environments will have shorter time horizons than those of cooperative hierarchies, but may be quite sizeable where market opportunities and technological learning possibilities seem attractive. The extent of their FDI in these kinds of location, then, is quite variable.

The risks of FDI in these contexts are likely to be managed differently by these three types of firm. Opportunistic ones have few organizational capabilities and are unwilling to enter into long-term commitments, so alliances and partnerships remain unusual for these sorts of company. Cooperative hierarchies, on the other hand, will probably try to develop such linkages, but slowly and incrementally as they learn about the new environment and adapt to it. This is especially likely when the host market is large and wealthy and its institutions are strong, as in Japan. Isolated hierarchies may also adapt to dominant mores, but are also likely to rely on market power to short-circuit the process of building alliances as well as on their firm-specific competitive advantages to attract local business partners. Where they do pursue local partnerships and adapt to local practices, as perhaps many US firms have done in Japan, they often find it difficult to integrate such subsidiaries into the global organization. This suggests that MNCs with major subsidiaries in a variety of strong collaborative environments will be limited in the extent of their organizational integration.

While these environments are not as uncertain and threatening as particularistic ones are, and so do not encourage high levels of direct control by the parent company, the pervasiveness of nationally based networks and alliances, and the generally uneven 'playing field', increase subsidiary dependence on the parent company, except of course for those taken over. Opportunistic firms will, in any case, continue to exercise strong direct control over foreign subsidiaries as they do at home, as long as their domestic environment remains unpredictable and particularistic. Cooperative hierarchies might be more willing to allow subsidiaries to 'learn' about their novel environment and adopt new ways of doing things, at least as long as they have not committed major resources to it, but are likely to try to control them through access to key resources.

Isolated hierarchies, on the other hand, are more experienced with formal control systems and also more confident of their ability to manage diverse activities in varied environments through such mechanisms. Granting considerable autonomy to units in collaborative environments that are seen as 'different', as long as they meet financial and other targets, will therefore seem quite reasonable to these kinds of firm, as seems to be the case in the firm discussed by Kristensen and Zeitlin in Chapter 7. Later on, of course, global integration may become more pressing as companies try to build on and extend their firm-specific advantages across major markets, but this will not be easy where foreign subsidiaries have successfully adapted to varied kinds of business environments.

This willingness to tolerate subsidiary autonomy means that local units of isolated firms will be more likely to adapt to collaborative host economy conventions and practices than those of cooperative and opportunistic firms. However, because these norms are more organized and institutionalized in these kinds of business environment than those of particularistic ones, they will have more sustained impact, albeit incremental, on foreign subsidiaries of both cooperative and isolated hierarchies. Both German and US firms, for example, can be expected to adapt more over time to Japanese practices and institutionalized expectations than they would in China and similar contexts. Both kinds of environment encourage accommodating behaviour to dominant conventions, but the more systemic and strongly institutionalized Japanese environment is more likely to lead subsidiaries to adopt organizational routines that fit local norms as major components of their organization and strategies than is the less systematically integrated and more volatile Chinese one.

The greater autonomy of isolated firms' subsidiaries enables them to develop distinctive organizational capabilities at an earlier stage than foreign units of cooperative hierarchies or opportunistic firms, especially if they have been acquired. As subsidiaries of cooperative companies become more integrated into host economies, they develop particular routines and linkages to local partners that differ from those of their parent and are more isomorphic with the host economy than those of isolated hierarchies. However, this seems likely to take quite a time for new business units. Similarly, the more autonomous subsidiaries of isolated MNCs can be expected to source more of their inputs from local suppliers, including technological services, as well as relying on local distribution channels. Those from cooperative hierarchies will rely more on products and technologies from the parent, as discussed above, or they may seek to reproduce domestic partnerships and connections with local subsidiaries of domestic allies. Opportunistic firms are likely to be governed by short-term price considerations in deciding where to buy supplies, and perhaps also by personal ties.

Overall, then, opportunistic firms seem least likely to adopt new routines and practices as a result of investing in collaborative environments. They are unlikely to commit major resources to such economies and, equally, are unwilling to enter into collaborative, reciprocal linkages with business partners, including workers. Cooperative hierarchies are also unlikely to commit substantial investments to such economies in the early stages of their internationalization, and will 'learn' only incrementally when they do so invest. Once established, and if subsidiaries do become integrated into the host economy, however, their tendency to integrate units across borders may well generate some more significant changes in routines than occurs in isolated firms.

Isolated hierarchies are the most probable to undertake major investments in these kinds of economies, often through acquisitions, and to grant subsidiaries considerable autonomy to develop their own ways of dealing with the local conventions. However, if these subsidiaries do become distinctive kinds of organizations with routines that are different from those of the parent company, it will be difficult to integrate these more collaborative ways of coordinating economic activities with the whole enterprise because both the domestic context of isolated hierarchies and the international business environment are antagonistic to such patterns. It seems unlikely therefore that such firms that have invested extensively in collaborative business environments and developed subsidiaries that are successful in them will radically change the basic characteristics of the whole organization. Learning in the sense of institutionalizing new routines based on these foreign subsidiaries, then, is unlikely to be highly significant in such firms.

Arm's length business environments are perhaps the most open to FDI because formal regulatory norms are quite institutionalized and, in theory, equally applicable to all enterprises. To a considerable extent, then, foreign firms compete on a 'level playing field' with local ones. Neither particularistic connections nor membership of local networks grant host economy firms especially strong competitive advantages in these kinds of economies—or at least not as major ones as they do in the other two contexts just considered. Opportunistic firms, though, are no more likely to commit major resources to them than to other ones because of their anxiety about control and flexibility. While some may invest in leading economies to obtain access to new technologies and markets, the ways they have managed the unsupportive, if not antagonistic, environment at home will limit the size and centrality of FDI.

Cooperative and isolated hierarchies, on the other hand, have considerable organizational competencies for coordinating economic activities and experience of making large-scale commitments. However, the former have less familiarity with adversarial environments and fewer firm-specific advantages that can be detached and transferred from their domestic environment. They are therefore unlikely to make major investments in these sorts of economy without gaining prior experience of their dominant conventions, and so will proceed cautiously. Isolated firms, on the other hand, will be more confident of managing significant activities in these kinds of context effectively and so be more willing to make substantial commitments.

Risk management strategies and parent control practices in arm's length environments often follow the logic of firms' domestic economies, since local institutional pressures to conform to a single dominant set of business practices in all functional areas are weak. The formality and pluralism of dominant governance mechanisms in such societies permit more variation across such areas than they do in more integrated environments, so that incoming investors have some scope for introducing their own practices in particular fields (Rosenzweig and Nohria 1994).

Thus, opportunistic firms develop personal networks, often amongst similar ethnic groups, while cooperative hierarchies may well encourage domestic partners to establish subsidiaries in the same locations so that they can share risks with them and rely on established relationships to reduce uncertainty in the new environment. This, of course, implies that such firms reproduce domestic connections in the major overseas subsidiaries and maintain a high level of international integration. Their involvement in local host economies remains relatively low, as does their adaptation to local practices and conventions in many functional areas. As a result, subsidiaries' development of distinctive organizational characteristics and capabilities is limited. The many studies of Japanese subsidiaries in the UK and the USA illustrate such behaviours (see, for example, Elger and Smith 1994; Kenney and Florida 1993).

Isolated hierarchies, on the other hand, are used to managing risks internally and have competitive advantages that are more firm-specific than shared with business partners. They are therefore likely

to manage risks in much the same way as they do domestically,
through their market power and organizational skills, and rely on
standard control procedures to integrate foreign units. Since these
environments are similar to their domestic one, these kinds of firm
will probably grant considerable autonomy to foreign subsidiaries,
provided they meet formal targets, and so they are quite likely to
become integrated into the local economy, adapt to host conventions,
and develop distinctive organizational capabilities.

In terms of organizational learning from establishing subsidiaries
in arm's length environments, this is clearly going to be limited in the
case of opportunistic firms, both because they are not likely to make
major investments and because when they do set up subsidiaries,
these will have limited autonomy and organizational capabilities.
Cooperative hierarchies also limit their subsidiaries' adaptation to
local norms and integration into host economies, but as they learn
more about operating in adversarial environments and integrating
operations across borders, they may well develop more novel routines and adapt to host contexts. Especially in internationally competitive economies where they can obtain access to new technologies
and markets, such firms attempt to develop new competitive advantages that will be firm-specific and so can be generalized throughout
the whole organization.

An example of this kind of learning—or intention to acquire new
knowledge and organizational capabilities—is provided by the investments by some German chemical and pharmaceuticals companies in
US medical research organizations and biotechnology companies,
and, to a lesser extent, by some Japanese banks' investments in London
and New York (Sakai 2000). Partly for regulatory reasons and partly
because these locations were seen to possess advantages that could not
be accessed domestically, firms from collaborative environments
made substantial commitments to the Anglo-Saxon economies in the
1980s. More recently, other German firms in different industries have
begun to seek New York Stock Exchange listings and acquisitions in
the USA as a way of gaining more autonomy from domestic institutional pressures, especially labour management restrictions, and to
develop new capabilities that, in principle, could be repatriated (Lane
1998 and Chapter 3 in this volume; Mueller 1996; Mueller and
Loveridge 1997).

As Lane discusses in Chapter 3, some of these investments have
been made in a different way from previous FDI by German and
Japanese firms, in that the parent companies have not sought to

reproduce largely their domestic practices in new local settings. They have, rather, attempted to learn new practices and routines from the novel environment that could be applied elsewhere, and/or to try out new managerial ideas in a more acquiescent context than their home economy. While some may have been successful in acquiring new scientific knowledge in the biomedical fields, many German firms were rather slow in reacting to the changed scientific and market conditions in pharmaceuticals during the 1980s, according to Casper (2000). They have also tended to develop different biotechnology strategies from their US competitors, largely as a result of their domestic institutional contexts.

Although these companies have deliberately focused on acquiring new knowledge and skills from a different environment, they have adapted to the changed nature of the pharmaceuticals industry by differentiating locations and functions in the production chain, rather than radically changing the nature of their domestic organization and governance structure. Hoechst and Bayer, for example, have committed considerable resources in accessing the US science base in biotechnology, through direct investment and collaborative agreements with universities and biotechnology companies, but retain the bulk of their resources in Germany where their organization and control remain much the same as before, despite some decentralization, according to Casper and Matraves (1999). Whether Hoechst will become transformed into a more 'Anglo-Saxon' enterprise as part of the Franco-German Aventis remains to be seen.

This separation of activities across environments is facilitated by the highly codified nature of the knowledge involved, much more so than development and manufacturing know-how. As Kogut and Zander (1993) have emphasized, codification and teachability of knowledge enable technologies to be more easily transferred between firms than when they are highly dependent on tacit knowledge, and this contrast affects the degree of internal integration of activities within firms as well (Howells 1998). Similarly, the German car companies that sought to use the greater scope of the arm's length business environment by developing novel managerial and organizational practices and routines have yet to demonstrate that these are compatible with their traditional strengths in the making of high value and innovative products (Lane 1998 and Chapter 3 in this volume). While, then, it may be possible in the longer term for cooperative hierarchies to learn from adversarial environments and then generalize their lessons to the whole organization, the strength of domestic institutions and continued ties to business partners will constrain the extent of such changes.

In the case of many Japanese banks, while they may have learnt how to participate in international financial markets, it seems that they largely bought market share in the late 1980s and 1990s by financing bond issues and similar instruments at a loss, and most focused the bulk of their activities on servicing their traditional Japanese customers (Sakai 2000). Indeed, according to Sakai, these companies continued to regard international activities and the people who managed these as less important than domestic ones, so that they were not really interested in 'learning' from their London and New York subsidiaries. This may, however, be changing as the result of the restructuring of Japanese banks and the financial system in general at the end of the 1990s (Morgan et al. 2000). In the case of much Japanese manufacturing FDI, many business partners in the USA and the UK are Japanese rather than local, and knowledge transfer has tended to be from the new investors to local firms rather than the converse.

Isolated hierarchies operating subsidiaries in arm's length environments are likely to assume that their firm-specific competitive advantages can be equally successful abroad as at home, and may be unwilling to 'learn' from foreign experiences. As they adapt to local conditions, though, subsidiaries will develop different routines and practices, which, if effective, will lead to distinctive organizational competences. Since these are firm-specific and not closely tied to particular links with local business partners and institutions, they could in principle be appropriated by the whole organization. Whether they will be depends, inter alia, on the strength of the domestic business system—and so the perceived need to change—and the extent to which the new practices would replace strongly entrenched practices that are closely tied to major domestic institutions such as the financial and legal systems. Just as learning from foreign firms investing in one's home economy is affected by the centrality of the practices concerned and their interdependent institutions, so too is learning from a firm's own foreign subsidiaries.

2.6. Conclusion

This discussion of how different kinds of firm from different business systems and institutional contexts are likely to conduct their FDI in contrasting business environments emphasizes the continuing importance of their domestic institutions and established ways of coordinating economic activities in their home economies. When these are cohesive and highly integrated, they have considerable impact on (1) the amount and type of FDI undertaken, (2) how much autonomy subsidiaries are allowed, (3) how much they become integrated into host economies, and (4) how much impact their learning from host economies has upon domestic routines.

Even when MNCs deliberately undertake major FDI in quite different business environments to gain knowledge and learn from contrasting ways of organizing economic activities, as in the case of the German pharmaceutical investments in US biotechnology research, it seems that this encourages organizational differentiation rather than significant restructuring and innovation in domestic routines. The home economy institutions and practices remain largely in place despite a considerable amount of research now being located in the USA and managed in line with US practices. This is an example of MNCs encouraging considerable learning at the local subsidiary level, but separating these organizational innovations from their domestic operations and so reducing the degree of integration in the firm as a whole. While the highly codified nature of much of the knowledge presumably means that such differentiation does not prevent its effective transfer between research and development, production and marketing—and so is a feasible strategy in this industry at a time of radical change—it remains to be seen how viable it would be in other circumstances.

In any event, this case, together with the German vehicle manufacturers discussed by Lane in her chapter, suggest that when cooperative hierarchies do invest major resources in arm's length business environments, and adapt to the conventions and practices of such environments, they may prefer to manage the subsequent organizational innovations by differentiating units and functions rather than by incorporating them into the parent organization and so radically transforming it. This is especially so where their domestic operations remain effective in key value-added functions and strong institutional pressures reproduce established routines.

Such a combination of segmented functions in varied business environments with some organizational integration represents a different kind of MNC from the four ideal types discussed above. It differs from the fragmented type by being more coordinated—necessarily so, since the subunits perform specialized functions within production chains—and yet is less dominated by standardized routines across all major subsidiaries. In this, it is highly dependent on the outputs from upstream units being sufficiently codified so that they can be transferred effectively to downstream ones across major institutional boundaries without incurring high transaction costs. While, then, codification and teachability of knowledge in general facilitate technological transfers across firm boundaries, in this case they enable cooperative hierarchies to operate major facilities in quite diverse environments without having to change domestic routines radically. Ownership integration here presumably enables sufficient control to ensure effective coordination and low spillover dangers, while differentiation across environments limits organizational upheavals and conflicts with key institutions and agencies.

A more common pattern of internationalization for firms in highly coordinated environments is to rely initially on exports because of their dependence on business partners and employees for competitive advantages, and hence the limited extent to which the managerial hierarchy can appropriate and transfer such advantages abroad. Additionally, their initial lack of experience of coordinating economic activities in anomic and adversarial environments inhibits managers in these firms from readily making major investments in distant foreign locations. When they do undertake significant FDI, the nature of the domestic business system and its associated institutions encourages risk-sharing with home country partners and close integration of foreign subsidiaries with parent operations. In general, then, subsidiaries of cooperative hierarchies located abroad tend to be only weakly integrated into host economies and to limit organizational innovations based on adaptation to local norms. In sum, without substantial changes in domestic institutions, these kinds of firm are unlikely to change their governance characteristics or organizational capabilities as a result of FDI, but may become more varied, differentiated, and complex organizations.

The influence of the home business system and institutional environment on FDI management and its consequences are equally important for opportunistic enterprises. As long as the domestic business environment remains highly particularistic and discourages long-term investments in building organizational capabilities and authority-sharing, FDI by these kinds of firms will be limited to relatively peripheral activities with short-term payback periods. Additionally, these activities will be located predominantly in environments where personal networks and common conventions facilitate high levels of direct control. When these firms invest in different kinds of business system, such as the compartmentalized one that develops in arm's length institutional contexts, any learning that does take place in subsidiaries is unlikely to impinge greatly upon the domestic organization because the institutional supports for predictable, formal procedures and control systems to manage activities are absent in the home economy. The transformation of Chinese family businesses in Pacific-Asia into Anglo-Saxon corporations as a result of investments in the USA is, then, improbable, and their key characteristics are unlikely to change significantly (Yeung and Olds 2000).

It is interesting to note in this connection that the developing linkages between Silicon Valley and firms in the Hsinchu Science Park in Taiwan are quite personal and particularistic according to Saxenian (1998, 2000). These Taiwanese firms have benefited considerably from state support and in some cases the personal patronage of leading figures in the political elite (Hung and Whittington 1997), and so have had a much greater public profile than the typical small firm in the export sector (see, for example, Hamilton 1997; Shieh 1992). Their owners have therefore felt more able to share risks and develop their own brands, as well as undertaking investments beyond the Asian region. Unlike many Japanese and Korean investors in North America, however, they have preferred to keep links with US firms flexible and tied to personal networks rather than hierarchically integrating them as directly controlled subsidiaries. Where a few Taiwanese firms have made relatively large-scale commitments to wholly owned subsidiaries in the USA—and in the UK—they have not been very successful. In other words, a major part of the success of this trans-Pacific integration of economic activities seems to be due to its consonance with the traditional Taiwanese way of managing transactions, although Saxenian also suggests that these science park firms have become partly 'Americanized' as a result of recruiting US-trained and experienced engineers and managers.

In the case of isolated hierarchies, their foreign subsidiaries are more likely to adapt to local ways of doing things and be relatively integrated into their local economies. These firms, then, become more complex and differentiated organizations as the result of investing considerable resources in different kinds of business system. However, the impact of such local learning on the basic governance and capabilities characteristics of the parent firms will be restricted by the weakly institutionalized international business environment and the largely arm's length domestic institutional context.

If, for instance, a US firm invests significant resources in Japan, and even makes that subsidiary the leading one for product development in a particular area, as Proctor and Gamble did for babies' nappies, the cohesion of the host business system and strength of its institutions will encourage the Japanese subsidiary to manage its internal and external relationships in different ways from those current at home. However, the transferability of such practices and routines to other subsidiaries or to the parent company will be discouraged by the varied labour market institutions, state structures and policies, and financial systems in different societies, and the difficulty of generalizing business partner commitments across institutional contexts.

To change the US firms' governance characteristics and capabilities significantly as a result of such investment would require substantial changes in domestic institutions, and probably the importation of its Japanese business partners to the USA in a similar manner to the Japanese transplants. This is not to say that no transfer of managerial technologies can occur, but to emphasize that these will be relatively codified and context independent, and will not make a significant impact on the sorts of basic firm features summarized in Table 2.1.

The overall conclusion to be drawn from this analysis, then, is that MNCs from distinctive and cohesive business systems with strong associated institutions governing economic activities may well become more complex and differentiated as a result of FDI—and so encourage novel forms of coordination to develop—but are unlikely to change their fundamental characteristics. Opportunistic firms are less likely to make significant foreign commitments in the first place, and so will change to an even lesser extent. The key variables here are the strength, cohesion, and integration of domestic institutions and their associated systems of economic coordination and control. As long as these domestic business environments remain distinctive and cohesive, and the international business environment is relatively anomic with weakly institutionalized norms and procedures governing business practices, FDI is likely to increase the organizational complexity without changing the nature of the firms engaging in it.

REFERENCES

Bartlett, C. A. and Ghoshal, S. (1989), *Managing Across Borders: The Transnational Solution*. London: Hutchinson Business Books.

Bartlett, C. A., Doz, Y. and Hedlund, G. (eds.) (1990), *Managing the Global Firm*. London: Routledge.

Braithwaite, J. and Drahos, P. (2000), *Global Business Regulation*. Cambridge: Cambridge University Press.

Casper, S. (2000), 'Institutional Adaptiveness, Technology Policy and the Diffusion of New Business Models: The Case of German Biotechnology', *Organization Studies*, 21: 887–914.

Casper, S. and Matraves, C. (1999), 'The Influence of Corporate Governance Structures on Firm Innovation Strategy in the Pharmaceutical Industry', unpublished paper, WZB and NIAS.

Dicken, P. (1998), *Global Shift*. London: Paul Chapman Publishing.

Dicken, P., Forsgren, M. and Malmberg, A. (1994), 'The Local Embeddedness of Transnational Corporations', in A. Amin and N. Thrift (eds.), *Globalization, Institutions and Regional Development in Europe*. Oxford: Oxford University Press.

Doremus, P. N., Keller, W. W, Pauly, L. W. and Reich, S. (1998), *The Myth of the Global Corporation*. Princeton, NJ: Princeton University Press.

Elger, T. and Smith C. (eds.) (1994), *Global Japanization?* London: Routledge.

—— (1998), 'New Town, New Capital, New Workplace? The Employment Relations of Japanese Inward Investors in a West Midlands New Town', *Economy and Society*. 27: 523–53.

Gates, H. (1996), *China's Motor: A Thousand Years of Petty Capitalism*. New York: Cornell University Press.

Ghoshal, S. and Westney, E. (1993), 'Introduction and Overview', in S. Ghoshal and E. Westney (eds.), *Organization Theory and the Multinational Corporation*, London: Macmillan, 1–23.

Hamilton, G. (1997), 'Organization and Market Processes in Taiwan's Capitalist', in M. Orru et al., *The Economic Organization of East Asian Capitalism*. Thousand Oaks, California: Sage, 237–93.

Hedlund, G. and Ridderstrale, J. (1998), 'Toward a Theory of the Self-renewing MNC', in W. G. Egelhoff (ed.), *Transforming International Organizations*. Cheltenham: E. Elgar, 168–93.

Heiduk, G. and Hodges, U. (1992), 'German Multinationals in Europe: Patterns and Perspectives', in M. W. Klein and P. Welfens (eds.), *Multinationals in the New Europe and Global Trade*. Berlin and New York: Springer Verlag.

Held, D., McGraw, A., Goldblatt, D. and Perraton, J. (1999), *Global Transformations*. Cambridge: Polity Press.

Hirst, P. and Thompson, G. (1996), *Globalization in Question*. Cambridge: Polity Press.

Howells, J. (1998), 'Innovation and Technology Transfer within Multinational Firms' in J. Michie and J. Grieve Smith (eds.), *Globalization, Growth and Governance*. Oxford: Oxford University Press.

Hu, Y.-S. (1992), 'Global Firms are National Firms with International Operations', *California Management Review*, 34: 107–26.

Hung, S. and Whittington, R. (1997), 'Strategies and Institutions: A Pluralistic Account of Strategies in the Taiwanese Computer Industry', *Organization Studies*, 18: 551–75.

Jones, G. (1996), *The Evolution of International Business: An Introduction*. London: Routledge.

Kenney, M. and Florida, R. (1993), *Beyond Mass Production*. Oxford: Oxford University Press.

Kenworthy, L. (1997), 'Globalization and Economic Convergence', *Competition and Change*, 2: 1–64.

Koechlin, T. (1995), 'The Globalization of Investment', *Contemporary Economic Policy*, 13: 92–100.

Kogut, B. (1993), 'Learning, or the Importance of Being Inert: Country Imprinting and International Competition', in S. Ghoshal and E. Westney (eds.), *Organization Theory and the Multinational Corporation*. London: Macmillan.

Kogut, B. and Zander, U. (1993), 'Knowledge of the Firm and the Evolutionary Theory of the Multinational Corporation', *Journal of International Business Studies*, 24: 625–45.

Lane, C. (1989), *Management and Labour in Europe*. Aldershot: Edward Elgar.

—— (1992), 'European Business Systems: Britain and Germany Compared', in R. Whitley (ed.), *European Business Systems: Firms and Markets in their National Contexts*. London: Sage, 64–97.

—— (1997), 'The Governance of Interfirm Relations in Britain and Germany: Societal or Dominance Effects,' in R. Whitley and P. H. Kristensen (eds.), *Governance at Work: The Social Regulation of Economic Relations*. Oxford: Oxford University Press, 62–85.

—— (1998), 'European Companies between Globalization and Localization: A Comparison of Internationalization Strategies of British and German MNCs', *Economy and Society*, 27: 462–85.

Lane, C. and Bachmann, R. (1996), 'The Social Constitution of Trust', *Organization Studies*, 17: 365–96.

Lazonick, W. (1991), *Business Organization and the Myth of the Market Economy*. Cambridge: Cambridge University Press.

Lazonick, W. and West, J. (1998), 'Organizational Integration and Competitive Advantage', in G. Dosi, D. J. Teece, and J. Chytry (eds.), *Technology, Organization and Competitiveness*. Oxford: Oxford University Press, 247–88.

Morgan, G., Kelly, W., Sharpe, D. and Whitley, R. (2000), 'Discourses of Freedom and Constraint: Japanese Expatriate Managers in the UK', presented to the International Conference on Organisational Discourse, Kings' College London, July.

Mueller, F. (1996), 'National Stakeholders in the Global Contest for Corporate Investment', *European Journal of Industrial Relations*, 2: 345–68.

Mueller, F. and Loveridge, R. (1997), 'Institutional, Sectoral and Corporate Dynamics in the Creation of Global Supply Chains', in R. Whitley and P. H. Kristensen (eds.), *Governance at Work*. Oxford: Oxford University Press, 139–57.

Penrose, E. (1959), *The Theory of the Growth of the Firm*. Oxford: Blackwell.

Porter, M. E. (1986), 'Competition in Global Industries: A Conceptual Framework', in M. E. Porter (ed.), *Competition in Global Industries*. Boston: Harvard Business School Press.

Redding, S. G. (1990), *The Spirit of Chinese Capitalism*. Berlin: de Gruyter.

Rosenzweig, P. M. and Nohria, N. (1994), 'Influences on Human Resource Management Practices in Multinational Corporations', *Journal of International Business Studies*, 25: 229–51.

Ruigrok, W. and van Tulder, R. (1995), *The Logic of International Restructuring*. London: Routledge.

Sakai, J. (2000), *Japanese Bankers in the City of London*, London: Routledge.

Sako, M. (1992), *Prices, Quality and Trust*. Cambridge: Cambridge University Press.

Sally, R. (1994), 'Multinational Enterprises, Political Economy and Institutional Theory: Domestic Embeddedness in the Context of Internationalisation', *Review of International Political Economy*, 1: 161–92.

—— (1995), *States and Firms: Multinational Enterprises in Institutional Competition*, London: Routledge.

Saxenian, A.-L. (1998), 'Silicon Valley's New Immigrant Entrepreneurs and their Asian Networks', presented to the International Conference on Business Transformation and Social Change in East Asia, held at the Institute of East Asian Economies and Societies, TungHai University, Taiwan, 22–3 May.

—— (2000), 'Transnational Entrepreneurs and Regional Industrialisation: The Silicon Valley and Hsinchu Connection', in T. Rueyling and B. Uzzi (eds.), *Embeddedness and Corporate Change in a Global Economy*. New York: Peter Lang, 283–302.

Shieh, G. S. (1992), *'Boss' Island: The Subcontracting Network and Microentrepreneurship in Taiwan's Development*. New York: Peter Lang.

Soskice, D. (1999), 'Divergent Production Regimes: Coordinated and Uncoordinated Market Economies in the 1980s and 1990s', in H. Kitschelt, P. Lange, G. Marks and J. Stephens (eds.), *Continuity and Change in Contemporary Capitalism*. Cambridge: Cambridge University Press, 101–34.

Teubner, G. (2001), 'Legal Irritants: Good Faith in British Law, or How Unifying Law Ends up in New Divergence', in P. Hall, and D. Soskice (eds.), *Varieties of Capitalism*. Oxford: Oxford University Press.

Tylecote, A. and Conesa, E. (1999), 'Corporate Governance, Innovation Systems and Industrial Performance', *Industry and Innovation*, 6: 25–50.

Westney, E. (1993), 'Institutionalization Theory and the Multinational Corporation', in S. Ghoshal and E. Westney (eds.), *Organization Theory and the Multinational Corporation*. London: Macmillan, 53–76.

—— (1999), 'Organization Theory Perspectives on the Cross-border Transfer of Organizational Practices', in J. K. Liker, W. M. Fruin and P. S. Adler (eds.), *Remade in America: Transplanting and Transforming Japanese Management Systems*. Oxford: Oxford University Press, 385–406.

Whitley, R. (1998), 'Internationalisation and Varieties of Capitalism: The Limited Effects of Cross-national Coordination of Economic Activities on the Nature of Business Systems', *Review of International Political Economy*, 5: 445–81.

—— (1999), *Divergent Capitalisms: The Social Structuring and Change of Business Systems*. Oxford: Oxford University Press.

Yeung, H. W. and Olds, K. (eds.) (2000), *Globalization of Chinese Business Firms*. London: Macmillan.

3

The Emergence of German Transnational Companies: A Theoretical Analysis and Empirical Study of the Globalization Process

CHRISTEL LANE

3.1. Introduction

German multinational companies (MNCs) have long stood out among companies from the most highly developed economies for their late start on the road to globalization and the relatively low degree of globalization attained (Doremus et al. 1998; Dörre 1996; Lane 1998; Ruigrok and van Tulder 1995). This fact has been connected with their exceptionally deep embeddedness in a highly cohesive business system and their dependence for factor creation and reproduction on the institutions which constitute this system (Lane 1998; Whitley 1999 and Chapter 2 in this volume). Whitley goes even further and suggests that companies from highly integrated and cohesive business systems—collaborative hierarchies—are unlikely to become transnational companies or, in his own terminology, do not become hybrid MNCs. He thus envisages systemic factors, namely constraints arising from deep domestic embeddedness and close inter-organizational ties, to constitute the reasons for this arrested development. During the later years of the 1990s, however, German companies' cross-border activities have begun to change in significant ways, indicating a move towards transnational status. Prompted by this apparent inconsistency between theoretical analysis and empirical developments, this chapter pursues two objectives: first, it critically examines Whitley's and other theoretical statements on companies' globalization activities and suggests a new approach to the study of such activities; secondly, it aims to show the utility of this new approach by applying it to in-depth case studies of globalization tendencies in seven German companies.

Globalization is a highly contested concept, and the degree to which it has been realized remains a contentious issue. This is true even when the object and focus of study are the same—MNCs and their changing structures and activities. The ideal-typical definitions of the MNC, operating in an international economy, and the transnational corporation (TNC), found in a global economy, provided by Hirst and Thompson (1996), serve as a useful starting point. MNCs spread their activity across national borders but remain, in most of their activities, embedded in the institutional environment of their home country. TNCs, in contrast, have become integrated into an autonomous world economic system, no longer have a national home base, but produce, source, and market on a global scale. Building on the latter definition, as well as on Hassel et al. (1999) and Morgan (1999), TNCs may be said to possess the following features: (1) a wide geographical dispersion of affiliates, indicated by a presence in all triad regions; (2) coordination of the stages of the value chain across locational sites; (3) the granting of a measure of autonomy and of resources to local affiliates by the parent company, in order to upgrade their activities; (4) financial integration of the company into the global economy, indicated by quotation on triad stock markets, adoption of international accounting standards, and a strategy of 'shareholder value', as well as some foreign ownership in the company; and (5) the development of a new organizational structure and process of interaction, with features of a 'differentiated network' (Nohria and Ghoshal 1997). Such organizational change may be a result of both growing complexity of coordination and the changed financial orientation, particularly the adoption of a strategy of 'shareholder value'.

The theoretical literature on the process of companies' globalization, i.e. transformation from multinational to transnational status, may be simplified to the following basic theoretical stances. The two extreme positions in the globalization literature either posit highly autonomous and footloose transnational companies, operating in a new global space, independent of any home country (Ohmae 1990) or view 'globalization as myth', with even MNCs remaining so deeply embedded in their home environment as to rule out the autonomous action and independence associated with transnational status (Hirst and Thompson 1996). Between these two extreme positions there now exist more nuanced theoretical stances. Authors adopting such an in-between position do not rule out the transformation of MNCs into TNCs but view such a process as the highly variable result of different causal influences. They see globalization activities either as responses to global contingencies where global competition generates isomorphic pressure to follow global 'best practice' (Bartlett and Ghoshal 1989) or as shaped by embeddedness in a particular domestic business system and developing in a largely path-dependent way (Doremus et al. 1998; Lane 1998; Ruigrok and van Tulder 1995; Whitley 1999 and Chapter 2 in this volume).

Although these approaches offer some useful insights into what shapes company strategies, on its own neither analysis fully encompasses the complexity of companies' globalization (Dörrenbächer 1999). Whitley's theoretical position is sociologically much more sophisticated than that of Bartlett and Ghoshal (1989) in that it envisages differing capacities for action in companies from varying home environments, depending on the degree of domestic embeddedness. But both sets of theorists, in very different ways, conceptualize the MNC as passively exposed to and constrained by either the domestic system in which it is located or by global contingencies. Both sets of analysts fail to allow for any independent capacity for strategic action that a company may possess. Although Whitley (in Chapter 2) now envisages that mature MNCs, with long experience of transnational activity, may engage in some activities that are not congruent with the logic of their national business system, he sees this as very exceptional behaviour.

Such independent strategic capacity should not, however, be excluded from the outset. Actors' responses are shaped by both constraints from the domestic business system and by new strategic openings, afforded by tensions and contradictions within that system, created by new global pressures and opportunities (Morgan 1999). Such strategic openings may even be used to circumvent the constraints imposed by the national business system and to engage in innovative activity. Moreover, such strategic action is not always internally coherent, nor is strategy necessarily consistent with actual behaviour. This lack of unity reflects not only conflicting constraints and opportunities, but also internal dissension over how to respond to them. It is useful to view international firms as organizations with complex internal processes of contradiction and conflict and a company's globalization path as the outcome of political negotiation between powerful actors in and around the company (see Morgan's contribution in Chapter 1). Powerful actors at both the central and subsidiary level of a company are responding to new global (often industry-specific) challenges, as posited by Bartlett and Ghoshal (1989) and within the constraints also of their national business system (Whitley, Chapter 2). But, in addition, actors also respond according to their own particular interests. Outcomes, in this approach, are the result of struggle and compromise between actors, constrained and enabled by their environment. Organizational order, as Morgan rightly observes in Chapter 1, is often contingent and precarious in nature. The degree and kind of constraint experienced by a company and its top managers vary with the nature of the business system (Whitley 1999 and Chapter 2 this volume), but in no case should the latter be viewed as making companies its passive captives, which act in a unified and predictable manner.

The position taken in this chapter is in contrast to both global contingency approaches and most institutionalist analyses. It conceptualizes companies as strategic actors, who, although constrained by the national business system, simultaneously possess some capacity for independent action. Such a theoretical understanding of TNCs is able to account for the complex mixture of strategic claims and activities present within individual TNCs, as well as explain the variety of structural forms and strategic orientations within the same business system and even the same industry.

Applying this theoretical approach to German companies' emergent globalization tendencies, this chapter aims to contribute to the debate on the following questions. Whether and to what degree German MNCs are changing in the direction of the transnational type; what routes are being taken; how this change comes about; and how identified patterns might be explained. Posed in terms of Whitley's theoretical approach in Chapter 2, this chapter explores how mature MNCs from a collaborative business environment expand their activities in contrasting business systems and how this impacts on company activity and on organizational and financial forms.

Companies that transform themselves from an MNC to a TNC change their structural and cultural characteristics. Whereas MNCs had their features shaped by the institutional environment of their home country, TNCs are additionally influenced by one or more host countries. Therefore, TNCs may experience hybridization. The latter is regarded as the outcome of the active process of integration into the global system of individual companies (Tolliday et al. 1998;

Whitley 1999 and Chapter 2 in this volume). Subsidiaries, which enjoy a high level of autonomy and of resources, become embedded also into their host countries. This will lead to learning processes and to the adoption of new organizational structures, practices, and competences. In so far as subsidiaries remain integrated into the company through ties with other subsidiaries and/or the parent company, their organizational and technological innovations will be channelled back into, and change, the company as a whole. Such hybrid companies, if they belong to the core companies of a country, may eventually affect the domestic business system, initiating a process of hybridization (Lane 2000). Whereas Whitley, in Chapter 2, does not envisage the process of hybridization affecting MNCs from a collaborative business environment, such as Germany, this chapter's emphasis on a degree of strategic freedom does not posit such a cast-iron logic.

The seven companies examined in this chapter are from three of Germany's core industries which are also among the most highly internationalized: Hoechst (since December 1999 Aventis), Bayer, and BASF—the Big Three in the chemical/pharmaceutical industries; Volkswagen, Mercedes-Benz (since 1998 part of Daimler-Chrysler), and BMW in the automobile industry; and Siemens in electrical/electronic engineering. The study utilizes public company documents and supplements them with secondary data from a range of recent case studies by mainly German social scientists.

A detailed examination of recent changes in globalization strategy and activity through a small number of case studies is well suited to the exploration of the complex company-internal dynamic of this process. This approach is able to capture the tension between strategic intent and institutional constraint. It makes evident the unresolved tensions between conflicting strategic goals, as well as the sometimes unstable compromise between innovative strategy and structural and cultural inertia and resistance. Additionally, this focus on the micro-level reveals the diversity both between and within industries and cautions against the homogenizing generalizations which prevail in much writing on globalization.

Despite the small size and lack of representativeness of the company sample, the case studies are intended to be more than merely illustrative. Although these companies are currently still exceptional in their degree of planned and realized globalization (as shown by a study of the one hundred largest German companies by Hassel et al. 1999), their impact is likely to be much larger than their

number suggests. Trends in 'flagship' companies in three core industries are bound to legitimize globalization tendencies as 'best practice' and, through isomorphic pressures, influence in a more general
way how German companies handle the growing tensions between
globalization and national embeddedness.

The chapter adopts the following structure. Section 2 briefly outlines patterns of internationalization, as well as emergent tendencies
of globalization at the macro-aggregate level. Section 3 presents
detailed case studies of the seven German companies, paying due
attention to the ideal-typical features of TNCs, as outlined in this
Introduction. This section indicates how globalization tendencies,
ascribed to TNCs, coexist with more traditional internationalization
features, associated with MNCs (as distinguished by Hirst and
Thompson 1996). Common 'industry' features are pointed out, but
significant divergent strategies within the same industry also receive
attention. The Conclusion summarizes the findings emerging from
the company studies and draws out the theoretical implications.

3.2. **Globalization Tendencies at the Macro-Level**

In Germany, the export strategy was still outweighing the foreign
direct investment (FDI) strategy in importance up until the end of the
1990s. FDI remains a much lower proportion of GDP than in comparable advanced economies (Deutsche Bundesbank 1997b). However,
since the mid-1980s FDI has grown in leaps and bounds, and its
importance has increased significantly in absolute terms. Between 1984
and 1995, the primary participating interests of German firms abroad
have more than trebled, and the increase was particularly strong in the
1990s (Deutsche Bundesbank 1997b: 64). At the same time, however,
Germany's share of the total of world FDI has remained virtually
unchanged between 1985 and 1995 (Dicken 1998: 44).

The increase in the volume of FDI has not only manifested itself in
the relocation of basic production activities but has also affected some
more high-value activities, including R&D. The pattern of geographical distribution of FDI also displays some significant changes.
Whereas the predominant West European investment location has
lost slightly in importance, FDI in the USA, Eastern Europe, and
South-East Asia (SEA) have gained in significance. Thus, whereas
German firms invested around half a billion DM per year in SEA in
the early 1990s, this had risen to between 1.5–2 billion DM by the

second half of the 1990s, despite the Asian crisis (Deutsche Bundes-bank 1998: 26).

In addition to FDI, international cooperations have gained in weight, indicating the increased significance to competitive success of advanced knowledge, as well as the much increased cost of R&D which exceeds the resources of even the larger firms (Becker et al. 1999: 13). The more protectionist political regimes of countries in SEA, and the necessity to gain market enlargement in this region through joint ventures, have provided an additional driving force (Wortmann and Dörrenbächer 1997: 36). Also significant has been the increased number of cross-border mergers and acquisitions, moti-vated by the perceived need to gain sufficient scale in highly com-petitive markets. Joint ventures and mergers have not only occurred with firms from culturally familiar European business systems but often with firms from more anomic and adversarial business envir-onments. Finally, foreign sourcing has increased significantly.

The above account of internationalization tendencies at the macro-level has shown that, despite strong acceleration of each tendency during the 1980s and 1990s, at this aggregate level talk about a glob-alized economy is premature. In terms of both the volume and the geographical dispersion of FDI, at the end of the 1990s the German economy remained internationalized, rather than globalized. This section confirms many of Whitley's claims in Chapter 2 about how firms from collaborative environments internationalize. But it also shows that, in recent years, German firms, lured by the opening up of large new markets, have begun to invest both in more adversarial and in particularistic business environments. Moreover, they have even entered into joint ventures and merged with firms from such environments—a development held by Whitley to be unlikely (see Chapter 2).

The next section will examine the cross-border activities of indi-vidual firms to establish whether or not globalization tendencies are more readily discerned at this level.

3.3. Globalization of Companies

Recent transformations in the global economic and technological environment have induced a number of large German firms to expand the volume of their foreign investment, increase its regional dispersion, and change their cross-border production and financing activities. They have also acquired more complex organizational forms, financial orientations, and, in some cases, reduced their product diversity. Affiliates are given more autonomy in R&D, design and production concepts, and greater implantation into host institutional and social networks is being sought. Such new developments, as expressed by Whitley in Chapter 2, are discernible not only in other collaborative environments, but also in arm's length and particularistic ones. Such globalization tendencies coexist in a complex way with persistent national and/or international ways of organizing business activity.

3.3.1. *The chemical/pharmaceutical industry*

The few already globally oriented firms in the chemical/pharmaceutical industries significantly stepped up their efforts to become 'global players' during the later years of the 1990s. They extended their geographical reach and regional spread and have established themselves also in SEA (Kädtler 1999; Tödter 1995). Hoechst and Bayer now have more employment on foreign sites than in Germany, and both now have more than half their sites outside Europe, while those proportions are just under 50 per cent in the case of BASF (Hassel et al. 1999: table 7; Kädtler 1999). Firms have engaged in organizational restructuring, with a view to facilitating global coordination and responsiveness. They have reduced the number of sites and, at the same time, established more complex central sites in each triad region (Kädtler 1999: 24). Patterns of control are subject to constant tensions between centralization and decentralization, and evolving networks often remain centrally coordinated (ibid.: 24). Finally, firms in the pharmaceutical industry have moved from local-for-local to some integrated production within the triad (Becker et al. 1999: 15; Dörre et al. 1997: 50). But beyond these common reorientations, the Big Three chemical/pharmaceutical companies have adopted strikingly different strategies to achieve their ends, expressed in divergent degrees of disembedding from the German institutional environment (Kädtler 1999).

3.3.1.1. *Hoechst*

During the 1990s, Hoechst participated in several large cross-border mergers and joint ventures both to change focus (from a mixed chemical/pharmaceutical to a life sciences company) and to acquire the size of a global player. To finance such massive enlargement, increased recourse to share issues on foreign stock markets became necessary, and Hoechst is now quoted on ten foreign stock exchanges (Hassel et al. 1999: 33). Global financial integration is also indicated by the adoption of international accounting standards, quarterly reporting, and the active pursuit of 'shareholder value'. But it is notable that German banks still control around 90 per cent of voting rights—a very German state of affairs, although German banks are said no longer to be the 'patient' shareholders they have been until recently (Jürgens et al. 2000: 58, 70).

Additionally, and partly in response to the changed financial orientation, the company has engaged in radical organizational restructuring, assuming some of the characteristics of a decentralized network structure (Becker et al. 1999). Since 1997, the Hoechst Group has consisted of a strategic management holding (the old head office) with only 250 employees and a number of legally and organizationally independent and financially self-responsible companies in each of its core businesses, which compete against each other in the market. The latter, in turn, have been internally divided into independent business units, each functioning as profit centres (ibid.), and the management holding no longer assumes any operational responsibility. Evaluation occurs according to financial results, expected profits, and development possibilities (Kädtler 1999: 26). The Holding's aim is a portfolio of a constantly changing mixture of new, growing, and mature businesses in the area of life sciences, oriented towards raising the profit potential of the value-creating network (ibid.; Hoechst 1998a and b).

Such radical decentralization, with central, financially guided overall strategic control, has enabled the management holding to engage in flexible de- and recoupling (Kädtler 1999: 24). At the same time, it renders the company more transparent to stock market investors (Becker et al. 1999: 14), turning it into what may be described as a financial combine with a predominantly industrial orientation. Hoechst's adoption of a network structure has not been motivated by concerns of production coordination and knowledge-sharing, but serves constantly to enhance the economic value of the whole network in terms of its innovative capacity. Additionally, restructuring has provided the company with a lever with which to initiate a reduction of the labour force, as well as a segmentation and flexibilization of employment relations (ibid.). Importantly, the company was not able immediately to lay off the many German employees made redundant by reorganization. The works council and unions managed to obtain a compromise, which postponed termination of employment by two years.

Hoechst has discontinued the traditional German *Verbundchemie* where there is a tight link between mass production for a broad spectrum of markets and an R&D centre, oriented towards incremental innovation (Becker *et al.* 1999; Kädtler 1999). Instead, the management holding seeks more radical innovation from its network of small science-based business units. The company's R&D is now organized from a centre in the USA. A division of labour between centres in Germany, the USA and Japan has been instituted (ibid.), and much of the research has been externalized. Recently, however, an important research facility has been opened in Munich.

All these developments combined indicate a dramatic transformation of Hoechst, away from the structure, production/innovation policy, and internationalization strategy which have been traditional in the German chemical industry. They are manifestations of a fairly unified and resolute strategy of transformation, away from the organizational features of a German 'collaborative hierarchy'. Such a strategy seems to go beyond the mere differentiation between locations and functions, leaving the German centre unchanged, as suggested by Whitley in Chapter 2.

Changes in strategy and structure are the end result of a learning process undergone in the more competitive and atomistic US environment. It is the outcome of an allegedly fierce internal struggle between different management factions, resulting in the ousting of the old guard (Kädtler 1999: 28). Shareholders are said not to have been involved. The winner in this struggle and the creator of the new Hoechst, the Chair of the management board, J. Dormann, is one of the new breed (in Germany) of financial specialists who, characteristically, never had any operational responsibility.

3.3.1.2. *Bayer*

Bayer is equally globally oriented and has also initiated some far-reaching changes in organization and production policy. Its strategic concept has been developed by top management. The company's structure and strategy are a kind of halfway house between the still deeply domestically embedded BASF and the Americanized Hoechst company. The company retains a broader spectrum of activities, combining chemicals and pharmaceuticals. The German site has now become secondary to its foreign sites, and it has assumed a decentralized structure. The central management board has surrendered operational responsibility but retains some functional and regional oversight. There remains a central R&D facility, although a high proportion of research activity has been shifted to the USA. Like Hoechst, Bayer has discontinued the principle of *Verbundchemie* (Kädtler 1999: 25), but still aims for synergy between its various activities.

In contrast to Hoechst, the Bayer central board (*Vorstand*) remains the centre of power and decision-making (ibid.). Its financial orientation is a complex mixture of American and German elements. On the one hand, it is the German company with the highest number (thirteen) of foreign stock market quotations (Hassel et al. 1999: 33) which champions the concept of shareholder value (Loehr 1996). On the other hand, Bayer still devises strategy for the company as a whole, and the product divisions are not genuine profit centres. Despite the introduction of market principles, the company only aims to make its traditional activity more profitable and retains a strong production orientation (Kädtler 1999: 27). It champions the maxim of shareholder value as a long-term strategy and has rejected any spectacular financial manoeuvres that might jeopardize employee security (Loehr 1996). Hence, its stock market orientation sits uneasily with its attempt to maintain synergy between its various product divisions and its effort to retain a long-term perspective in employee development. Control of around 90 per cent of voting rights on the supervisory board by German banks (Jürgens et al. 2000: 59) also sits somewhat incongruously with attempts at global financial integration.

3.3.1.3. *BASF*

BASF, in contrast to its old industrial rivals, has deliberately retained its traditional chemical product spectrum and aims for profit from the entire range. The principle of *Verbundforschung* (research networks) continues to be the basis for profit accounting, organization, and control. Geographically, embeddedness in the European area and the German site have remained important, although expansion into SEA is beginning to challenge the supremacy of its European centre (BASF 1996a). R&D is located in the German centre and top managers still emerge from here (Kädtler 1999). BASF has, however, tried to combine this policy with a strategy of enhanced globalization, as well as introducing some modest organizational innovation. The company is quoted on the stock market. Some market principles have been introduced which sit uneasily with the traditional profit control.

80 *Christel Lane*

Thus, the three chemical/pharmaceutical giants have combined globalization efforts with changes in production policies, principles of control, financial orientation, and organizational forms. Whereas Hoechst has become thoroughly Americanized, Bayer has followed this pattern only some of the way, and BASF has largely remained a traditional German chemical company. The latter two now contain a complex and contradictory mix of strategic orientations. Despite efforts by all three to disembed from the German business system, in the case of Bayer and, more so, BASF, this has only happened partially, and even Hoechst has been unable to turn its back totally on Germany. Finally, these strategic reorientations are all still fairly new, and it remains to be seen whether they ensure competitiveness and acquire a degree of stability.

3.3.2. *The automobile industry*

In the auto industry, the two hitherto largely domestically and/or European-oriented firms (Mercedes-Benz and BMW) made concerted efforts during the 1990s to widen and deepen their global involvement, combining globalization with a modernization offensive (of production and company organization) (Eckardt et al. 1999: 179; Riehle 1996). Eckardt et al. describe this rapid and far-reaching change, as 'a leap into the future' (*Flucht nach vorn*) (1999: 170), indicating the dramatic nature of the change. Volkswagen (VW), by comparison, internationalized much earlier and has merely accelerated its already initiated globalization activities (Eckardt et al. 1999; Pries 1997; Riehle 1996). Cross-border mergers and acquisitions have increased notably in recent years. All auto firms have established multiple cooperations and joint ventures, going beyond familiar European cultural environments (Köhler 1999: 43).

Auto companies have changed from MNCs, with a clear core in Germany and more peripheral affiliates in foreign locations, to TNCs with globally differentiated production networks (Pries 1997). This has been accompanied by organizational restructuring at both company and plant level. Production facilities abroad in many cases are no longer mere assembly operations, but have become relatively independent 'local players', with full responsibility for a whole model (ibid.: 78f.). Extensive organizational restructuring has also entailed the adoption of the principle of cost and profit centres by all firms in the industry (Köhler 1999: 41). Despite continuing central direction on some aspects of strategy, affiliates are now given a high degree of autonomy on how to configure production arrangements (Pries 1997: 92, 94).

All three auto companies have greatly reduced vertical integration, which in the new plants in Latin and North America now amounts to between 20 and 25 per cent (ibid.: 88). Given the rules on local content in the North American Free Trade Agreement (NAFTA) region, this means a much greater involvement with local suppliers than has been the case in the past. Even in Germany, a significant proportion of components is now outsourced to neighbouring countries where lower wages are the norm, particularly the more standardized parts, requiring lower-skill input. The companies can no longer claim that their cars were 'made in Germany'.

Adaptation to local conditions and market requirements, however, are now meant to be the springboard for innovation in the company as a whole (ibid.: 84). In contrast to the chemical companies, increased global integration in the auto industry has been primarily production-related and involves much less financial integration. Moreover, the prime example for production modernization has been the Japanese 'lean production' model, rather than any American influence.

Although the three car companies have globalized at different speeds, they share more commonalities in strategy and structure than the chemical companies. This may be partly a result of their converging product spectrum, with VW diversifying upmarket and the other two companies downmarket.

3.3.2.1. *Volkswagen*
Despite an historically deep embeddedness in German institutional structures and economic networks, VW was nevertheless the first of the Big Three to develop globalization tendencies (Jürgens 1998b) and still leads the field in this respect today. Although the company continues to rely heavily on German and European markets, recent FDI and new cooperations by VW constitute a massive expansion into new and growing markets, particularly in the USA, Latin America, and SEA and China, but also in Eastern Europe (Eckardt et al. 1999: 174; Jürgens 1998b; Kiefer 1998). Car production on foreign sites (62 per cent in 1997) now outstrips that in Germany, but employment in Germany still stood at 52 per cent in 1997 (Volkswagen AG 1997: 17, 18). Global expansion was followed, in the mid-1990s, by corporate reorganization according to brand and region. The latter became profit centres (Jürgens 1998b: 300).

VW's financial orientation is a curious mixture: on the one hand, it is quoted on eleven foreign stock markets (Hassel et al. 1999: 33). On the other, there is the remaining part-ownership by the regional state of Niedersachsen which, until 1994, had a majority of votes in the shareholders' assembly (Volkswagen AG 1997: 20). This political tie, it will be shown below, has strongly shaped the company's governance structure and industrial relations traditions in Germany, albeit not on foreign sites. While these had long exerted a constraining influence on both productive modernization and globalization, more recently such constraints have become attenuated (Jürgens 1998a).

Global strategy, since the early 1990s, became expressed in process-oriented integration of production, linked to an international or regional supply and development network (ibid.), as well as being oriented towards utilization of cost advantage on a global scale (Volkswagen AG 1998: 8). The company has begun to integrate its production sites in different parts of the globe into a uniform platform concept (Eckardt et al. 1999: 169, 174). Against this, however, 77.5 per cent of parts still were supplied by German firms in 1997 (Volkswagen AG 1997: 16).

Although core strategic functions—such as R&D and design—remain mainly in Germany, affiliates have become 'technical, organizational and social laboratories in the development of new production configurations and concepts' (Pries 1997: 81). Each affiliate is meant 'to maximize the exploitation of local idiosyncrasies and to optimize intra-consortium competition and learning processes' (ibid.). The upgrading of the Mexican plant at Puebla, making the new Beetle model, has exemplified this changed strategy. This event has been the beginning of a new phase within the company of a wider process of restructuring of relations between German and foreign sites, initiating mutual competition and learning (ibid.). Jürgens (1998b: 304) goes as far as to say that the key vector of VW's modernization and restructuring strategy ran from the periphery to the centre.

Another equally innovative venture has been the Brazilian truck plant opened in Resende in 1996. Resende is a modular consortium, or 'fractal factory', in which different modules are entirely operated by different suppliers who use their own labour, equipment, and work organization methods. Volkswagen contributes only engineering, sales, quality, and overall coordination (Fleury and Salerno 1998: 288f.). The concept is linked with the name of Lopez—who was appointed as supplies manager in the shake-up period during the early 1990s—and has been regarded as a more general vision for the company's future productive model.

A different pattern of localization, due to pressure from foreign political elites, is exemplified by the joint venture in China, described as 'fundamentally Chinese, but foreign whenever it suits the purpose better' (Kiefer 1998: 342). Moreover, the foreign elements in the production concepts used do not come only from German plants, but from sites 'all around the world' (ibid.: 352). The model primarily produced in China, the Santana, uses technology from VW's development centre in Brazil, rather than from Germany (ibid.: 350)—evidence of a differentiated network structure. VW's acceptance by the Chinese authorities and its subsequent domination of the Chinese market for cars have been due, in large measure, to its willingness to transfer modern technology, management, and training methods to the Chinese (ibid.: 349, 351). Except for a small number of managers, employees in the Shanghai factory are Chinese. VW's experience in China would be difficult to understand from the perspective of Whitley's theoretical approach, which rules out successful venture by 'collaborative hierachies' in 'particularistic' business environments.

This rapid expansion and far-reaching change, introduced in a relatively short time, were partly made possible by the appointment of a new and much tougher top manager—Ferdinand Piëch—during VW's crisis years of the early 1990s. He promptly removed many of the old guard and was responsible for Lopez's appointment, whom he took from General Motors where he was known for his tough policy towards suppliers (Jürgens 1998b: 299). Not surprisingly, this process of multiple changes initiated increasingly bitter internal competition between the different national sites, mostly over which plant would get a share of producing the best-selling models (Jürgens 1998a: 297). One prominent example of such conflict has been over Puebla's new role and enhanced responsibility within the company. These were conceded only after a long negotiation process and extensive struggle within the company (Eckardt et al. 1999: 175).

3.3.2.2. *Mercedes-Benz*
Mercedes-Benz (MB), a late starter on the road to internationalization, has begun to aim for globalization (Riehle 1996). In the second half of the 1990s, following the arrival of a new chairman of the management board, MB made a giant leap from a mainly domestically oriented exporting company to a globally operating one, embracing some daring new product and organizational strategies. The merger

with Chrysler in 1998 and quotation on the New York Stock Exchange (NYSE) clearly signalled global ambitions and a changed financial orientation. This new image was further reinforced by abandoning the old MB tradition of having a bank representative as chair of the supervisory board. The company's home-centredness was, however, still evident in the late 1990s in the enduring high concentration of employment in Germany—78 per cent—and by the retention of most high-value functions in Germany.

In the mid-1990s, nearly 70 per cent of the company's turnover still came from Europe and only 6.3 per cent from Asia-Pacific. But MB's intention was to increase their presence in the latter region (Riehle 1996: 249). In 1997, the plan was to increase the company's foreign production from a proportion of only 3 per cent to 30 per cent by the year 2000 (Eckardt et al. 1999: 177). The company is now well established in the USA (Tuscaloosa, Alabama) and in Brazil and Argentina, has established joint ventures in China and Kazakhstan, and it also has a cooperation with the Swiss company SWATCH in Hambach, France (Eckardt et al. 1999: 175f; Riehle 1996: 256, 258).

MB has adopted similar, though less advanced, shifts in strategic and structural orientations to those initiated by VW (Pries 1997: 81). MB's plant at Tuscaloosa, with full responsibility for making the M-class, and its cooperation with SWATCH in France, to produce the Mini-Swatch-Car, are two examples of the new production strategy. It is also notable that, contrary to its German policy, MB has gone for a union-free site in the USA. Outsourcing has been dramatically increased, particularly in Tuscaloosa and Hambach, where more than 70 per cent of model components now come from suppliers. These affiliates are seen as playing a pioneer role vis-à-vis German production sites, and outsourcing is being progressively increased with each new model and each new site (Eckardt et al. 1999: 181).

MB has tried to adapt its organizational structure to its more globally oriented activity. Headquarters are still centralized, but have been reduced from a top managerial staff of 500 to around 300, concerned only with top management (*Leitung*) functions. Service functions have been externalized into a centralized service centre. To achieve greater focus, business units, which were reduced from thirty-five to twenty-three (Schlie and Warner 2000), have been made self-responsible profit centres with around 1,000–2,000 employees each, and overall employment was cut drastically. Procurement of materials became globally coordinated for each group of materials in 1995 (Eckardt et al. 1999: 161).

Financial integration into the global economy has also been pursued, even if largely at the symbolic level. The company has adopted international accounting standards and quarterly reporting. Its chief executive counts as one of Germany's most ardent champions of shareholder value and introduced a value-oriented controlling system (Jürgens et al. 2000: 69, 74). The company's quotation on the NYSE, however, is considered to constitute more of a signal to shareholders than global financial integration.

Integration of MB affiliates into host societies has deepened through the placement of direct production, more consultancy and engineering functions, and also some development tasks (Riehle 1996: 250). MB envisages 'a pronounced local commitment with considerable value creation locally', as well as 'a give-and-take game with local cooperation partners, oriented towards the longer-term' (ibid.: 251). But MB has also greatly profited from foreign investment. For the Alabama work, for example, the company received large subsidies to build a new and exclusive training centre.

It is planned to render top management in the centre more multinational in composition and to recruit more indigenous top managers in affiliates (Eckardt et al. 1999: 180; Riehle 1996: 255). By 2000, however, this latter goal had been realized only very partially. Promotion to higher management and board membership in foreign affiliates still requires that a candidate be either of German origin or has cultural/linguistic affinity to Germany, so the proportion of indigenous top managers remains low. Moreover, such indigenous top managers are not rotated between affiliates in different countries (Kotthoff 1999; oral communication from an employee in a foreign affiliate, 2000).

MB thus emerges as a company where a bold new global concept and increased globally oriented activity coexist, in uneasy tension, with a persistent embeddedness in the German home site. The strategic and structural innovations have been closely associated with Jürgen Schrempp, the chief executive who developed much of his managerial experience in one of the company's US sites. However, cultural inertia has been difficult to overcome, and global pretensions and traditional German attachments form a contradictory and unstable mix.

3.3.2.3. BMW

Of the three auto companies, BMW has been the most German-focused. In 1998, more than half of the company's workforce was still in Germany where the company also realized its highest sales (BMW 1998). Recent transformations of the company have been explained by both the extension of its product range away from solely luxury class vehicles and its recognition that new markets have to be secured by a stronger local presence. Minimizing the exchange risk has been a further consideration (Eckardt et al. 1999: 175).

BMW has acquired (and now sold off) the British Rover Group, as well as the Rolls-Royce brand name (from 2003). It has opened green-field production sites in Spartanburg, USA and Rosslyn, South Africa, as well as assembly works in several Asian countries, which exemplify the new focus on this triad region. Although R&D remain highly centralized in Munich, the company now has smaller design and development centres in the UK, Japan, and the USA (BMW 1999: 111). Thus, the new technology/engineering office in Palo Alto, California, through collaboration with leading US companies in the fields of electronics and new materials, is intended to feed into early development processes in Germany (ibid.: 21).

BMW has adopted similar, though more modest and cautious, strategic and structural reorientations to those initiated by VW (Pries 1997: 81). Spartanburg makes a complete vehicle, the Roadster Z3. This constituted the first step in the new strategy, and, according to the then chief executive, Pieschetsrieder, any further new full production sites will be opened only in foreign locations (quoted in Eckardt et al. 1999: 178). BMW's strategic plan for future globalization envisages: (1) complete vehicle production in the main markets of Europe, North America, and Japan; and (2) assembly operations for market development in countries where local assembly is at least 20 per cent cheaper than importing the cars.

Like the other car companies, BMW has restructured both its overall organization and that of production in order to cope with more complex global processes. Cost and profit centres were already introduced in the 1980s, and an international office for global procurement was also introduced during that time. Outsourcing has greatly increased, enabling concentration on core processes (Eckardt et al. 1999: 182). Like MB, BMW uses its American subsidiary to try out new organizational forms and practices (ibid.: 183–4).

Such a leap within only one decade from a localized Bavarian company to one with global aspirations has not occurred without conflict. This became very public in 1999 when the then chief executive, Pieschetsrieder, was forced out over differences in policy towards the formerly British-owned Rover company, after twenty-five years of service with BMW (BMW 1999). Several other top managers with a long service record were replaced at the same time (ibid.). The struggle also revealed that, in a very German fashion, the works council took a decisive role in the appointment of Pieschetsrieder's successor. The decision, in 2000, to sell the Rover works after continued big losses, again was finalized only after further conflict and resignation at top management level. Whether BMW's main German shareholder, the Quandt family, will retain loyalty in the face of this severe setback and the return to an internationally vulnerable small size remains to be seen.

BMW's more cautious advances in global integration of production have been combined with a relatively low degree of financial integration (Hassel et al. 1999) and a highly traditional ownership structure. The majority of shares remain in the ownership of the Quandt family, and stock market quotation so far has not been an issue. BMW clearly remains the most Germany-focused company of the three auto companies discussed here. It is global only in its aspirations, rather than in its actual activities.

In all three auto companies, contradictory tendencies coexist, resulting from a mixture of traditional German ways of running companies with bold global moves, which are no longer congruent with the features of 'cooperative hierachies'. In all three cases, there now exists an unresolved tension between the new measures of global decentralization and the still-important German corporate centre. Foreign sites have provided opportunities for experimentation and innovation. It is, however, still problematic whether and to what extent experimental practices on foreign sites can be reintroduced into Germany (Eckardt et al. 1999: 187). The traditional striving for high-quality standards also poses problems in some foreign sites (see, for example, ibid. 186) on the problems in this area for MB and the closing of VW's first American plant at Westmoreland, Pennsylvania). All this is evidence of the fact that a hybrid model is emerging, which, at the current time, carries within it unresolved tensions.

3.3.3. *The electrical/electronic/telecommunications industry*

3.3.3.1. *Siemens*
Siemens, until recently a quintessentially German company, has been trying to shed this image and has developed a more global orientation (Dörrenbächer 1999). The company now has a strong presence

in the two Americas. It has developed a strategic plan, envisaging successive increases in global integration, multiple global cooperations, and a significantly increased presence in SEA, particularly in China. Foreign acquisitions and cooperations have been stepped up (Siemens 1998). Increased relocation of production has been followed by greater relocation of R&D activity and employment (ibid.). Employment has recently been expanded abroad at the expense of the German location and is now as high abroad as in Germany (von Pierer 1998: 3). Siemens, like the other German MNCs, emphasizes the wish to become embedded in host societies, through local content and local partnership (von Pierer 1996: 9). Global aspirations are also evident in the company's telecommunications division. Here, significant foreign expansion and increased regional spread have taken place. But in comparison with telecommunications giants from other countries, Siemens's progress towards globalization appears modest (Dörrenbächer 1999: 35f.).

Restructuring started in the late 1980s, when downsizing, greater specialization, and decentralization of responsibility were initiated, but the more radical change came only in the 1990s, after a change in chief executive (Naschold 1997). The most recent process has been oriented towards further 'de-conglomerization', as well as the optimization of the value chain on a global level, with the aim of achieving more favourable cost structures and better access to specific know-how. It has entailed the adoption of production concepts, replacing the focus on Germany with what the company calls 'world regional mandates', i.e. having production centres in all the triad regions (Dörrenbächer 1999: 98; Siemens 1998). Siemens, like Hoechst, now wishes to discard the German vision of 'integrated technology concerns' where profitable units subsidize the poorer performers (Schlie and Warner 2000).

In the area of financial integration, Siemens takes only a moderately high place, according to the index for German companies developed by Hassel et al. (1999: 55, diagram 2). This expresses the increase in foreign ownership through recent acquisitions, rather than presence on international stock markets. Siemens has adopted a diluted concept of shareholder value, reflected in quarterly reporting, the adoption of a scheme of management stock options (Jürgens et al. 2000: 69), and a generally much stronger emphasis on performance (Siemens 1998).

Siemens well exemplifies the difficulty of transforming a deeply domestically embedded company into a globalizing one. Despite strategic intent from the mid-1980s onwards, the transformation of organizational culture and cumbersome and highly centralized structures has proved a formidable task. Until the mid-1990s, the company was still being described as having a conservative and ethnocentric globalization style (Naschold 1997). More recent developments, however, indicate greater effort to achieve the integration of foreign affiliates. However, this process is still being described as 'more hesitant, than radical' (Dörrenbächer 1999: 99). Whether this slow transformation reflects internal resistance or active opposition is not clear.

The above survey of developments in seven German flagship companies makes it evident that globalization tendencies are progressing. Although strategies differ between sectors and companies in the extent and kind of globalization pursued, there are some common tendencies. In all cases, a progressive reduction of presence both in the German and European sites is under way, and much of the new FDI has been placed in less collaborative business environments. With the exception of Volkswagen, companies no longer emphasize their German identity and the advantages this has for marketing. Both Mercedes Benz and Hoechst have engaged in cross-border merger activity which, in any case, puts this identity in question, and all the other companies have made major foreign acquisitions. With the exception of Hoechst, disembedding from the German site has not been drastic in the firms examined, but globalization tendencies are nevertheless unmistakable.

Production is no longer Germany-centred but increasingly integrated within world regions. FDI is being placed into geographically and culturally more remote countries, and affiliates in these countries are no longer of the 'transplant' type. Organizationally, most have adopted aspects of the 'differentiated network' structure, and decentralization and recentralization of control are exercised simultaneously. Greater implantation into host country networks, primarily through increased outsourcing and more local recruitment of managers is being pursued, although it is not clear how much has been accomplished in these respects. Global financial integration has been progressing, albeit at a modest pace and mostly in a symbolic manner. In this respect, German TNCs still differ significantly from core Finnish companies, which as Tainio et al. show in Chapter 6, how much deeper and more consistent global financial integration, brought about by foreign institutional investors.

In several of the German companies discussed here, bold globalization moves on some aspects coexist with persistent domestic
embeddedness on others as a result of which the tensions between
global aspirations and national constraints have become very apparent. Although the companies' routes towards transnational status
share many common features, some notable divergencies are also
evident. These are due to both 'industry' factors and to strategic
choices made within individual companies. Thus the much greater
advance towards transnational status by the three chemical/phar-
maceutical companies is clearly an 'industry' factor. This is equally
apparent in the electrical/electronic engineering industry, where the
very hesitant advance towards global status by Siemens may be
partly explained by domestic monopolies and close relations to the
state, which lasted until the very recent past.

But the differences in strategy within industries are equally
notable. In the auto industry, the cautious globalization strategy of
BMW contrasts with the more daring 'leaps-and bounds' strategy of
MB. But the greatest 'outlier' within an industry is undoubtedly the
Hoechst company, with its thoroughgoing adaptation to an US strategy and structure. Its adoption of a concept of a financial combine
with an industrial orientation is not only alien in its industry context
but is difficult to reconcile with the German business system. Its
merger with a French company and adoption of a new name, Aventis,
completed this denationalization process.

The analysis of company strategies also shows that, although the
choice of investment site is partly influenced by the cost factor,
German companies have not become truly global footloose companies without ties in either home or host society. Instead, their strategy is one of 'glocalization' (Ruigrok and van Tulder 1995), i.e. a
tendency to establish networks also in foreign sites and to make
efforts to become recognized as local by the adopted region (Kiefer
1998, on VW in China; Pries 1997; Riehle 1996, on MB strategy;
Siemens 1997). To this end, more and more valuable resources and
competences are being transferred, and local needs are given greater
consideration. In this respect, they attempt to become 'collaborative
hierarchies' (Whitley 1999 and Chapter 2 in this volume) also in their
host countries—a stance that is very different from that identified by
Moen and Lilja in Chapter 4 in the case of Finnish and Norwegian
TNCs.

3.4. Conclusion

The above account has shown that the German economy is not yet globalized. Instead, it has been argued that the German business system is currently experiencing significant globalizing impulses from the emerging and, in some cases, accelerating globalization tendencies in a small number of economically important and highly influential companies. Their vanguard status makes it inadvisable to ignore globalization tendencies and their current and future effects on the German business system.

The examination of changing company strategies in section 3 has made it clear that companies should be viewed as actors who are partly constrained by their domestic business system but, in pursuing new opportunities in a changed global environment, nevertheless have scope for strategic action. The latter transforms not only the company itself but may impact also onto the business system. Such strategic action is the outcome of a political process of negotiation which may be shaped by a variety of shifting contingencies. Hence company strategies and activities are not usually internally consistent but form a complex mix, reflecting internal company negotiation and struggle, shaped by managerial (and, in Germany, much less shareholder) interests, as well as by global competition and the national business system.

The case studies have thus shown the usefulness of a focus on internal complexity and conflict, as recommended by Morgan in Chapter 1. The hesitant and ambivalent transformation bears out Whitley's observations in Chapter 2 on the constraining effects of a collaborative business environment. But the many radical innovations—in locational choice, organizational and financial form, and relations with affiliates—also show that firms do not follow a compelling logic, as Whitley suggests in Chapter 2, but have some strategic choice. Moreover, this choice is exerted very consciously to escape the constraints of the domestic business system—a freedom that is an integral part of the globalization process. Firms are clearly weighing up the costs of breaking domestic ties against the opportunities believed to exist in culturally less familiar business environments and their large markets. This finding may indicate that firms from collaborative business environments have a broader corridor of choices than surmised by Whitley in Chapter 2. Alternatively, it may point towards a weakening of institutional constraints and a lessening of lock-in effects, in the wake of greater global interconnectedness, as claimed by recent German commentators such as Streeck (1997).

It might be objected that these seven companies are still exceptional and that one should not generalize from such a small number. But their 'vanguard' status means that political elites will respond to their concerns and pressures and that their global image will encourage companies of lesser size and status to emulate their practices and/or use the notion of a new global space of action to lever concessions from domestic actors. These companies, in varying degrees, have become hybridized. Contrary to what Whitley argues in Chapter 2, it is thus concluded that even companies from highly integrated and cohesive business systems do not consistently follow 'the similar integrated' strategy, but that, in recent years, they have systematically turned towards investment in particularistic and arm's length environments, as well as seeking alliances/mergers with firms from them.

Hybridization may be the result of managerial learning from what is perceived as global best practice, as, for example, in the auto firms' implementation of lean production. Alternatively, hybridization may be the consequence of learning from experience in foreign affiliates, as has been the case for Hoechst and MB. Such learning may be applied to effect a gradual process of hybridization, or it may initiate hybridization in an accelerated manner through cross-border mergers and acquisitions. The latter process is more destructive of coherence and identity if, indeed, the new entities manage to survive the abrupt process of hybridization. The transformation of the former Hoechst company into Aventis through a merger with Rhône-Poulenc will be watched with interest.

How have these hybridization processes come about, and in what circumstances will they be more widely effective? As shown in section 3, affiliates of German MNCs have been allocated more and more valuable resources and competences, as well as being granted more organizational and financial autonomy. Networks in host societies are being systematically built up and extended. New developments have necessitated the establishment of local networks with supplier companies, as well as research institutions and government agencies. Glocalization is becoming prominent at the level of strategy, although it is too early to judge how consistently it is being adopted.

Glocalization—the very antithesis of the footloose company—means that German managers and scientists will be spending much more time in foreign locations. They will have to interact with new bargaining partners, construct new reciprocities, and will be establishing and cultivating a host of local networks. The ensuing gradual acculturation of individual employees will translate itself into the creation of hybrid organizational mental maps. (Existing evidence on the interaction of German with foreign affiliate personnel suggests that the alternative strategy of attempted Germanification is not common (Child et al. 1999; Ferner and Varul 1999; Pauly and Reich 1997), except perhaps in relation to skill training (Jürgens 1998a: 322).) But it is clear, as Whitley argues in Chapter 2, that the extent of organizational learning also depends on the perceived value of the experience undergone in various host countries.

Organizational learning from host country experience by managers of affiliates will, in integrated TNCs, initiate organizational learning and hybridization at company level. Once such processes have achieved a critical mass in a number of leading TNCs, this will, in turn, initiate the institutional transformation of the German business system in the direction of hybridization. But more and better data will be required to explore to what extent emergent hybridization creates fissures which ultimately destabilize the company or, alternatively, will settle into a new and broadly diffused pattern, changing the German business system of the future.

REFERENCES

Bartlett, C. and Ghoshal, S. (1989), *Managing Across Borders: The Transnational Solution*. London: Hutchinson Business Books.

BASF (1996a), 'Ausführungen von Dr. J. Strube'. 44th Shareholder Assembly, 9 May.

—— (1996b), 'Presse-Information', 13 November: 450.

Becker, S., Menz, W. and Sablowski, T. (1999), 'Ins Netz gegangen: Industrielle Beziehungen im Netzwerkkonzern am Beispiel der Hoechst AG', *Industrielle Beziehungen*, 6(1): 9–35.

BMW (1999), *Annual Report*. Munich: BMW.

Child, J., Faulkner, D. and Pitkethly, R. (1999), 'Foreign Direct Investment in the UK 1985–1994: The Impact on Domestic Management Practices', *Journal of Management Studies*, January.

Deutsche Bundesbank (1997a), 'Shares as Financing and Investment Instruments', *Monthly Report*, 49(1): 27–40.

—— (1997b), 'Development and Determination of International Direct Investment', *Monthly Report*, 49(8): 63–75.

—— (1998), 'Recent Trends in Germany's External Relations with the South-East Asian Economies', *Monthly Report*, 50(7): 17–32.

Dicken, P. (1998), *Global Shift*, 3rd edn. London: Paul Chapman.

Doremus, P. N., Keller, W., Pauly, L. and Reich, S. (1998), *The Myth of the Global Corporation*. Princeton: Princeton University Press.

Dörre, K. (1996), 'Globalstrategien von Unternehmen—ein Desintegrations-phenomen? Zu den Answirkungen grenzüberschreitender Unternehmensaktivitäten auf die industriellen Beziehungen', *SOFI Mitteilungen*, 24 (November): 15–28.

Dörre, K., Elk-Anders, R. and Speidel, F. (1997), 'Globalisierung als Option—Internationalisierungspfade von Unternehmen, Standortpolitik und industrielle Beziehungen', *SOFI Mitteilungen*, 25 (July): 43–70.

Dörrenbächer, C. (1999), *Vom Hoflieferanten zum Global Player*. Berlin: Edition Sigma.

Eckardt, A., Köhler, H. and Pries, L. (1999), 'Die Verschränkung von Globalisierung und Konzernmodernisierung oder: Der "Elchtest" für die deutsche Automobilindustrie', *Soziale Welt*, Sonderband 13: 167–93.

Ferner, A. and Varul, M. (1999), *The German Way: German Multinationals and Human Resource Management*. London: Anglo-German Foundation. Report presented at a workshop at the University of Warwick, 12 December.

Fleury, A. and Salerno, M. (1998), 'The Transfer and Hybridization of New Models of Production in the Brazilian Automobile Industry', in R. Boyer et al. (eds.), *Between Imitation and Innovation*, Oxford: Oxford University Press, 278–95.

Hassel, A., Höpner, M., Kurdelbusch, A., Rehder, B. and Zugehör, R. (1999), 'Dimensionen der Internationalisierung: Ergebnisse der Unternehmens-datenbank "Internationalisierung der 100 grössten Unternehmen in Deutschland"'. Paper presented at the workshop on 'Dimensions of Firms' Internationalization', Max-Planck-Institut für Gesellschaftsforschung, Cologne, 16–17 December.

Hirst, P. and Thompson, G. (1996), *Globalization in Question*. Cambridge: Polity Press.

Hoechst AG (1997), *Geschäftsbericht*. Frankfurt.

—— (1998a), Bericht des Vorsitzenden des Vorstands, J. Dormann. Shareholders' Assembly. Frankfurt, 5 May.

—— (1998b), Statement by J. Dormann, Chief Executive. Press Conference. Frankfurt, 7 November.

Jürgens, U. (1998a), 'Implanting Change: The Role of "Indigenous Transplants" in Transforming the German Productive Model', in R. Boyer et al. (eds.), *Between Imitation and Innovation*. Oxford: Oxford University Press, 319–41.

—— (1998b), 'The Development of Volkswagen's Industrial Model, 1967–1995', in M. Freyssenet, A. Mair, K. Shimizu and G. Volpato (eds.),

One Best Way? Trajectories and Industrial Models of the World's Automobile Producers, Oxford: Oxford University Press, 273–311.

Jürgens, U., Naumann, K. and Rupp, J. (2000), 'Shareholder Value in an Adverse Environment: The German Case', *Economy and Society*, 29(1): 54–79.

Kädtler, Jürgen (1999), 'Am Netz oder im Netz? Zu neuen Unternehmenskonfigurationen in der chemischen Industrie', *SOFI-Mitteilungen*, 27: 23–30.

Kiefer, T. (1998), 'Volkswagen's Shanghai Plant: Between Chinese Tradition and Modernization Strategy', in R. Boyer et al. (eds.), *Between Imitation and Innovation*, Oxford: Oxford University Press, 342–60.

Köhler, H.-D. (1999), 'Auf dem Weg zum Netzwerkunternehmen? Anmerkungen zu einem problematischen Konzept am Beispiel der deutschen Automobilkonzerne', *Industrielle Beziehungen*, 6(1): 36–51.

Kotthoff, H. (1999), 'Mangement Prozesse und Unternehmenskultur'. Paper presented at a workshop of the Max-Planck-Institut für Gesellschaftsforschung, Cologne, 16–17 December.

Lane, C. (1998), 'European Companies Between Globalization and Localization: A Comparison of Internationalization Strategies of British and German MNCs', *Economy and Society*, 27(4): 462–85.

—— (2000), 'Globalization and the German Model of Capitalism—Erosion or Survival?' *British Journal of Sociology*, 5(2): 207–34.

Loehr, H. (1996), 'A German Approach to Shareholder Value', in *The Future of European Business. The German or British Way?* London: Robert Fleming Ltd, 15–17.

Morgan, G. (2001), 'Transnational Communities and Business Systems', *Global Networks*, 1(2):113–30.

Naschold, F. (1997), *Die Siemens AG: inkrementale Anpassung oder Unternehmenstransformation?* Discussion Paper FS II 97– 201. Wissenschaftszentrum Berlin.

Nohria, N. and Ghoshal, S. (1997), *The Differentiated Network: Organizing Multinational Corporations for Value Creation*. San Francisco: Jossey-Bass.

Ohmae, K. (1990), *The Borderless World: Power and Strategy in the Interlinked Economy*. London: Collins.

Pauly, L. and Reich, S. (1997), 'National Structures and Multinational Corporate Behaviour: Enduring Differences in the Age of Globalization', *International Organization*, 51(1): 1–30.

Pries, L. (1997), 'Production Configurations and Production Concepts in Globally Operating Companies: Outline of a Comparative Analysis of Volkswagen, Mercedes-Benz and BMW in the USA, Mexico and Brazil', in G. Schmidt and R. Trinczek (eds.), *Regulierung und Restrukturierung der Arbeit in den Spannungsfeldern von Globalisierung und Dezentralisierung*. Arbeitspapiere II. Kolloquium, 25–26 April, Erlangen/Germany.

Riehle, W. (1996), 'Globalisierung als unternehmerischer Entwicklungsprozess. Das Beispiel Daimler-Benz', in U. Steger (ed.), *Globalisierung der Wirtschaft*. Berlin: Springer Verlag, 245–65.

Ruigrok, W. and van Tulder, R. (1995), *The Logic of International Restructuring*. London: Routledge.

Schlie, E. H. and Warner, M. (2000), 'The "Americanization" of German Management: Embracing a New Shareholder Value-Society?', *Journal of General Management*, 25(3): 33–49.

Siemens (1997), *Research and Engineering Education in a Global Society*. Proceedings of an international symposium, Berlin, October.

—— (1998), *Annual Report*.

—— (1999), Personal communication, 20 January.

Streeck, W. (1997), 'German capitalism: Does it Exist? Can it Survive?', in C. Crouch and W. Streeck (eds.), *Political Economy of Modern Capitalism*. London: Sage, 33–54.

Tödter, N.-U. (1995), 'On BASF', in OECD (ed.), *Foreign Direct Investment, Trade and Employment*. Paris: OECD.

Tolliday, S., Boyer, R., Charron, E. and Jürgens, U. (1998), 'Introduction: Between Imitation and Innovation: The Transfer and Hybridization of Productive Models in the International Automobile Industry', in R. Boyer, et al. (eds.), *Between Imitation and Innovation*. Oxford: Oxford University Press, 1–20.

Volkswagen AG (1997), *Geschäftsbericht*. Wolfsburg.

Volkswagen AG (1998), *Ein globales Unternehmen*. Wolfsburg.

von Pierer, H. (1996), Summer Press Conference. 15 July, Cernobbio/Lake Como, Italy.

—— (1998), 'Ein Konzern setzt auf den globalen Markt', *Neue Ruhr Zeitung*, 2 December.

Whitley, R. (1994), 'Dominant Forms of Organization in Market Economies', *Organization Studies*, 15(2): 153–82.

—— (1999), *Divergent Capitalisms: The Social Structuring and Change of Business Systems*. Oxford: Oxford University Press.

Wortmann, M. and Dörrenbächer, C. (1997), 'Multinationale Konzerne und der Standort Deutschland', in W. Fricke (ed.), *Jahrbuch für Arbeit und Technik*. Bonn: Dietz, 28–42.

4

Constructing Global Corporations: Contrasting National Legacies in the Nordic Forest Industry

ELI MOEN AND KARI LILJA

4.1. Introduction: Systemic Modes of Economic Action

The strong drive towards forming Euro corporations and even corporations that are claimed to have a global presence (Bartlett and Ghoshal 1989; Ohmae 1987) has led scholars to suggest that firms are becoming similar with respect to their operations, managerial styles, and work systems. Such a thesis has support from various sources. One obvious source of evidence is the car industry, which has entered into cross-continental mergers and transformed its ways of operations at the global level (Womack et al. 1990). Another source of evidence towards homogenization is derived from the increasing importance of new managerial techniques designed and diffused by the international management consultant firms, business media, and business schools (Abrahamson 1996). A parallel development is caused by international organizations that are launching new standards and regulations. Such standards homogenize activities inside and between firms (Braithwaite and Drahos 2000).

However, studies of firms originating from different countries have shown that there are significant differences as to their sectoral specialization, forms of ownership, modes of managerial coordination and control, types of work systems, mechanisms of risk-sharing, and ways of internationalizing (Hirst and Thompson 1996; Whitley and Kristensen 1996, 1997). In Chapter 2 Whitley summarized these interrelated tendencies of governance systems and bundles of capabilities by constructing three ideal types of firm that he calls opportunistic, collaborative hierarchies, and isolated hierarchies (see also Whitley

1999). Accordingly, firms from contrasting business systems are likely to internationalize their activities differently, and internationalization is assumed to have a varying effect on governance systems and organizational capabilities.

In this chapter we will show that, despite some apparent convergence in the management of modern corporations, a specific effect from the national business system can still be traced (cf. Lane 1998). The Finnish-based forest industry corporations have, until very recently, clearly resembled the type of collaborative hierarchy embedded in a collaborative national business system (Lilja and Tainio 1996). In Norway, by contrast, the forest industry firms have been embedded in a more compartmentalized business system. Together with predominantly family ownership and control, this delayed the vertical and horizontal integration of companies at the national level. A process of decline occurred in the industry in the 1960s and 1970s, and only one forest industry corporation—Norske Skog—has been able to grow and become international (Moen 1998).

During the 1990s, the Finnish-based corporations internalized multifunctional operational and managerial competencies, many of which were earlier pooled in jointly owned firms, industry level associations, and cooperatives (Lilja et al. 1992). This inter-organizational structural change within the industry has meant that the leading corporations can be characterized as meeting the profile of an isolated hierarchy (see Whitley's contribution in Chapter 2). Such a characterization also suits Norske Skog. But the relevance of a national business system perspective can still be traced, because managerial actions during the ongoing phase of rapid regionalization and even globalization of production systems tend to have path-dependent features, derived from the nationally specific business systems.

This chapter is based on historical studies on Nordic paper industry companies, especially the Finnish-based UPM-Kymmene, StoraEnso based on the Swedish/Finnish cross-border merger, and the Norwegian company Norske Skog. Interviews and documentary data from these corporations are complemented by secondary sources and studies on the recent strategic moves and management recipes of these firms (Laurila 1998; Lilja and Tainio 1996; Lilja et al. 1992; Melander 1997; Moen 1998; Näsi et al. 1998).

4.2. **The Outcome of the Internationalization Process in Finland and Norway**

Since the mid-1990s Nordic pulp and paper companies have significantly increased their turnover and extended the geographic span of their business operations. The growth process has taken place through mergers, acquisitions, and joint ventures, as well as through green-field site investments. Managers in the industry describe the situation with metaphors such as 'the game is to eat or to be eaten'. This mentality has replaced the old rule of the game that was based on the principle of 'live and let live'. The latter principle gained its strength from the fragmentation of the industry: there were huge numbers of firms producing relatively standardized products without many opportunities for market dominance. Due to tariffs, import quotas, and transport costs, producers in national markets had significant competitive advantages with respect to exporting firms (Melander 1997: 180–6, 215–16). However, by 2000 Nordic-based corporations were among the largest corporations in the forest industry (see Table 4.1) and were leading the global list of paper producers ranked according to the production capacity in the printing and writing grades.

Table 4.1 *The top ten forest industry corporations by turnover, based on 1999 figures*

Rank	Europe	$US (millions)	World	$US (millions)
1*	StoraEnso & Consolidated Papers	13,200	International Paper & Champion International	30,395
2*	UPM-Kymmene	8,790	Georgia-Pacific & Fort James	24,802
3*	SCA & Metsä-Tissue	7,533	StoraEnso & Consolidated Papers	13,200
4*	Metsäliitto & Modo Paper	6,790	Kimberly-Clark	13,005
5	Arjo Wiggins Appleton	5,445	Weyerhauser + Macmillan	12,260
6*	Norske Skog & Fletcher Challenge Paper	4,165	UPM-Kymmene	8,790
7	Jefferson Smurfit Group	3,925	Smurfit-Stone Container & St. Laurent	8,065
8*	AssiDomän	2,965	Nippon Paper	7,960
9*	Ahlstrom	2,300	SCA & Metsä-Tissue	7,533
10	Haindl	1,760	Oji Paper SCA	7,415

* Nordic firms
Source: Finnish Forest Industries Federation

The current internationalization process started during the second part of the 1980s. Western Europe became the battlefield for acquisitions and market share competition due to the implementation of free trade and the European Community (EC) decision in 1985 to complete the unification of the common market by 1992 (Fligstein and Mara-Drita 1996: 9). In the competition for growth and market shares, forest corporations from the Nordic countries were amongst the most aggressive. National waves of mergers among these businesses provided a platform for such an expansion. The corporations combined their financial resources and also started to divest unrelated divisions from which further funds could be accumulated for international operations. At that time neither Finland nor Sweden were part of the European Union (EU). In Norway the political climate was, and still is, against joining the EU. This exclusion from the European integration process was clearly a major worry for the forest industry corporations that based their operations on exports. Such a concern could be counteracted by acquisitions and green-field site investments in the EU area.

By the end of the 1980s, mergers between Finnish-based forest industry corporations had already made them among the largest in Europe (Näsi et al. 1998), but the concentration process continued at an accelerating pace during the 1990s. The process culminated in 1995 in a merger of the two largest corporations, United Paper Mills (UPM) and Kymmene. This created a financial leverage to extend their horizons of action beyond Europe, but it has proved to be more difficult than anticipated. In 1997 UPM-Kymmene acquired Blandin Paper Corporation, a US-based firm. In February 2000, UPM-Kymmene made a bid for Champion International, a large forest industry corporation based in the USA. International Paper, a US company, which is the largest forest corporation in the world, saw this as a threat and in two successive stages raised its bid and won the competition for the takeover. UPM-Kymmene has been forced to proceed in North America with a more step-by-step approach in order to establish its system of production. In autumn 2000, it acquired Repap, a Canadian pulp and paper company. In Asia the experience has been even more traumatic. In 1997 UPM-Kymmene entered into an alliance treaty with an Indonesian pulp and paper company, April Ltd. Because of April's liquidity crisis, the alliance treaty, which covered only the fine paper segment, was terminated in autumn 1999. The only benefit from this venture was the continued ownership of a fine paper mill in China.

Compared to UPM-Kymmene, Enso has been more dynamic in its attempt to consolidate the global forest industry. In 1998 it entered into the first cross-national merger with the Swedish-based Stora. For a while this combination was the largest pulp and paper corporation in the world in terms of production capacity. StoraEnso had production units both in North America and in Asia, and thus became a cross-continental corporation in several product lines. In February 2000 StoraEnso finalized an acquisition in the USA by buying Consolidated Papers, thus securing its position as the second largest forest industry corporation in the world.

Several other internationalized forest industry groups originate in Finland. Metsäliitto Group, as the majority owner of Metsä-Serla, is among the largest European forest corporations. Ahlstrom is a global producer of speciality papers and Myllykoski is a large cross-continental producer of printing and writing papers, having, in addition, an alliance with Metsä-Serla, which is a minority owner of Myllykoski.

Norske Skog either acquired or merged with what was left of relevant firms in Norway with the result that the company controlled about 70 per cent of all pulp and paper activities in the country by the end of the 1980s. During this time, the company also started developing plans for greenfield-site investment in France. A new newsprint mill in Golbey came onstream in 1992 and in 1995 Norske Skog acquired a magazine paper mill in Austria and a newsprint mill in the Czech Republic. A third step occurred in 1998, when Norske Skog acquired two newsprint mills in Asia. The same year the company formed a strategic alliance with Hansol Paper, a Korean-based corporation, and with Abitibi-Consolidated, based in North America. The alliance, called Pan Asia Paper Company, owns four newsprint mills in China, Thailand, and Korea. It supplies almost 30 per cent of newsprint demand in the Asia Pacific region outside Japan. The decisive step in the process of becoming a global corporation was the acquisition of Fletcher Challenge Paper, a New Zealand-based corporation. It had also established a cross-continental system of production, covering, besides New Zealand, such countries as Canada, Brazil, Chile, Australia, and Malaysia. By simultaneously entering into a joint venture with a Brazilian-based company Klabin, Norske Skog has become a dominant newsprint producer in South America. As a result of these acquisitions, Norske Skog is now a truly global corporation, with production operations on five continents. It is the second largest producer of newsprint in the world.

The most important motivation for internationalization has been the search for market power in selected product groups. This is considered to be the key to profitability in an industry that is very capital-intensive and in which over-investment has been a periodically repeated disease. Competitive investments and over-capacity ensuing from the investments have eroded profitability during the recessions. For this reason forest industry corporations have not been considered attractive investment targets for international investors. Consolidation and improved economies of scale and scope are considered crucial to raise the level of profitability in this sector.

Mergers and acquisitions are the quickest way to gain market power. Because the stock values of the corporations are used in deciding new ownership ratios, both the managers and the owners have become interested in attracting the attention of international investors. This can be done by appearing to be a global corporation. Market power is also one criterion that international investors use when evaluating their placements.

Additionally, new types of raw materials have encouraged the internationalization of the Nordic forest industry corporations. This development applies first and foremost to the replacement of virgin fibres by recycled paper in the newsprint sector, as well as the use of new species of short fibre pulps in fine papers. The use of recycled paper has radically changed the preferred location of newsprint production. Both supply of raw material and distribution and sales now favour locations close to densely populated areas. From 1985 to 1995 the percentage of recycled paper in newsprint increased from about 20 to 40 per cent. However, it was only in the early 1990s that newsprint made entirely from recycled paper became feasible. Subsequently, a strong greenfield site expansion based on recycled paper occurred in Western Europe.

Table 4.2 presents a schematic overview of the leading paper industry corporations in the Nordic countries and their geographic presence. Though the transformation of the corporations has been in many ways dramatic, it has proved to be difficult to create global production systems for distinct product segments. In newsprint, Norske Skog's production facilities cover five continents. UPM-Kymmene has also production operations on three continents in one of its speciality paper divisions. Otherwise, the process of internationalization has reached the stage where the product divisions have only cross-continental learning opportunities.

The corporations from the Nordic countries share, then, a number of similarities in their overt strategies of internationalization. This similarity is due to the pressure to gain market shares that are used as an

Table 4.2 *Geographic presence of the leading Nordic paper industry corporations*

Product segment	Corporations		
	StoraEnso	UPM-Kymmene	Norske Skog
Newsprint	Cross-continental	European	Global
Magazines	Cross-continental	Cross-continental	Two countries
Fine papers	Cross-continental	Cross-continental	None
Boards	European	None	None
Speciality papers	One country	Global	None

Key:
One country: mills specialized in a product segment only in one country
European: mills in at least two European countries producing similar grade
Cross-continental: mills in at least two continents
Global: mills in at least three continents alone or through alliance

indicator of profitability. The similarity is also due to isomorphic tendencies stemming from pressures to meet period-specific criteria of being modern. Underneath these apparent similarities there are, however, important differences. Some of these can be detected by looking at quantitative indicators of the corporations, such as turnover and available production capacity. But to ground further the thesis of an underlying difference reflected in the product portfolio, a considerable amount of industry-specific knowledge of products and technologies is required. In simple terms, the difference between the Finnish and the Norwegian case is twofold. First, there is a company cohort effect in the Finnish case; several international corporations have emerged from the Finnish context, but only one from Norway. Secondly, the Finnish-based corporations have upgraded their product portfolios. Besides standard products such as pulp and newsprint they are market leaders in technically more sophisticated products such as uncoated and coated printing and writing papers, liquid packaging board, and speciality papers. In addition, three of the largest Finnish companies have a wide assortment of mechanical wood-processing products (Pajarinen et al. 1998: table 4.3). The demand in these more advanced papers is forecast to grow faster than for more standard grades.

4.3. National Business System-Based Reasons for the Differences in Strategic Positioning

The main source of difference between the current strategic positioning of the corporations from the two contexts is the constellation

of collective actors in the nation-state and the degree of their commitment to the forest sector from a long-term perspective. The distinct
Finnish development path is characterized by aggressive patterns of
investment for economies of scale and movement into the upgraded
product segments. This can only be understood if the various collaborative linkages, mobilization, and risk-sharing mechanisms beyond
the level of the corporation are outlined. In Norway, on the other
hand, the family-owned firms were stuck in isolated phases of the
value chain. There was low commitment on the part of the state and
the political parties to the forest sector. Collective institutions that
could have served as mobilization mechanisms for corporate growth
did not emerge.

In the Finnish case, collaboration has many forms. An important
feature of Finnish economic history is the development of social
movements that combined both economic and political aspirations
and initiated a wide set of interlinked businesses. These supported
each other through ordinary business relations, cross-ownership,
interlocking directorships, and commitment to joint activities in various kinds of interest associations. One of the social movements was
the so-called *fennomanic* movement, which emphasized the interests
of Finnish-speaking businesspeople and ordinary consumers in an
economy that was dominated by a Swedish-speaking business elite.

The economic core of the *fennomanic* movement was formed at the
beginning of the 1890s around a commercial bank and two insurance
companies. This financial group became one of the dominant players
in the Finnish economy for about hundred years, until the middle of
the 1990s (Kuisma 1993). As an extension of their political movements, both farmers and blue-collar workers were also able to create
an economic arm by entering into a variety of businesses. In addition,
the state was used as a source of finance and as an owner of businesses that were capital-intensive and involved high risks, such as
the forest, mining, chemical, and energy industries. All the above-
mentioned groups used the state through their political arms as an
alliance partner in starting up and extending businesses. Periodically,
the state-owned bloc has acted very independently of the spheres
of economic influence based on social movements. The Swedish-
speaking economic elite also formed its own bank group that could
coordinate economic action across industries through their flagship
companies, business, and personal relations. The basic distinguishing
feature of this system of economic, political, and social spheres of
influence is that even the core firms in each of the blocs observed bloc-

specific interests and collaborated in risk-sharing (Lilja et al. 1992; Lilja and Tainio 1996). Because the forest industry was, until the middle of the 1990s the core industry in Finland, the firms within it were most important flagship corporations of the financial groups.

This system of coordinated economic interests beyond individual firms provided the context for the concentration of economic and intellectual resources and their strategic mobilizations. The forest industry corporations were able to grow through mergers and acquisitions at the national level, becoming in the process, step by step, significant players in Europe. They were also active in unrelated diversification until the middle of the 1980s. This gave them a strong foothold in mechanical engineering firms linked to forestry and forest industries. They also held minor stakes in electronics and chemistry businesses. This was especially the case with Nokia, which began as a mechanical pulp firm in 1868 (Lovio 1993: 214–26).

In the forest industry the development and implementation of a new generation of technological processes are dependent on the harmonization of a wide range of technologies. In the Finnish case, there is a long tradition of sharing experiences across corporate boundaries in both formal and informal ways. Such experiences have been institutionalized through workshops where suppliers, users, researchers, and technological consultants have participated. The engineers' professional associations have also been active in maintaining such knowledge-sharing institutions. Additionally, some engineering consulting firms have had integrator roles. The most notable of them is Jaakko Pöyry Consulting, which has become the largest in the world in the area of engineering consulting in the forest industry.

There has also been considerable circulation of managers and experts from one corporation to another. This sharing of insights in the innovation networks has formed the basis for upgrading the technological competence of the whole forest sector (Lilja and Tainio 1996). The business bloc structure, ownership of businesses in related and linked industries, and the facilitating role of highly prestigious engineering associations have helped to create visions for technological breakthroughs and to generate the knowledge and competences needed in a series of cumulative development projects (Laurila 1998).

In the 1950s and 1960s, it was the Swedish-based companies that were the first to respond to the American challenge in the pulp and paper industry. In this period Sweden also held a leading position in pulp and paper technology. A strong network of pulp and paper companies, supplier industries, and national R&D institutions constituted the base for this leadership. Sweden was known as the 'Northern Star' in the field of research and development (Moen 1998). Parallel to the development in Sweden, Finnish companies also upgraded their product portfolio, first by moving forwards from pulp to paper. Due to technological developments in the printing and publication industries, in paper chemistry, pulping technology, paper machine-making, and with the emergence of electronic process control devices, new types of paper products were developed.

Although many of the inventions were made in the USA, it was the Finnish-based corporations that took the lead by rapidly investing in more sophisticated paper machines that were capable of producing new printing and writing paper grades. This move rejuvenated the Finnish paper industry in the 1980s and opened a window of opportunity for internationalization: the demand for these paper grades was growing at two to three times the rate of the more traditional paper grades such as newsprint. In addition, these upgraded products gave better surface properties to paper and replaced wood fibres with cheaper minerals. To respond to the supply gap, Finnish-based paper corporations also started to launch new machines within the EC at a quicker pace than their competitors. Through collective learning, the capability for mill-planning, construction, and start-ups accumulated. This shortened the implementation phase of mill construction projects and helped to establish other timing-based advantages, like the one deriving from the opportunity to keep the planning teams together over several projects.

The state functioned as the final risk-sharing institution. Its contribution came via macro-economic policies: during recessions the devaluation of the Finnish currency acted as the final method to restore the competitiveness of Finnish forest industry firms. The westward-orientated free-trade policies adopted by Finland and the application for membership of the EU were strongly shaped by the interests of the forest industry (Heikkinen 2000: 276–95, 384–8). The influence of the forest industry has been secured via strong social networks, co-option of diplomats, leading political actors, and also, as a last resort, political compromises.

In several respects Norway forms a striking contrast to Finland in terms of systemic modes of coordinating and organizing economic activities. The Norwegian companies restricted their operations to a single stage of the value chain. These units demonstrated an unwillingness to merge and to establish cooperation with other firms. Mergers and acquisitions took place only in cases of insolvency.

Companies had a production focus and risk-averse strategies: new products were rarely introduced on a large scale and the industry failed to develop a strong customer orientation. This was partly because of large wholesalers who controlled the sales of paper and in this capacity were able to occupy a dominant position vis-à-vis producers. Some companies took high risks in foreign direct investments and failed (Moen 1998). These are the main reasons why more than two-thirds of the companies disappeared during the 1970s and 1980s.

Norske Skog is the only exception in the Norwegian population of pulp and paper firms. One reason for this is its ownership structure: in contrast to the majority of the old firms that were mainly owned by families, it has had forest owners as major shareholders. For the forest owners, growth of the corporation was a desirable target because it secured the demand for their raw material. In addition to acquiring pulp and paper mills in Norway, Norske Skog also diversified into related businesses such as sawmills, building materials, particle board, etc. (Moen 1998; Norske Skog, Annual Reports).

The sort of sectoral and intersectoral collaboration that distinguishes the Finnish economy never evolved in Norway. For one thing, there are few links between industry and finance: credit institutions played a minor role in the financing of industry and an even more limited role in framing industrial policy. This pattern goes back to the forming of the industrial society in the nineteenth century. The emerging banking system consisted of small and autonomous units with limited resources for industrial investment. This decentralized system established itself as a unit bank system in strong opposition to any form of concentration process. As a result, no branch banking system evolved in Norway. The decentralized dimension of banking was even formally institutionalized in the first Norwegian Bank Act of 1924. In this way banks were debarred from the possibility of creating powerful financial institutions (Lange, Knutsen and Nordvik 1992; Nordvik and Knutsen 1990). Moreover, legal regulations restrict the investment behaviour of financial institutions. Currently, a parliamentary act forbids banks to invest more than 4 per cent of their total assets in the shares of one company. The act also regulates the representation of banks on boards where they have shareholder interests. This lack of institutional interrelatedness prevented the financial system in Norway from developing inside knowledge of the industry, which could have supported a proactive approach in competitive strategy.

In essence, the Finnish and Norwegian economic systems reflect different norms and values concerning legitimate horizons of action. Whereas top managers in Finnish firms had to observe long-term bloc-specific interests and collaborate, Norwegian actors distrust anyone who would act beyond his or her own immediate interests. This was the dividing line between the Finnish and Norwegian business systems, to the detriment of the pulp and paper industry in Norway.

The gaps in the inter-organizational and social networks can also be detected in the national systems of innovation. In Norway, the pulp and paper firms kept an arm's length distance from suppliers of technology. The main reason for this was their risk-averse stance towards investments. In this way firms were debarred from the informal gathering of information about future developments from their suppliers. Moreover, the pulp and paper firms did not consider R&D as an investment but as a cost. Such an attitude to R&D restricted the development of capabilities in the mills and excluded the exploitation of potential resources generated by the national innovation system. This inability to develop multifunctional competencies has also hampered Norske Skog in its endeavour to catch up technologically. It is the main reason why the company has largely stuck to newsprint production.

In Finland, forest firms and machinery suppliers together developed technological innovations. Close connections were partly conditioned by the constant wave of investments of the forest firms. This constituted a platform for informal contacts and circulation of engineers from the supplier side to the user side and back again. Deep and wide connections between forest and engineering firms were also partly facilitated by the strong ownership linkages between them (Laurila 1998: 111–30).

For various reasons the Norwegian pulp and paper industry did not enjoy high status in the political system, although it was the dominant export sector until the mid-1950s. Historical antagonisms between management and the labour movement were revived in the postwar years over the direction of economic policy. As early as the immediate postwar years, the Labour government treated the forest industry as though it was outdated and on the decline. A sort of 'armistice' was reached in the early 1950s, to the effect that joint policy-making was delegated to a type of corporatist arrangement, bringing together the industry and the state bureaucracy (Moen 1998). However, within this arrangement, no political will was demonstrated to force changes through in the industry. The Labour government chose instead to favour and support the electro-metallurgical and electro-chemical industries. Due to low interrelatedness between the pulp and paper industry and the political system, there were few channels for industrialists to influence the economic policy. In the case of Norway, there were few intersectoral networks which either could have exerted pressure to change the priorities in industrial policy or help the industry to internalize existing societal resources.

In relation to Whitley's (1999) typology of business systems (also see Chapter 2), the Finnish case conforms to that of a collaborative or a coordinated type. The Norwegian business system is not readily classified. To some extent, it resembles that of a compartmentalized business system. Characteristic features are the dominance of self-reliant firms, institutional differentiation, and pluralism. This sort of system has a low degree of risk-sharing. But the Norwegian system diverges from the compartmentalized type by the fact that the low degree of risk-sharing has not resulted in a diversified economy. Nor can the Norwegian business system be characterized as capital market-based. Moreover, its strongly personalized features obstruct economic coordination. For these reasons, investments in long-term innovation strategies did not evolve.

4.4. Contrasting Coordination Initiatives in the 1990s

The previous section has demonstrated that the characteristics of the Finnish and Norwegian national business systems have had both a cohort and a product portfolio effect on the internationalized forest corporations. In this section we describe the nature of managerial coordination initiatives in corporations originating from Finland and Norway, summarized in Table 4.3. In the managerial coordination initiatives, there appear to be nationally specific differences.

4.4.1. *Capacity management and discipline on pricing*

The main difference with the past is that the Finnish-based firms have been signalling very strongly that they are subject to strong restraints on new investments. This has been done in industry conferences through the speeches of the Chief Executive Officers (CEOs) and in

Table 4.3 Coordination initiatives and managerial stances of the Finnish-based consolidators and the Norwegian specialized corporation

Areas of coordination initiatives	UPM-Kymmene StoraEnso	Norske Skog
Capacity management	Restraint on investments Access to North America via acquisitions Divestments of non-core businesses	Global grip on markets through rapid implementation of alliances and acquisitions. Divestments of non-core businesses
Greater pricing discipline	Fostering a climate for partnership with customers; counteracting business cycles	Fostering a climate for partnership with customers and differentiating of the product offering
Signals to financial markets	International board members Commitment to higher dividends Stock Exchange listing at NYSE by UPM and StoraEnso	Only national board members Commitment to higher dividends
New layers to the product offering	Logistics centres close to customers Branding of product families Wide scope of the offering Electronic information services to the customers Hesitation to use environmental standards in marketing communication	Logistics centres close to customers Early mover in the branding of products Narrow scope of the offering Electronic information services to the customers Enthusiasm in the adoption and use of environmental standards in marketing communication.
Shaping of international regulations and standards	Involvement in the European level interest organizations and the policy-making in the EU	Concentrating on business-related networks

articles written by strategic planning experts. Despite the growth in demand, allocation of capital to investments has dropped by one-third. The pressure for that has come from investment banks and from international investors. The latter have, after every new investment announcement, sold shares, with the effect that the prices of stocks fell. This was contrary to the earlier experience of Finland, the tradition of which favoured aggressive investment behaviour. The emphasis on restraint in investment from the Finnish-based firms can be understood as an attempt to secure higher profit margins after they have secured a stronger market share in several product segments. This mutually reinforced limitation on investment has had serious repercussions on the supplying engineering firms. A strong piece of evidence for this is the fact that in 1999 the former technological leader in the paper machine business, the US-based Beloit, announced that it would close down its operations in ordinary paper machines and concentrate only on tissue paper machines.

In terms of market behaviour, the Finnish-based corporations are urging a new approach to production planning and pricing. When demand for paper products decreases, they traditionally agreed restrictions on production by keeping mills at a standstill for a certain period. These periods have been used for maintenance and for training the workforce. In this way the firms have shared losses in proportion to their production capacity. Such industry-level 'solidarity' has not been the case in the USA and Canada, where production capacity is largely old, and capital investments paid back. Even lowered prices give a margin over variable costs. Also, for newcomers in newly industrialized countries restraint in production is inconceivable for a different reason: cash flow is necessary to maintain the liquidity of the corporation, though production might cause losses due to low prices.

In Norway, from the point when Norske Skog was controlling about 70 per cent of all pulp and paper activities, such a regulation of production has not been an issue. At the international level, Norske Skog has less relative weight compared with the Finnish-based corporations and on the global scale the newsprint segment is still rather fragmented. Moreover, Norske Skog is in a catching-up situation as regards size and positioning among the top-ranked paper industry corporations. For this reason it has accelerated its rate of growth and also moved to upgraded magazine paper products. To finance its growth, Norske Skog has sold its mechanical wood division.

4.4.2. *Financial markets and corporate governance*

In the early 1990s, bank control of the forest firms in Finland withered away. The main triggers for this process were the banking crisis in the first half of the 1990s (see Tainio, Lilja and Santalainen 1997), allowance of unrestricted international ownership of Finnish firms since the beginning of 1993, and the growth of the forest firms. Due to the recession, several banks collapsed and were merged with other banks. The remaining banks have abolished the policy of keeping controlling ownership stakes in their former flagship corporations of each industry. The risk concentrations would have been too high. As a result, Finnish-based forest firms' dependence on the domestic financial market came to an end. In early 2000, the figures for foreign ownership were as follows: UPM-Kymmene 59 per cent, StoraEnso 70 per cent (due to the Stora merger), and Metsä-Serla 35 per cent (*Helsingin Sanomat*, 3 February 2000). Even for Metsä-Serla, the figure is rather high, because the corporation is owned by the cooperative of forest owners via a parent corporation (Metsäliiton Teollisuus) which is not quoted on the Stock Exchange. Thus, the two largest corporations are no longer Finnish from the ownership point of view. In the case of StoraEnso, the higher degree of international ownership has also had an impact on the composition of the top management team, which consists of eleven Finns and ten Swedes. In order to get a grip on the cross-continental integration process and to facilitate the recruitment of international managers, StoraEnso has set up in London an administrative extension to its Helsinki-based headquarters.

Norske Skog's situation resembles that of Metsä-Serla, because their roots are in the joint operations of forest owners to secure a demand for their raw material base. In Norske Skog, a change in the structure of ownership took place in the late 1980s when the share of foreign ownership increased as a result of the greenfield site investment in France. However, by comparison with the two largest Finnish-based corporations, the share of foreign ownership in Norske Skog is low. At the beginning of 2000, it made up 24 per cent of the equity capital with voting rights. In Norway, foreign shareholders were given equal rights to the national ones in 1995. However, this alteration has not changed the percentage of ownership. Norske Skog is, to some extent, suffering from Norway's closed political culture, which is accused of being too nationalistic.

The increased significance of international investors as owners has changed the agendas of the CEOs dramatically. Much more time is now allocated to investor relations. Also, other measures have been taken to increase visibility in the international financial community. For instance, the stocks of UPM-Kymmene are quoted on the NYSE (New York Stock Exchange). Shareholder value has been adopted in the management rhetoric as the overriding goal. This has been translated to a commitment to higher dividends than previously, and such a policy has been implemented consistently since 1996. Managers, owners, and analysts evaluate strategic actions from the point of view of how they influence the value of stocks. An example of this is the fact that Norske Skog was characterized as the most dynamic pulp and paper company at an investor conference in New York in spring 1999 (Norske Skog, Avis for Norske Skogsindustrier ASA 3/1999). This was due to the alliance treaty negotiated in Asia with Abitibi and Hansol Paper.

The composition of the boards has been renovated both in UPM-Kymmene and StoraEnso. In the spring of 1999 they appointed foreign members to their new boards for the first time. The nomination of external board members has strong signalling effects. StoraEnso has inherited two outside directors from the board of Stora—Marcus Wallenberg, because the Wallenbergs had a share in Stora, and Harald Einsmann, a director and board member of Procter and Gamble (a leading company within the household paper segment). UPM-Kymmene has two new international board members: Anton Lenstra, a director of Unilever, and Carl H. Amon III, a lawyer from the USA (Lilius 1999). Independent outsiders as board members signal to the financial markets that insider rules are observed and minority shareholders are not treated in an unjust way. Bank control of corporations kept international investors away from national stock markets because there was a danger that majority owners could influence the stock values in their favour. In contrast, Norske Skog and Metsä-Serla have only national members nominated to their boards. Thus, both companies are missing the contact and information interface provided by international board members.

4.4.3. *Branding of products and product families*

Moving away from pure commodity production is the key to the competitiveness of the pulp and paper industry corporations. Conscious efforts are being made to turn bulk products into brands through technological innovations and/or by adding services to the product which differentiate the offering from standard products. A further way to increase the value of the product to the customer is to offer the whole product range that the customer needs. This lowers the transaction costs in the buyer–seller relationship. To facilitate customization of products and other operations, considerable efforts have to be invested in managerial coordination between production units, functions, and value chain processes. For instance, it is very difficult to meet similar technical standards in different paper mills over long periods of time, due to raw material supplies, skills of the operators, differences in the production technology, etc. However, invariance in the quality of the product is a minimum requirement for multiple sourcing of the same product brand.

Here, we can point to one significant difference between the leading paper industry corporations originating from Finland and Norske Skog. The latter has been very quick to establish a product brand for newsprint (Nornews) which can be supplied from many mills. Norske Skog has the advantage of further developing an established sales and distribution system that over the past decades has achieved a worldwide span. It has a logistics system called GLOSS ('on time—in full'), based in Antwerp in order to better serve customers. The branding process is being extended to the adoption of quality and environmental standards and certification (ISO 14001, EMAS). For instance, the newsprint mill in Norway, Skogn, was the first processing industry plant in the world to achieve the ISO 14001 certificate. An example of creative marketing is Norske Skog's cooperation with Springer Verlag on the environment. Springer shows in its homepage (*http://www.familie.de/nbaum/*) that its publications are printed on paper based on ecologically sustainable forestry in Norway. Also, the World Wildlife Fund has expressed a positive attitude towards this measure. Norske Skog is currently restructuring the firm in order to match various functions better with a customization policy. This implies a shift of control within the management system from the mills to the divisional level.

The Finnish-based corporations, on the other hand, have been involved in post-merger integration processes, which have retarded the launching of product families that would reflect the new merged corporate identity. They are also strengthening the power of the divisional level over the mills in many product segments to reap the internal synergies available within the corporate system. In the market for intermediate industrial products the uncertainty linked to a customer interface is considerable: suppliers are kept in a competitive relationship with each other. Although there is much talk in the paper industry about becoming market- or even customer-driven, the corporations have apparently still a long way to go. It will take time before diversified forest corporations can capitalize on the wide scope of their product portfolio and the geographic spread of their production operations at the level of individual products from the point of view of branding.

The competitive edge which can be gained from technical innovations, quality standards, and certifications is relatively short, ranging from half a year to two or three years at the maximum. Thus, the lesson from the latter half of the 1990s has been that commodity producers that intend to differentiate their product offering by adding services, guarantees, and creative marketing communication have to keep up with such a development track over a longer period of time. Otherwise, differentiation efforts do not become visible in the markets. Such a long-term commitment towards differentiation is dependent on the support of the top management. For this reason there is a tendency for focused corporations to be more consistent in this type of developmental work. This is very clear in the case of Norske Skog.

4.4.4. *Institutional management at the international level*

In the formation of cross-national systems of production and sales, international regulations are of utmost importance. For the forest industry, the most urgent regulatory issues are the certification procedures of forestry practice, regulations for the usage of tropical forests, implementation of quality standards, standards for environmental management systems, and the ways in which product life-cycle analyses are standardized for the forest industry. Another important regulatory practice is related to decisions of anti-trust authorities. A major difference between the Finnish and Norwegian-based forest corporations is the amount of effort invested in the arena of international institutional management.

Since Austria, Finland, and Sweden joined the EU, it has become a net exporting region of forest products. This provided a platform for the Finnish-based corporations to change the view of the European Commission on the role of forests and the forest-based industries. The main breakthrough at the EU level has been the acceptance of a policy document by the EU Commission. The document specifies initiatives for the competitiveness of the whole 'cluster' linked with the forest industry. The main aim is clearly to support the formation of transnational epistemic communities in various areas of knowledge management, technological foresight, and R&D. The Commission and interest associations related to the forest-based industries are committed to organizing a yearly discussion forum. This is designed to become a major platform for discussing EU-level policy-making within the forest-based value chain constellation (European Commission, DG 3, 1999; Forest Cluster Database 1999). The Finnish Forest Industries Federation has shifted its focus of action from Finland to the EU. It contributes to the activities of the Confederation of European Paper Industries (CEPI). CEPI has started to build connections to about fifty industry associations linked with the forest cluster. Before the initiative of CEPI few connections existed between these associations (Hyvärinen 1999).

The relevance of the role of the EU competition authorities can be perceived in the case brought up by the StoraEnso merger. Together, they had a 70 per cent market share in the production of liquid packaging carton board. The merged corporation was allowed to keep all its units in this product segment. Its argument was that their product was competing with other packaging materials, such as glass and aluminium, and consequently the whole packaging material segment should be taken as the relevant competitive context. Such precedents of regulative practice have a strong conditioning role in forming cross-continental systems of production and for the possibility that European-based corporations are able to become globally significant players.

Environmental protection and the setting up of norms for best available technology (BAT) are similar types of regulatory issue. The Finnish-based corporations have been active in contributing to the formation of EU norms for BAT for the forest industry (Honkasalo 1999). Being technological leaders, the Finnish-based corporations can demonstrate in practice how challenging demands for environmental protection can be met. By contrast, neither Norske Skog, nor the national industry association, nor the Norwegian state have been active in promoting the industry-level interests of the forest industry on the international scene.

4.5. Explaining the Differences in Coordination Initiatives

The differences in coordination initiatives are related to the types of stakeholder that can be linked to the coordination activities of the firms. The Finnish-based corporations rely on extended inter-organizational networks in a number of arenas, while Norske Skog puts its emphasis on generic managerial skills and time-based competitive advantage. The first contextual factor to explain the above difference is the type of professional labour markets typical for the forest sector in Finland and in Norway. The second contextual factor is the difference in the sectoral specialization of the Finnish and Norwegian societies. The third contextual factor is Finland's and Norway's different choices as to EU membership. This differentiates also the managerial attention and action of the Finnish- and Norwegian-based forest industry corporations.

In Finland there has been a relatively large professional labour market in the forest sector due to the specialization of the Finnish economy in forest sector businesses. The scope and scale of these businesses have been exceptionally wide, covering all sorts of activity, from the production of forest products to the supplying industries, to specialized merchant houses, consulting firms, and even investment banking. These firms have supported each others' internationalization. Because the sector has been in the economic core, unlike in most other countries of the world, it has enjoyed a high status in Finland and attracted talented people.

The top managers of the Finnish-based corporations have had long careers in the forest industry corporations, typically a lifetime employment beginning in one of the smaller corporations which, over the last few decades, have become amalgamated into the remaining giants of the industry. Most of the top managers have an engineering background. Due to the strong emphasis on engineers and the cross-fertilization of a broad range of technologies, the Finnish-based corporations are characterized as technology-focused in their management style. Their competitive strength has been built on the optimization of the usage of raw materials and the building of mill combines to maximize the economies of scale and scope. However, since the middle of the 1990s, considerable investments in management training have been made to improve general management capabilities. The nominations to the CEO positions signal this change in orientation: the CEOs of both UPM-Kymmene and Stora-Enso have a business school background. Also changes in the internal and external environment of the Finnish-based corporations support a more finance-driven managerial culture. Having divested themselves of divisions in the pulp and paper machinery industries, forest corporations have no corporate-specific incentive to give orders to the engineering firms. It is now easier to turn down suggestions for investments made by engineers and in this way respond to the priorities of international investors. The opening up of the market for company acquisitions in Continental and Northern Europe has helped both the process of consolidation and the divestment of non-core businesses.

In Norway, by contrast, the long history of family ownership in the pulp and paper industry did not facilitate active professional labour markets in the forest industry. Nor was there a labour market open at the wider sectoral level, because of the compartmentalized nature of the Norwegian industry. It is quite natural that Norske Skog, as the sole representative of the Norwegian forest industry at the international level, is less affected by management traditions in the forest industry corporations. Because of the lack of internal candidates to manage an internationalized forest industry corporation, Norske Skog's current CEO was recruited from Scandinavian Airlines (SAS). In addition to activities in the areas of branding, the corporation is currently experimenting to develop cross-national management cultures in some of their divisions. One aim is to create a communicative space within which alternative trajectories for the future can be discovered, evaluated, and chosen. Organizational practices are reformed with new mindsets, through the support of new recruitment and training. In general, there is openness to adopt new management tools and practices.

As to the setting up of industry-level conventions, Norske Skog is adopting a pragmatic, business management approach. Instead of being involved in extensive signalling and lobbying activities, it has implemented on a global scale an impressive specialization in the newsprint segment. This will give a long life expectancy for its business concept because a learning curve effect can be diffused to less demanding markets. Moreover, Norske Skog is in a good position in the market for corporate control when the newsprint segment is experiencing the next steps of restructuring. According to a consultancy report, the number of newsprint producers is currently 95 and a reduction by 15–20 per cent is expected to happen in ten years time.

Although the Nordic forest firms have started to act according to Whitley's characterization of an 'isolated hierarchy' (Whitley 1999: ch. 3), the Finnish-based corporations are exporting their style of institutional management to the international level. The cluster-based industrial policy initiative taken up by the EU Commission is very similar to the one that has been implemented by the Finnish Ministry of Trade and Industry since 1993. The Finnish chairmanship of the EU provided a platform for the Finnish interest organization of the forest industry to introduce a new EU policy document.

The decline of the Norwegian forest industry has left Norske Skog alone on the international scene. The company has few opportunities to mobilize allies and resources from the national context in the formation of transnational communities relevant to the forest industry. From a sectoral point of view, Norske Skog is less nationally anchored than the Finnish-based firms. Because Norway is debarred from participating in EU decision-making, Norske Skog has not invested any energy in influencing its regulatory practices. This is one reason why Norske Skog has concentrated on internal managerial measures and on business and alliance relationships to build its competitive edge.

4.6. Conclusion

The European pulp and paper industry is now dominated by large multinational corporations that have internalized multifunctional managerial capabilities. These companies have set up cross-continental and even global systems of production and sales. This implies a radical structural change to the situation prevailing in the mid-1980s. The dominant firms meet the criteria set by Whitley (1999) for isolated hierarchies as a specific firm type. However, this overt similarity in corporate evolution hides important structural differences as to the nature of strategic positioning and types of period-specific coordination initiatives.

This chapter has demonstrated how differences in national business systems in Finland and Norway have had radically different outcomes as to the number and size of the internationalized forest industry firms originating from these countries. Two of the Finnish-based corporations have turned out to be among the major global consolidators in the pulp and paper industry. In addition, one Finnish-based corporation has become a global player in a niche market and another one a dominant player in Europe. Norske Skog, the only Norwegian survivor on the international level, has shown surprising vigour in becoming the second largest newsprint producer in the world.

In its coordination initiatives, Norske Skog is relying on intra-firm managerial capabilities and business-to-business relationships. The Finnish-based corporations have been active in promoting new recipes for industry-level coordination in new regions, mobilized European-level interest organizations for a variety of industries to construct sector-based competitiveness strategies at the level of the EU policy making, and have co-opted international investors to corporate governance. This difference in the profile of coordination initiatives of the Finnish-based firms is very much related to the cohort effect and the related spill-over effect derived from the societal specialization into the forest sector in the Finnish case. Norske Skog has demonstrated that it has been able to overcome national disadvantages and experience rapid growth. Here, we have provided evidence for the thesis that the differences in the national business systems have long-term structural effects on the nature of firm population, their product portfolio, and for period-specific managerial coordination initiatives.

REFERENCES

Abrahamson, E. (1996), 'Management Fashion', *Academy of Management Review*, 21: 254–85.

Bartlett, C. A. and Ghoshal, S. (1989), *Managing Across Borders. The Transnational Solution*. Boston: Harvard Business School Press.

Braithwaite, J. and Drahos, P. (2000), *Global Business Regulation*. Cambridge: Cambridge University Press.

European Commission, DG 3 (1999), The State of the Competitiveness of the EU Forest-based and Related Industries. *http://europa.eu.int/comm/dg3/*

Fligstein, N. and Mara-Drita, I. (1996), 'How to Make a Market: Reflections on the Attempt to Create a Single Market in the European Union', *American Journal of Sociology*, 102(1): 1–33.

Forest Cluster Database (1999), *www.database.forestcluster.com*

Heikkinen, S. (2000), *Paper for the World: The Finnish Paper Mill's Association Finnpap 1918–1996*. Helsinki: Otava.

Hirst, P. and Thompson, G. (1996), *Globalization in Question*. Cambridge: Polity Press.

Honkasalo, A. (1999), 'On Implementation of the IPPC-Directive in Finland'. CEPI Seminar on IPPC. Brussels, 20 April.

Hyvärinen, J. (1999), *R&D in EU Forest Cluster*. Helsinki: Finnish Forest Industries Federation.

Kuisma, M. (1993), *Metsäteollisuuden maa*. Helsinki: SHS.

Lane, C. (1998), 'European Companies between Globalization and Localization: A Comparison of Internationalization Strategies of British and German MNCs', *Economy and Society*, 27(4): 462–85.

Lange, E., Knutsen, S. and Nordvik, H. W. (1992), *Bankstruktur og kunde-forhold i langtidsperspektiv*. Oslo. Norges råd for anvendt samfunnsforskning. Rapport/Det nye pengesamfunnet: 31.

Laurila, J. (1998), *Managing Technological Discontinuities*. London: Routledge.

Lilius, A-L. (1999), 'Impivaaran aika ohi hallituksissa', *Talouselämä*, No. 11.

Lilja, K. and Tainio, R. (1996), 'The typical Finnish firm', in R. Whitley and P. H. Kristensen (eds.), *The Changing European Firm*. London: Routledge, 159–91.

Lilja, K., Räsänen, K. and Tainio, R. (1992), 'A Dominant Business Recipe: The Forest Sector in Finland', in R. Whitley (ed.), *European Business Systems*. London: Routledge, 135–54.

Lovio, R. (1993), *Evolution of Firm Communities in New Industries: The Case of the Finnish Electronics Industry*. Helsinki: Helsinki School of Economics and Business Administration, Series A: 92.

Melander, A. (1997), *Industrial Wisdom and Strategic Change: The Swedish Pulp and Paper Industry 1945–1990*. Jönköping: Jönköping International Business School, Dissertation Series No. 1.

Moen, E. (1998), *The Decline of the Pulp and Paper Industry in Norway, 1950–1980*. Oslo: Scandinavian University Press.

Näsi, J., Ranta, P. and Sajasalo, P. (1998), *Metsäteollisuuden megamuutos*. Jyväskylä: Jyväskylän yliopisto. Taloustieteellinen osasto. Julkaisuja No. 114.

Nordvik, H. W. and Knutsen, S. (1990), *Bankenes rolle i norsk industriell utvikling*. Oslo. Norges råd for anvendt samfunnsforskning. Rapport/Det nye pengesamfunnet: 10.

Ohmae, K. (1987), *Beyond National Borders*. Homewood, IL: Down Jones-Irwin.

Pajarinen, M., Rouvinen, P. and Ylä-Anttila, P. (1998), *Small Country Strategies in Global Competition*. Helsinki: ETLA & SITRA.

Tainio, R., Lilja, K. and Santalainen, T. (1997), 'Changing Managerial Competitive practices in the Context of Growth and Decline in the Finnish Banking Sector', in G. Morgan and D. Knights (eds.), *Regulation and Deregulation in European Financial Services*. London: Macmillan, 202–15.

Whitley, R. (1999), *Divergent Capitalisms*. Oxford: Oxford University Press.

Whitley, R. and Kristensen, P. H. (eds.) (1996), *The Changing European Firm*. London: Routledge.

—— (eds.) (1997), *Governance at Work*. Oxford: Oxford University Press.

Womack, J. D., Jones, P. T. and Roos, D. (1990), *The Machine that Changed the World*. New York: Rawson Associates.

PART II

CONSTRUCTING AND DECONSTRUCTING THE VISIBLE HAND

5

Between National and International Governance: Geopolitics, Strategizing Actors, and Sector Coordination in Electrical Engineering in the Interwar Era

HENRIK GLIMSTEDT

5.1. Introduction

In this chapter, we follow the continuous efforts from the 1890s to the Second World War of a transnational community in electrical engineering to construct a world market through cartelization of oligopoly. What the argument reveals is that the process of internationalization in this period was highly political, driven by individual actors and firms aiming to construct a specific set of market relationships. The chapter therefore reinforces the need to have both a political and an historical perspective on processes of internationalization. Forms of markets and international economic coordination emerge from the actions of individuals and firms seeking to deal with complex technological, economic, and political environments. In order to grasp these processes, it is necessary to examine the interactions between national and international forms of social embeddedness and how these give rise to forms of transnational communities (within and across firms).

In the period under consideration, as will be discussed in what follows, the 'Big Four' electrical engineering companies (General Electric, AEG, Siemens, and Westinghouse) worked jointly with financial circles to construct a world monopoly. The process they were engaged in was experimental, as they tried to construct both

national and international sectoral governance mechanisms. Their
vision was to integrate production, distribution, and use of electrical
power into one integrated business system. To achieve this end they
needed to have joint access to a number of resources: they needed a
huge pool of financial resources to enable power plants to invest in
central stations with turbine-based generators; they needed to control
a huge pool of patents for suppliers of equipment; and they needed
to be able to build an association that could control competition so
that corporations, financial investors, and power plants could reduce
the financial risks involved in the technological aspiration of electri-
fying the 'world'. Achieving this involved a range of actions over the
period from the 1890s to the 1930s, as economic and political conditions changed. However, perhaps the high point of these endeavours
was the ability, at the height of the disintegration of most international orders under the impact of the Wall Street Crash, the Great
Depression, and the rise of Nazism in Germany, to create a private
agreement across firms from different countries to manage the
world's markets for electrical engineering. By signing the International Notification and Compensation Agreement (INCA) between
1930 and 1933, an international tool for both national and international cooperation was created, enabling firms both within and
between countries to negotiate over technological specialization,
exports shares on different markets, and prices. With growing political tensions and demands on industry, the industrialists had a body
where they could negotiate how to respond to the national demands
of different political regimes, especially in Nazi Germany.

The history of governance of the electrical engineering sector is,
therefore, one that oscillates between international and national forms
of governance. In this story, it is the interwar period that constitutes
the watershed. According to the standard view, the pre-1913 period
was extremely favourable to economic internationalization. As
Foreman-Peck writes 'By 1913 . . . Europe's international trade/gross
national product ratio, at a peak not achieved until the late 1970s and
1980s, indicated that the late nineteenth century liberal international
order supported markets at least as free as those created by the post-
1945 institutions of GATT and IMF' (1983: 316). Yet it cannot be denied
that the very same liberal international regime resulted in the Great
War, representing the very essence of international fragmentation.
The postwar settlement failed to re-establish a stable international
order, instead leading through increased economic rivalry and growing disputes over territory to a widespread fragmentation of economic

activity into national and imperial blocks. To the extent that international trade and international investments occurred in the interwar era, it was not because of but in spite of the political conditions that typified the international order in the 1920s and 1930s.

Yet, it was the case that there were significant actors seeking to construct a relationship between national and international governance systems in spite of the fragmentation and integration of international markets. This approach raises a series of much thornier and more complicated issues: how do international governance mechanisms emerge? What are the relations between international and national governance structures over time? How do alternative architectures of international economic interaction, or the actor's visions of international agency and governance, define internationalization? How do we explain the shifts between associative (cartel-type) of governance to governance based on ownership and foreign direct investment?

Naturally, the nationalist turn of the interwar period had a clear and restricting impact on foreign industrial economic activity. But it would be a mistake to conclude that managers and other key actors of the private sector were completely trapped by the deterioration of international relations. Even at the height of disintegration of the interwar period, it would be inaccurate to portray international business life as entirely stifled by political and economic nationalism. What I argue, in short, is that efforts to establish governance structures and integrate economies at the national level interplay with the emergence of new forms of international sector governance. Managers of the electrical engineering industry experimented with both national and international sector governance to stabilize the business during the volatile first part of the century in what can be described as a reflexive learning process. In most cases, electrical manufacturers and their financiers clearly realized the need to replace the withering political support for a stable international trade and investment regime with private governance mechanisms—mostly in the form of international cartels. Fearing US dominance in technology and the deep financial resources of the leading firm, General Electric, participation in international cartels was seen as risky by the European industrialists in that it might lead to US retaliation. British and German managers were thus no less torn between an international and national approach to economic policy than the interwar politicians were. Against this background, they began to experiment with a combination of national and international governance mechanisms as a way of strengthening the national industry before taking part in international governance efforts. According to this view, the drift towards increased national governance of technology and business activities in the electrical engineering industry was related to, and in fact a way to prepare national manufacturers to participate in, efforts to build private international governance mechanisms.

In the first part of the chapter, I examine how the governance of this industry was managed in different countries in the period leading up to the First World War, a period when developments in the USA and Germany were of crucial significance to the broader internationalization of this industry. The second part of the chapter concentrates on the interwar period, when the fragmentation of political order and economic activity intersected with the perception amongst key actors in the industry that the potential for profits from the international coordination of the expansion of firms within this sector was high. The actors sought to create a structure of governance which within the constraints of the wider political and economic environment would enable some form of coordination for mutual benefit.

5.2. The Construction of Governance in Electrical Engineering before 1914: Challenges and Solutions

In the 1880s, a wide range of technical options typified the electrical industry. In the USA at this point, Edison was beginning his work to develop the incandescent electric light system. Alternatives to Edison's electrical system were, however, already established. Homes and factories were lit by natural gas. Small electric lighting systems, serving only one building or a block, were commercialized in the late 1870s. By 1885 they were a booming business, involving more than 1,500 arc and incandescent systems, operating in homes and factories. Alongside these 'stand-alone' or isolated generator units, privately owned central electric stations emerged as an industry. From fewer than two dozen firms in 1882 to almost 500 in 1885 and almost 2,000 independent local firms by 1891, the central station business industry grew, using different technologies and organizational structures.

Central station electric systems were a major commitment for Thomas Edison, who mobilized his personal financial and patent-based resources and those of his subordinate co-workers and their families to create and manage the Edison (later General Electric) electrical equipment manufacturing firms. The first incandescent station was brought on line by Edison himself, on 1 October, at Pearl Street, in New York's financial district; it served no more than about a square mile. Arc lighting stations existed from 1879 on, but it was only incandescent stations that provided residential service and which eventually displaced arc lighting stations entirely. While others, such as Britain's Thomas Swan, had invented isolated components, Edison's real achievement was to integrate producing, distribution, and the use of electrical power into a *system* (Hughes 1983; Passer 1953).

Closely linked to the systemic dimension of electrical engineering, one central management issue that arose early in the industry was thus the creation of an organizational structure that met the requirements of both technological invention (scope) and marketing of the electrical system (scale). According to the key historical analyses, the large electrical engineering firms constitute instructive examples of the virtues of vertical integration since the mid-nineteenth century. Through restless investments and mergers, they controlled unrivalled technological capabilities; the decisions to develop a wide variety of related electrical and electronically based processes for both industry and household required the balancing of many technological, marketing, production, and financial variables. As in the chemical firms, many new products were realized only years after the initial investment in development had been made (Chandler 1990: 212–22; Hughes 1983, ch. 1)

The same coordination problem vexed the German 'first movers' in electrical engineering. Solutions were, on the one hand, akin to the American strategy. The German manufacturers integrated horizontally through a series of mergers in which firms like Helios, Schuckert, and Union became parts of AEG and Siemens. Thus, German entrepreneurs put the electrical industry under a leadership that made the necessary investments and developed strategic skills. On the other hand, they integrated forward into both financial institutions and electrical utilities, resulting in a greater role for the German banking system in the formation of electrical trust (see Chandler 1990: 463–67, 538–53; Feldenkirschen 1997).

However, as pointed out by Harold Passer as early as 1953, to understand the governance of electrical engineering and the emergence of the central station concept, which came to dominate the electrical energy industry, it is important to place in context how the managers, engineers and financiers within Edison's group began in the late 1880s and early 1890s to look for ways to consolidate electrical manufacturing and the central station concept (Passer 1953). Apart from learning how to master the new technologies involved in the generation, distribution, and use of electric energy, the entrepreneurs and financiers in the industry thus faced a dual complication. First, they had to create a market for electricity, which interlinked local politics, finance, and entrepreneurship in building energy systems for metropolitan areas. Secondly, the electrical manufacturing business required huge investments not only in new technologies, organizational solutions, and marketing, but also in financial solutions for undercapitalized power plants. The manufacturers tackled this problem head-on.

5.2.1. *Governance of competition: the General Electric merger*

Edison's preference for central stations set off a move from the small flexible forms of generators that in many places constituted the backbone of electrical systems before the 1890s. The central station concept, resulted from intensive Edison lobbying and, since the mid-1890s, also from Samuel Insull's efforts to reorganize the energy market through horizontal integration in big, densely populated areas such as Chicago. In engaging in the organization of the market, both manufacturers and central stations manufacturers simultaneously aimed to go beyond the existing generators based on cyclic motion, which were too small and inefficient to serve a large metropolitan area. The successful expansion of the central station strategy, hence, required new technological achievements. The necessary technological inputs came from Charles Parson's steam turbine technology, which operated on high pressure steam that propelled a rotating turbine (Hughes 1983). Therefore, the necessity to develop turbine-based generators hit manufacturers at the same time as they had to shoulder the financial burdens of financing and organizing the market.

It is thus in this setting, typified by the creation of central stations, new technological demands, and costly R&D challenges, that it became clear to the industry's leading actors that the fierce competition that existed, however good in theory, constituted a very real threat to the firm's limited financial resources. In an economic environment, where huge financial resources were needed for the upkeep of technological development and organizational capacities, it seemed to the top managers that thin margins due to fierce competition among the manufacturers threatened the business as a whole. In particular, the financiers and managers became increasingly convinced that price competition and patent litigation, the two main competition tactics, would undermine the large firms. Concerned about soaring costs of competition and problems in raising sufficient capital, the business leaders started to explore and apply collaborative efforts, such as cartelization and patent pooling (Carlson 1991: ch. 6). One of Edison's top managers, Henry Villard, acted to promote collaboration between the leading US firms in a more organized manner. Charles Coffin, Thomson-Houston's respected leader, responded to Villard's initiatives with a bold proposal to consolidate the electrical engineering business through a merger between the leading firms in the central station business. Thus, Carlson concludes, the process that led to the merger between Thomson-Houston and Edison's group, resulting in General Electric (GE) in 1892, was first and foremost a reflection of the desire to limit competition and, to a lesser extent, an outcome of the dynamic between technology and organization (ibid., esp. 290–4).

5.2.2. *Governance of the volume of demand*

Another basic governance innovation to deal with the problems of this sector was invented by S. Z. Michell, an engineer with Edison's New York company (Hirsch 1989). While early industrial users had been able to finance their investments in stand-alone electrical systems, the central station approach developed under Insull required larger investments. Thus, as the American electrical pioneers developed their central station technology, they also discovered that the major potential customers—the municipalities—in most cases lacked financial resources to build and operate power plants. In response to the customers' shortage of capital, the major producers of electrical equipment were forced to raise capital for the construction and initial operation of the plants. Manufacturers thus took two steps towards forward integration of electrical engineering into power stations (Federal Trade Commission 1928). In the 1890s, GE started to accept the power companies' bond securities as collateral for bond issues for a larger financial company, United Electrical Securities. Through the establishment of 'electro-finance' firms, the manufacturers were able to sell 'bundled' securities of small utilities, making the investment somewhat less risky. Thus, a large holding company, Electric Bond and Securities, which purchased stock and bond of individual electric utilities and issued its own more marketable securities, became the second governance innovation in electrical manufacturing (ibid.: 99; for Europe, see Segreto 1994).

5.2.3. *Governance of the structure of demand*

Providing customers with the financial means to build the plants was far from enough. While the manufacturers sought to resolve the matter of credits to their customers, Edison's central station strategy faced even more severe hindrances. The central station strategy involved huge investments, requiring not only deep pockets but also a large and stable market to carry the investments. Drawing particularly on Arthur Wright and John Hopkinson's insights into the cost structure of producing electricity, Insull (working in the Chicago area) realized that he needed to combine large day-time users of energy to balance the night-time residential use of electricity (Platt 1991). Having promoted the use of electric power in urban services and integrated smaller energy users into a large network served by one central station, Insull's task involved the creation of a 'natural monopoly' in the Chicago area. In essence, the central station strategy was not only based on increased demand through the expansion of electrical services, but also a process in which smaller networks were integrated into a large grid covering the Chicago area (ibid., esp. 74–82 and ch. 5).

The organizational structure of the industry was, despite Edison's preferences for the central station strategy, not given. First, the electrical trade was strongly under the influence of the virtues of vertical integration. By the 1890s, for example, the telephone trade had opted for vertical integration under the Bell system, integrating the manufacturing arm under Western Electric with the telecom-operator function. Secondly, decentralized systems, ranging from small isolated plants serving a neighbourhood of a few urban blocks and generators serving a specific industrial plant to entrepreneur Homer Yaryan's chain of dedicated steam and electrical plants, built and operated in more than thirty cities stretching from Cleveland to LaCrosse. The viability of these systems was striking; they represented as late as 1918 around 50 per cent of all installed energy supply in the USA. According to contemporary observers, such as financier Henry Doerty, who specialized in the energy sector, these small and flexible, multi-use systems were the hardest to replace because of their efficiency (Hirsch 1989).

The technical merits of these systems were variable, locally specific, and debatable. Insull's real mission after leaving GE, was to mobilize his network of collaborators within the company and the industry associations to the end of promoting the central station concept across the industry. Insull's circle drew on local and national contacts. They spearheaded lobby efforts in Washington; they took control of the industry organizations; and they set up labs which played an increasingly important role in the setting of standards. Crucial to the embedding of their collective template of industry development was domination of the electric industry trade associations as a method of transferring technical and organizational norms. In combination with the technical experts from the big six central stations (New York, Philadelphia, Brooklyn, Detroit, Boston, and Chicago Edison), Insull's circle of influential collaborators were capable of institutionalizing the central station concept in the US power industry (Granovetter and McGuire 1998). The privately owned 'natural monopoly' expanded, even if the small flexible plants still were as important.

5.2.4. *Governance of international sector coordination mechanisms*

In sum, the rapid development towards a US–German oligopoly in electrical engineering was based on the creation of a number of governance solutions and coordination mechanisms beyond the firms themselves (for a general overview, see Schröter 1977). The combination of these solutions, furthermore, provided the entrepreneurs with a platform for foreign expansion. In 1885 Edison had established Edison Continental to license its technology in Europe, resulting not only in the Deutsche Edison Gesellschaft (AEG's predecessor), but also in French and Italian start-ups based on Edison's system. Thomson-Houston and Westinghouse followed suit. Investments and licence agreements in France were soon followed by parallel moves in Britain and Germany, where Thomson set up Union Electrizität with Ludwig Loewe. At the time of the world exhibition in Paris in 1900—a highly symbolic event in the European electrification process—the degree to which the electric utilities in Europe depended on US and German technology became apparent. In France, for example, the French affiliates of the American firms controlled around 40 per cent of the French electric utilities and were responsible for some 60 per cent of the electrical manufacturing that supplied the utilities. While licence agreements provided a vehicle for combinations of European financial resources and US technology, the German and US electromechanical industries became even more interdependent through German investments in America. The stabilization of the US electrical manufacturing required, in addition, foreign financial support. In her history of foreign direct investment in the US industry, Mira Wilkins (1989) has examined how the financial stabilization of Edison General in the late 1880s, as well as the first stages of the GE merger in the early 1890s, involved Deutsche Bank. Given the increased level of international interlinkage in the industry, the leading financiers and managers in electrical engineering, such as Henry Villard, were preoccupied with and quite explicit about the need to organize a world cartel (for pre-1914 cartels, see Federal Trade Commission 1928, 1948; League of Nations 1927; Liefermann 1932; Pribram 1935; Schröter 1977).

The complexities of the system of international licence agreements and international finance made the idea of a global order in electrical engineering—an international governance mechanism—seem logical to the dominant players. All it took was one small change in the complicated network of international ties that jeopardized the balance of power between the main actors. In particular, when AEG in 1903 absorbed one of GE's German licence-holders, Union Elektrizität, this changed the balance of power in the European market, given that AEG was competing with GE's affiliated licence-holders in the European markets. Thus, by the turn of the century the actors tried to resolve this type of concern, including exploring the possibilities of establishing an institution for ongoing cooperation in electrical manufacturing. As a result, GE signed a bilateral agreement with AEG concerning exchange of patents, formal recognition of each other's markets, and a clause which specified how both parties should maintain the same distribution of market shares on the markets outside their respective exclusive spheres of influence. While AEG's move and the subsequent agreement with GE threatened to undermine the position of the other key actor on the European market—Siemens—the latter entered into a similar cooperative arrangement with GE's chief competitor, Westinghouse (Schröter 1977).

5.3. **National and International Governance During the Interwar Years**

Before the First World War, the electrical engineering industry had reached its familiar structure of twofold vertical integration. Insull's vision of a market dominated by large private energy producers loomed large in the electrical industry. Manufacturing was dominated by four large firms. It was combined with an international regime, which integrated world electrical engineering beyond national economies. It was, however, the interwar period, after the complete breakdown of the international contacts between the leaderships of the USA and the German electrical manufacturers during the First World War, that witnessed the coming of a global multilateral cartel (Epstein and Newfarmer 1980).

No single explanation has a clearer bearing on the steps towards the institutionalization of international governance of electrical engineering during the interwar period than the breakdown of the international market equilibrium after the First World War. Above all, the rise of economic nationalism in the interwar period, including soaring tariff measures, discouraged international investments, and volatile exchange rates, furthermore, made international business riskier. However, the breakdown of the international regime in the 1920s motivated the managers of the large electrical manufacturers, with ample backing from their financiers, to construct industry-wide governance mechanisms. As Reid (1989) has shown, there is a connection between the unstable international environment that typified the interwar era and GE's efforts to re-establish and consolidate global governance in electrical engineering. Faced by protectionism and trade uncertainties after the war, GE took steps to find new strategies for international expansion that would not further exacerbate the outbursts of economic nationalism that were increasingly common in European markets. GE wanted in particular to avoid a heavy-handed approach, such as offensive direct investments and penetration of Europe's markets through US export. According to the American view, it would be good business for GE to assist its foreign associates in matters of technology and production, since that would accelerate the pace of electrification in the export markets. Given the associates' dependency on American know-how and financial resources, GE estimated that it would generate more foreign business.

In addition, GE paid particular attention to the structure and performance of British electrical engineering, which the leadership of GE believed, in sharp contrast to Germany's electrical firms, was fragmented and disorganized, crippled by its inability to understand the importance of managerial coordination. Therefore, GE developed a dual strategy for collaboration with the two other major nations in electrical engineering. While GE's leaders were inclined to build an alliance with AEG and Siemens on the basis of a cartel, they came to the conclusion that they needed to take the lead in the restructuring of British electrical engineering (Reid 1989) While the major actors, thus, saw good reasons to renew their prewar international state of international affairs, they developed an ambivalent attitude towards closer integration at the international level. Lagging behind in technology and organizational capabilities, the British industry in part welcomed closer ties to their more advanced competitors, but in part also worried about the British industry's independence. The German firms were, despite their inclination to break out of isolation through an alliance with the Americans, also less willing to enter a global cartel under GE's leadership unless AEG and Siemens were able to re-establish their pre-1913 position in the international trade.

5.3.1. *Britain's experience with national governance*

Britain's electrical engineering before 1914 has been characterized as chaotic, rendering entrepreneurs incapable of reaping returns from early scientific achievements. That picture is well documented. The developments during the First World War changed the face of the industry in a number of important ways (see the discussions in Catterall 1979; Davenport-Hines 1984; Jones and Marriot 1970). First, industrialists such as Dudley Docker paved the way for organizational changes. Docker successfully orchestrated the merger of three leading British electrical manufacturers—his own Metropolitan, Vickers, and British Westinghouse—into Metrovic, with the explicit purpose of starting a national trust movement in British electrical engineering. Secondly, Docker was also instrumental in forming an international patent exchange with Westinghouse to safeguard access to better technology. Thirdly, Docker took steps towards improving the industry organizations with the aim of forming a national policy for closer economic and technological cooperation in British electrical engineering, including increased technological interchange between firms. Fourthly, to reinforce the weak links between British electrical manufacturing and the financial sector, Docker also forged links with international sources of finance. In particular, SOFINA, the Belgian financial institute controlled by Heinemann, was the target for the British plans to close the gap between manufacturing and finance (Segreto 1994).

However, it seemed to both foreign as well as domestic observers that these efforts were far from adequate. Whereas GE's management, for example, asserted that Germany's primary problem arose from a lack of financial resources, it characterized the problems in Britain's manufacturing as being predominantly organizational, resulting in lagging technology. In their reports on the state of British electrical engineering, the British Electrical and Allied Manufacture's Association (BEMA) concluded that collaboration with foreign firms promised better technology and, above all, better access to parts of the European markets. Nonetheless, closer ties with American and German competitors threatened the independence of British industry, and the British therefore opted to secure the integration of the national skill base in order to avoid long-term dependency on foreign actors (Davenport-Hines 1984: 200).

It was Dudley Docker, as Davenport-Hines points out, who came closest to combining the recommendation to mimic Germany's industrial structure with economic nationalism. Germany served as the main model for the British manufacturers. In its recommendations to British industry, Sir Charles Parson's *Committee on the Electrical Trades After the War* pointed directly towards German rationalization, combination, and consolidation of electrical manufacturing (quoted in Reid 1989). Throughout the 1920s, the BEMA, was involved in organizing British manufacturers into both price and market cartels, known as 'industry rings', as well as helping closer technological cooperation. What furthermore fuelled the formation of the industry rings under BEMA's guidance was the observation that the British electrical manufacturers were left outside the closed circle of German and US collaboration, leaving British industry outside the allocation of market shares. On this view, national cartels were set up as national hubs of the industry, integrating private as well as public actors at the national level in order to enable them to participate in the governance of international markets. In addition to the formation of a national governance system amongst the manufacturers, the restructuring of the domestic demand side also helped to revitalize the industry. Beginning in 1926, the creation of the Central Electricity Board and the construction of the national energy grid contributed to increased sales and the technological revitalization of UK manufacturers. These reforms cut through the complicated system of regulations, ownership, and mix of technologies that hampered the aggregate level of energy demand.

There is little doubt that improvements in national governance spilled over into the performance on export markets. Britain saw export shares develop favourably between 1922 and 1926. In insulated cables (electric and telecom), the British remained the leading exporter. Likewise, in the heavy segments, Britain's sales soared to

around 45 per cent of the global market, making the UK the dominant exporter of transformers, generators, and related goods. At the
same time, however, the effects of these efforts were limited. First,
per capita consumption of energy lagged well behind Germany,
France, and Italy throughout the 1920s, and the rise in consumption
during the 1920s was disproportionately concentrated in the pros-
perous areas of the south of England. Secondly, mergers and acquisitions had only limited effects. As the many accounts of the mergers
in British electrical engineering show, vertical integration failed
because the resulting firms were run like loose holding companies.
For example, the English Electric mergers, which pulled together the
resources of several British electrical manufacturers with Siemen's
British manufacturing arm and AEG's British sales organization, was
carried out without subsequent development of organizational capabilities (Chandler 1990: 349–50).

However, the British advantage in trade depended on access to
markets outside Europe, such as India and South Africa, which were
held to be technologically less demanding than the European
markets. Under Docker's leadership, Britain had been incapable of
gaining access to the most advanced markets in Europe. Performance
in the most advanced segments of light electrical engineering, a lucrative area that was increasingly dominated by Siemens, was also poor.
Despite the growing negative attitudes towards Docker's strategy,
BEMA still advised against an alliance with GE:

The British electrical industry has two possible moves left–either to form
closer associations with German and American manufacturing concerns,
and so become absorbed in the international combine which may be formed
ultimately, or to tighten up its own organization, to form a compact group
of manufacturers with a common policy both in manufacturing (prices and
orders) and in finance . . . The future prosperity of the industry is sufficient
justification for close cooperation in prices, manufacturing and market conditions. (BEMA 1927: 96–7)

Nevertheless, what the contemporary actors viewed as the limited
success of national governance persuaded Docker himself to rethink
the possibilities of international governance and, in particular, collaboration with GE. In order to revitalize the British industry, Docker
hence turned to Gerald Swope, previously CEO of Western Electric
and the electricity industry's most capable manager. As Jones and
Marriott (1970) show, to save British electrical engineering, Docker
abandoned his national strategy and orchestrated a merger between

Metrovic and GE's British subsidiary, BTH, as a first step towards linking the British governance system to GE's plans for a globalized governance system.

5.3.2. *Germany's revival*

AEG and its main domestic rival, Siemens, lost ground on foreign markets during the war: foreign assets were confiscated and German manufacturers were stripped of foreign patent rights. After the Versailles Treaty the German electrical manufacturers were threatened by both imminent isolation and general anti-German sentiments throughout the European continent (Schröter 1977). International isolation, combined with the unstable domestic situation that characterized the young Weimar Republic, provided a clear motive for Siemens and AEG's leaderships to consider strategies to renew the prewar alliance with American industry. Despite their inclination to break out of isolation through an alliance with the Americans, the German key actors were reluctant to enter a cartel under GE's leadership unless AEG and Siemens were allowed to re-establish their pre-1913 position in the international trade. Although the strengths and weaknesses were unevenly distributed, there were similarities in the strategic assessments made by British and German firms. Just like the British, the Germans arrived at the conclusion that international collaboration had to be based on the regaining of their prewar market position.

The unexpected strength that the German industry revealed between 1919 and 1923 put them on a more equal footing in the negotiations with GE, making international agreements more feasible. In particular, AEG was successful in taking advantage of the weak German currency on export markets because of its early shift from military to civil production. Thus, when the mark declined in 1919, AEG was one of the few manufacturers that were able to meet postwar demand. With the head start in plant reconversion to civil production, AEG was capable of re-establishing itself in the Scandinavian countries, France, and Belgium. Hence, German resistance to GE's initiatives broke down gradually, as AEG and Siemens began to experience the regaining of their former 'rightful' market shares and greatly expanded their part of international trade leadership during the growth period. By the end of the German inflation in late 1923, German firms were prepared for cartelization and bilateral agreements with GE, in both the allocation of markets and the exchange of technology and manufacturing experience.

However, the increased international antagonism between Germany and the Allied nations in 1922 had far-reaching effects on AEG's estimation of its relationship with GE. The failure at the Genoa Conference to generate an agreement among Allied powers to grant Germany a moratorium on reparation payments triggered the period of hyperinflation in the German economy. The preconditions for a peacetime accord with Germany were crumbling in this period, as illustrated by France's unilateral occupation of the Rhineland in its demand for war reparations. The sudden breakdown of German industrial activity after the French occupation and the hyperinflation made the shortcomings of the German energy system obvious. In important industrial areas such as Mannheim, coal-fired utilities had to import expensive imported coal and force already strained industrial customers to participate in an advance payment scheme to raise foreign currency (Schott 1997: 184–9). Large industrial customers, which were balanced against household consumption to achieve an even load factor, threatened to return to self-generation or to relocate to areas with hydroelectric power sources. In the face of these turbulent events, the key actors in Mannheim concluded that energy policy could not be handled on a local basis. As in many other cases, Mannheim thus aimed for a regionally integrated grid integration that would involve the state of Baden and several larger utilities.

Naturally, the collapse of the Reich Mark created serious liquidity problems for German manufacturers. According to Reid (1989), AEG, the more financially vulnerable of the two major German electro-groups, took actions to form a closer alliance with GE to secure financial aid. The altered attitude of AEG and the efforts to form closer financial ties to the American industry marked an important juncture in the German–American relationships. By the end of 1924, AEG and GE had activated the 'Principal Agreement', which stipulated exclusive markets, terms of cooperation with GE's licence-holders in Europe, and collaboration in manufacturing.

To reconstruct the German war reparations in the wake of hyperinflation, the victorious powers appointed Charles Dawes, a US banker, to propose a plan for currency stabilization in Central Europe. Dawes was appointed to lay down the principles for a rapid return to gold-based currency stabilization. A return to gold was generally seen as the key to the increased flows of foreign funds into the German economy, faciliating Germany's economic recovery. Being very much the political twin of the Dawes Plan, the Locarno Treaty of 1925 marked the end of coercion of Germany in favour of more cooperative international relations. Locarno's chief contribution was to stimulate hope for the future. Germany was on its way towards membership status in the League of Nations and the League contributed to the early removal of the occupation forces from the Rhineland, signalling Germany's confirmation of its western borders. The twin international relations landmarks of the mid-1920s—the Dawes Plan and the Locarno Treaty– proved to be of importance to German electrical manufacturers, as they provided the financial foundations for the integration of the relatively fragmented German electrical system, which had already before 1914 proved to be very vulnerable to the business cycle. The proclamation of the Dawes Plan not only promised hope for recovery for Mannheim's industry, but also provided a financially more solid foundation for the tendency towards regional integration and large-scale utilities.

Supported by AEG, the government started to prepare a scheme for central control by a state agency, arguing that only a national agency could adequately design and run an energy system for the whole nation. But the large private and semi-publicly owned power companies, such as REW, Electrowerke, and Preussen-Electra, were already far down the road towards integration, as exemplified by the grid that connected the Rhine and Westphalian districts, operated by RWE (Rheinisch-Westfälische Elektrizitätswerke). Other significant links connected brown coal districts in central Germany to hydro-stations in the Bavarian Alps (Brady 1933: 196: 217–219; Lucas 1985: 178–82).

The reorganization of the German energy system resulted in a period of rapid growth. The installed capacity increased by around 10 per cent per year between 1924 and 1929, resulting in a dramatic increase in German energy production. The increase reflects the move towards greater presence of public governance, larger units, and increased regional interlinkage (Brady 1933: 197). To meet the staggering demand, at home as well as abroad, German manufacturers looked towards the USA both for new efficiency models and for capital to sustain new investments. Financed largely by American capital, the rationalization movement contributed to soaring productivity and output levels in parallel with a great increase in electrical trade. Siemens was particularly responsive to what they saw as American production methods (see Homburg 1983 and Reid 1989, ch. 5, for a somewhat different interpretation).

Yet, scientific management was only one side of the rationalization movement. In addition, the German manufacturers explored mergers and cartel arrangements to settle the differences on the domestic markets to boost their international firepower. In his classic work on the rationalization movement and governance in German engineering, Brady (1933) showed the centrality of intra-industry coordination to the electrical engineering industry. On the one hand, R&D and the establishment of industry standards were carried out in cooperation between the large firms, the technical institutes, and the general interest organizations, such as Zentral Verband Elektrotechnischer Industrie, Vereinigung der Elektrizitätswerke, and the VDMA. Here, again, the leading firms were able to construct a solid foundation. Although advanced ideas to merge Siemens and AEG's marketing and selling activities into a joint company to reduce competition on the domestic market were shelved, the firms revitalized the prewar cartels. Also, the Zentral Verband Elektrotechnischer Industrie proved to be an effective vehicle for technical inter-firm cooperation. In particular, it institutionalized the dialogue between the full-line firms and the specialized suppliers. On the other hand, the network in the electrotechnical industry was brought into close contact with other German industries that faced the challenges of electrification. The various interconnections in the electrotechnical industry thus came more and more to take on the character of a general 'service' to nearly all branches of manufacturing and commerce in the German economy.

Thus the Dawes Plan underpinned the developments that led to the restructuring of both the demand and the supply side of German electrical manufacturing. To turn more effective domestic governance solutions into revenues, the manufacturers were, however, dependent on German diplomacy to open up European markets. Compared to their American competitors, AEG and Siemens were ultimately limited by the structure of the European market. Together with SOFINA's executive manager, Heinemann, executives of AEG and Siemens were for, example, instrumental in drawing up a plan for an integrated European energy grid that would eventually become the German 'home market'. While this bold plan lacked a firm footing in the realities of interwar international relations, German diplomacy was instrumental in re-establishing AEG and Siemens in the European market. Following the Locarno Treaty, German diplomacy succeeded in winning ratification of trade agreements across Europe, with particular emphasis on the French and the Soviet markets (Reid 1989).

5.4. Towards Multilateral Governance in International Markets

Between the mid-1920s and 1929, the establishment of national governance mechanisms and the increase in international trade initiated changes in the balance of power between the main actors. By the end of the decade, the largest European electrical manufacturers, the Germans and the British, had regained their previous spheres of interest in the global markets. In particular, the German firms showed a great readiness to form regional blocks involving the French, Swiss, and Scandinavian firms to inhibit the smaller firms' capacities to capture market shares through slashed prices. British industry controlled the trade with the Dominions, including Canada.

Despite the sign of efforts to build national industries, enhance corporate firepower, and to protect 'natural' market shares against penetration through bilateral agreements, the large players remained committed to the idea that there was a need for international governance of the relations between the main competitors in electrical engineering. The breakthrough came with the October Crisis and the second economic slump of the interwar period. Initially, the sudden collapse of German internal demand in 1929 made GE's leadership aware that Siemens and AEG would be likely to try to substitute domestic sales with exports, resulting in increased competition if not outright price wars in world markets. GE thus turned to German and British manufacturers with a new proposal to form a more effective coordination mechanism agreement based on bilateral agreements, which re-established the idea of a global cartel on the agenda of international electrical engineering policy. After intensive negotiations between the main actors between autumn 1929 and late 1930, the President of BTH, William Lusk, put forward a proposal for a multilateral cartel based on the principles for allocation of production quotas developed by the BEMA. (According to Jones and Marriott (1970), Lusk was regarded as GE and Swope's 'hatchet man' in British electrical engineering.) By December 1930, the large firms had signed the INCA (International Notification and Compensation Agreement), modelled on the internal British approach to regulation of competition on the domestic market (see Epstein and Newfarmer 1980). Being set up to achieve price stabilization, reduction of competition, and to help compensate the signatories for the heavy costs involved in designing and planning bids for contracts, the INCA was seen favorably by the large electrical manufacturers, which signed the agreement between the end of 1930 and 1933. The INCA did not regulate prices; it was built on the large number of bilateral understandings of the respective spheres of interest developed during the 1920s. Given the notification arrangement, however, it provided the industry with a forum that regulated competition to a limited extent, which helped keep the prices from collapsing. It was also viewed as a body for the promotion of joint interests, such as the financing of electrical trade and sharing of technology. What finally brought the competitors together into a multilateral cartel was thus a combination of reinforcing events that made GE's long-term plan for a multilateral cartel compatible with both the long-term and short-term interests of British and German electrical manufacturers.

5.4.1. *Britain*

Although access to technology and the need to use US organizational skills to improve British manufacturing contributed to Docker's reorientation in the late 1920s, it was again the concern for market shares that finally drove the British industry into GE's camp. Some of the evidence supports the notion that British manufacturers were concerned that the decline in Europe's demand for electrical equipment in 1929 would lead to new efforts by their competitors to penetrate the British spheres of influence in the imperial markets (Reid 1989). According to this line of argument, the British supported Lusk's proposal because it would protect Britain's market share in these areas. Whilst this might hold some water, it runs against the claim that Britain's manufacturers had concluded by 1927 that the technological gap between Britain and her competitors was actually caused by Britain's orientation towards the imperial markets. Nevertheless, the prospects of entering the European markets played a greater role in the British decision to participate in Lusk's plans than did the protection of existing markets. The British view on what restricted Britain's access to the European market was spelt out quite explicitly in 1927:

We find . . . that Saxony raising £750,000 in London to equip power stations where all the contracts have already been placed with German firms, and the City of Berlin obtaining with ease £3,500,000 to extend its underground system, the contracts again having been placed with German firms. . . . We can go through the list—the Republic of Estonia, Danzig, Finland, Greece— and discover that, out of £10,550,000 placed in London by six countries, nothing or practically nothing represents increased trade for British manufacturers. ... At the same time, the United States have advanced over £12,000,000 to electric supply undertakings in Italy—directly productive capital expenditure, which will be reflected in increased exports from American manufacturers. (BEMA 1927: 100)

Without narrowing the gap between British manufacturing, foreign competitors and their financial backers, British electrical manufacturers would remain too isolated to participate effectively in the big European deals. Lusk's plan certainly promised British access to those circles. For as Reid himself acknowledges, GE's vision was to create an 'investment trust that would assume an aggressive role in channeling capital from London and New York into electrification projects world wide. The trust was to be co-owned and controlled by the world's leading manufacturing firms' (1989: 258). Participation in a global cartel that chiefly aimed at protecting the existing allocation of markets would, on the views expressed by BEMA, have cemented the British strategic disadvantages in world trade in electrical goods.

5.4.2. *Germany*

GE's new proposal to set up a global coordination system to curb increased international competition started a trend towards increased coordination of activities between AEG and Siemens. In particular, they moved together to consolidate their export markets through a series of coordinated cartel agreements. By July 1930, the two firms had reached an understanding with the largest French manufacturers, which would serve as the basis for an expanded Continental cartel agreement under German leadership, including Sweden's ASEA and the Swiss manufacturer, BBC. To the German manufacturers, the overshadowing problem was the weak demand of electrical goods after 1929. As Reid describes, the German view of the prospects for the 1930s was in fact so pessimistic that particularly AEG began to favour a cartel agreement with GE that would protect the German-led cartel agreements and the formal trade treaties from penetration. While price maintenance always played a prominent role in the cartel negotiations between the large manufacturers during the interwar years, in 1930 the German manufacturers particularly favoured the principle of trade quotas as the basis for the multilateral cartel. To base the cartel on allocation of trade quotas instead of price fixing was judged by the Germans to better serve their short-term interests in defending their market share.

Siemens was less willing to join such a club. What finally made Siemens reconsider its position was a series of events that were akin to the circumstances under which AEG had decided to sign the general agreement with GE in 1924, i.e. lack of financial resources to rescue the firm in the deep economic crisis. Thus, when Siemens were caught in the midst of the October Crisis in 1929, GE's management received help from one of the financiers that had previously helped Siemens finance its rationalization in the mid-1920s. Dillon, Read & Co. now arranged for GE to buy securities in Siemens in order to restore the latter's financial standing. In essence, it was a very good deal for Siemens in that the securities financed Siemens's debts without giving GE the same influence in Siemens as stock.

Swope's success in building a financial bridge between GE and Siemens was followed by Lusk's proposal. What made Siemens rethink its previous strategy was the fact that the INCA agreement served Siemens's interests very well. Rather than superseding the pre-existing cartel agreement, the INCA proposal built on the existing institutional structure of bilateral cartel agreements that had developed during the course of the 1920s. Accordingly, the German markets were not up for grabs, but designated as exclusive territories under existing bilateral agreements. In essence, Germany 'got' the contested Continental markets, while large chunks of the American and British overseas markets were covered by the agreement and therefore not exclusive territories. Thus, the proposal was tailored to meet the combination of German export dependency and its fear of a prolonged stagnation in the export markets.

5.4.3. *The INCA and national governance before 1939*

Although the Depression caused a major decline in world orders and drove prices down, the INCA agreement at the international level inspired more cooperation at the domestic market level as a way to enhance national influence in international negotiations. In all three major producing countries, firms united in close cooperation, which paved the way for an even larger consensus around the international cartel. In the American market, GE and Westinghouse settled most of their differences and established a joint export association under the Webb Act, with the explicit ambition of coordinating and promoting their foreign activities. In particular, the export association provided the two main US manufacturers with a vehicle for coordinating US participation in INCA (Federal Trade Commission 1948: 54).

Concerning the outcome of the cartelization process in this period, a recent study of technological specialization in electrical engineering during the interwar period suggests that the large American firms involved in cooperative arrangements, namely GE and Westinghouse, became increasingly more focused and technologically specialized in different areas. Cross-licensing under the cartel agreement invoked some kind of division of labour between the firms, which reflects the fact that the cartel had a positive effect on technological specialization.

The militarization of the German economy under the Nazis resulted in mixed consequences for electrical manufacturers. While domestic demand soared as a consequence of government spending, the new regime set out to incorporate the large German manufacturers into the planned economy. The Nazi government's commitment to turn these manufacturers and their cartel organizations into instruments for the Nazi military economy, as exemplified by the amendment of the German Cartel Law in 1933, changed the rationale of national cartels. After 1935, the Nazis installed restrictions on price-setting and involved the manufacturers of electrical equipment more deeply in military programmes, which translated into costly reorganizations of productive resources and changes in the division of labour (Reich 1990). In addition, the new government put the electrical manufacturers under pressure to increase their exports in order to meet the increased demand for foreign currency that occurred as the Nazis realized their plans for German rearmament. Increased domestic political pressure on the German manufacturers spilled over into the arena of international electric engineering. According to US sources, the non-German members were not insensitive to the new situation facing the German manufacturers. It had, for example, been established by the Federal Trade Commission (FTC) that the US and British members of INCA were willing to accommodate the Germans by giving AEG and Siemens an increased share of orders from the British Imperial markets (Federal Trade Commission 1948: 43–8).

In the eyes of contemporaries, Docker's plans for national governance solutions did not provide British manufacturers with the necessary organizational capabilities. Even if the manufacturers themselves were less convinced about the effectiveness of the 'Groups' by the late 1920s, the economic slump of the 1930s helped revitalize the infrastructure for industry cooperation. As the slump deepened, as documented by the Monopolies and Restrictive

Practices Commission, large full-line producers re-established their collaborative arrangements in order to be able to coordinate activities, resulting in effective price maintenance in the domestic market (UK Monopolies and Restrictive Practices Commission 1957: 47–56). In addition, increased cooperation in the home market was followed by cooperative efforts at the international level. The British manufacturers were particularly keen on linking Siemens and AEG's quest for increased market shares to the British interest in the price issue. This was an area of importance, since British manufacturers had been less successful in the profitable light-current sector than their German and US competitors. Once concessions were made to Siemens and AEG through giving the Germans a share of the British markets, the British took the opportunity to pave the way for negotiations with the German manufacturer's industry association concerning world market prices in the electric trade. The British government supported the negotiations in order not only to help the British manufacturers negotiate higher prices in export markets but also to reduce the domestic pressure on tariff barriers and special trade privileges in the Dominions (Reid 1989: 292–3). Thus, the participation in the multilateral cartel reinforced the national industry infrastructure, since both British manufacturers and the British government saw participation in the cartel as a way of defending British trade interests.

5.5. Conclusion

At the turn of the twentieth century, the electrical industry had acquired its familiar structure, with close ties between vertically integrated manufacturing firms and finance, its characteristic mechanisms to build natural monopolies, and international cartels to organize competition, regulate prices, and pool technologies. These ties were effectively destroyed by the First World War. Above all, the rise of economic nationalism in the early interwar period, including soaring tariff measures, discouraged international investments, and volatile exchange rates made international business riskier. The volatile political climate in early interwar Europe promised, in addition, very little public institutional support for measures that would stabilize international business. Basing their research on well-known tendencies towards disintegration, unilaterism, and economic nationalism after 1919, historians have treated the interwar era as perhaps the most significant case of international fragmentation in the industrial era. The question asked in this chapter is how the key actors in an industry, such as electrical engineering, which was already heavily internationalized before 1900, dealt with international fragmentation. How did managers and other influential actors react to disintegration of the international market? How did they develop strategies and experiment to build the mechanisms that recreated the international market that existed before 1913?

This chapter points towards a surprising conclusion: given the uncertain environment with weak political support for governance of international business, managers on all sides of the electrical engineering industry concluded as early as 1919 that the new political and economic circumstances made a revitalization of private governance mechanisms necessary. To all of the large manufacturers, collaboration had a particular appeal. US manufacturers were concerned with the rise of economic nationalism and soaring trade barriers. In 1919, GE seemed strong enough successfully to capture larger market shares from its major competitors and, perhaps, drive some of the minor European manufacturers out of business. Swope feared, however, that such an aggressive strategy would backfire and that Europe would defend its markets through tariffs or other measures of economic nationalism. Swope's vision of the organization of economic relations after 1919 was one based on associational governance where cartel 'deals' could be a substitute for the aggressive export of US-produced goods to Europe. In essence, Swope's ambitions to build an international organization to safeguard the well-being of the industry appealed to European industry leaders for different reasons. In the British case, collaboration with GE promised access to improved technology, whereas the Germans were attracted by the opportunity to break out of postwar isolation as well as by GE's financial stability. While both British and German manufacturers saw good reasons to join GE's club in 1919, they were nevertheless reluctant to enter into collaboration on GE's terms. In both cases, managers began to experiment with intensified national governance structures to build technological and organizational capabilities. Between 1919 and the late 1920s, thus, European manufacturers involved themselves more deeply with national efforts to boost their capability to win market shares through exports.

It was during this era that the actors constructed a clear vision of improved national governance as an alternative to international governance solutions. However, the European strategies were not completely incompatible with GE's plans for international governance.

On the contrary: the late 1920s witnessed a convergence in the different US and European strategies, resulting in the International Notification and Compensation Agreement. Despite the European success in the foreign markets in the 1920s, both British and German manufacturers saw good reasons to forge a closer relationship with GE. In the British case, there was an emerging consensus that the British had been unsuccessful in their efforts to organize the links between the financial sectors and the manufacturers, resulting in a dependence on colonial markets and weak penetration of the more advanced European markets. Meanwhile, the two deep recessions and financial turbulence that typified the interwar period revealed the limitations of the German system of national governance. While Siemens and AEG's technological edge and capabilities to build foreign markets remained unquestioned, the lack of financial stability and capability to endure the crises in 1930s made the need for collaboration with the US manufacturers acute.

Actors developed a strategic vision of the advantages and disadvantages of building private governance mechanisms in order to sustain the operability of the international market. Both national and private international governance mechanisms were explored. Ultimately, actors identified a critical interlinkage between national and international governance mechanisms. On this view, the way that governance and market were shaped during this critical historical phase depended on the ability of actors to strategize and form colloborative networks. The creation of the visible hand of managerial hierarchies went along with processes of economic coordination that crossed national boundaries.

REFERENCES

BEMA (British Electrical and Allied Manufacturer's Association) (1927), *Combines and Trusts in the Electrical Industry*. London: BEMA.

Brady, R. A. (1933), *The Rationalization Movement in German Industry: A Study in the Evolution of Economic Planning*. Berkeley: University of California Press.

Carlson, W. B. (1991), *Innovation as a Social Process: Elihu Thomson and the Rise of General Electric, 1870–1900*. Cambridge: Cambridge University Press.

Catterall, R, (1979), 'Electrical Engineering', in N. K. Buxton and D. H. Aldcroft (eds.), *British Industry Between the Wars: Instability and Industrial Development 1919–1939*. London: Scholar Press.

Chandler, A. D. (1990), *Scale and Scope*. Cambridge: Harvard University Press.

Davenport-Hines, R. H. (1984), *Dudley Docker: Life and Times of a Trade Warrior*. Cambridge: Cambridge University Press.

Epstein, B. and Newfarmer, R. (1980), *International Electrical Association: The Continuing Cartel*. Washington, DC: US Government Printing Office.

Federal Trade Commission (1928), *Report on the Electric Power Industry: Supply of Electrical Equipment and Competitive Conditions*. Washington, DC: US Government Printing Office.

—— (1948), *Report on International Electrical Equipment Cartels*. Washington, DC: US Government Printing Office.

Feldenkirschen, W. (1997), 'Competition and Cooperation in German Electrical Industry in the Home and World Markets', in H. Pohl (ed.), *Competition and Cooperation of Enterprises on National and International Markets*. Stuttgart: Franz Steiner Verlag.

Foreman-Peck, J. (1983), *A History of the World Economy: International Economic Relations Since 1850*. Totowa, NJ: Barnes and Noble.

Granovetter, M. and McGuire, P. (1998), 'Making of an Industry: Electricity in the United States', in M. Callon (ed.), *The Laws of the Market*. Oxford: Blackwell.

Hirsch, R. (1989), *Technology and Transformation in the American Electric Utility Industry*. Cambridge: Cambridge University Press.

Homburg, I. (1983), 'Scientific Management and Personnel Policy in the Modern German Enterprise 1918–1939—The Case of Siemens', in H. Gospel and C. Littler (eds.), *Managerial Strategies and Industrial Relations*. London: Heinemann.

Hughes, T. P. (1983), *Networks of Power*. Baltimore: Johns Hopkins Press.

Jones, R. and Marriott, O. (1970), *Anatomy of a Merger*. London: Jonathan Cape.

League of Nations (1927), *Monograph on the Electrical Industry*. Geneva.

Liefermann, R. (1932), *Cartels, Concerns and Trusts*. London: Methuen.

Lucas, N. (1985), *Western European Energy Policies: A Comparative Study of the International Influence of Institutional Structure on Technical Change*. Oxford: Clarendon Press.

Passer, H. C. (1953), *The Electrical Manufacturers, 1875–1900*. Cambridge: Harvard University Press.

Platt, H. (1991), *The Electric City: Energy and the Growth of the Chicago Area 1880–1930*. Chicago: Chicago University Press.

Pribram, K. (1935), *Cartel Problems: An Analysis of Collective Monopolies in Europe with American Application*. Washington, DC: Brookings Institution.

Reich, S. (1990), *The Fruits of Fascism: Postwar Prosperity in Historical Perspective*. Ithaca: Cornell University Press.

Reid, P. R., (1989), 'Private and Public Regimes: International Cartelization of the Electrical Eqiupment Industry in an Era of Hegemonic Change, 1919–1939.' Ph.D. thesis, Johns Hopkins University, Baltimore.

Schott, D. (1997), 'Power for Industry: Electrification and Its Strategic Use for Industrial Promotion: The Case of Mannheim', in D. Schott (ed.), *Energie und Stadt in Europa*. Wiesbaden: Franz Steiner Verlag.

Schröter, H. (1977), 'A Typical Factor of German International Market Strategy: Agreements Between the US and German Electrotechnical Industries up to 1939', in A. Teichova, H. Lévy-Leboyer, and H. Nussbaum (eds.), *Multinational Enterprise in Historical Perspective*. Oxford: Oxford University Press, 161–9.

Segreto, L. (1994), 'Financing the Electrical Industry World Wide: Strategy and Structure of Swiss Holding Companies, 1895–1945', *Business and Economic History*, 23(1).

UK Monopolies and Restrictive Practices Commission (1957), *Report on the Supply and Export of Electrical and Allied Machinery and Plant*. London: HMSO.

Wilkins, M. (1989), *The History of Foreign Investment in the United States to 1914*. Cambridge: Harvard University Press.

6

The Internationalization of Capital Markets: How International Institutional Investors are Restructuring Finnish Companies

RISTO TAINIO, MIKA HUOLMAN,
AND MATTI PULKKINEN

6.1. Introduction

The internationalization of capital markets is having a significant impact on corporate restructuring worldwide (Useem 1996). By restructuring, we here mean mainly portfolio restructuring, including divestitures, liquidations, asset sales, and spin-offs, and organizational restructuring, including redesigning corporate governance systems and streamlining organizational structures (Bowman and Singh 1993).

At the company level, the internationalization of capital markets has encouraged the increase in foreign ownership and control of shareholdings (Whitley 1999). New, active, and demanding foreign shareholders have entered the scene, and challenged local managers as well as local, often patient or passive, owners. American institutional investors are the most visible and influential representatives of these new global actors. Unlike individual shareholders, they invest 'other people's money', and therefore they are prone to take proactive steps to protect or to increase the value of the companies they have invested in (David et al. 1998). Since the institutional investors often represent Anglo-Saxon governance norms and priorities, they have played a central role in disseminating the so-called 'shareholder view' to the management of companies in many countries.

The internationalization of capital markets has also reduced companies' dependence on domestic financial institutions (Whitley 1999). Companies frequently grow nowadays through mergers and acquisitions, and increasingly they use their own stocks, instead of cash or domestic bank debts, to finance these operations. It is in the international capital markets where the 'right' market value of the companies' stocks is determined.

Finnish companies have only recently become a part of the dynamics of the global capital markets. It was not until 1 January 1993 that foreigners were allowed to buy shares of Finnish companies without restrictions. Since then, foreign share ownership has increased rapidly, and by now the major Finnish companies have become foreign-owned to a substantial extent. By the end of 1999, 65 per cent of the stocks at the Helsinki Stock Exchange and one-third of all the stocks of Finnish companies were foreign-owned. Nokia, which dominates the Helsinki Stock Exchange, had 86 per cent of its stocks in the hands of foreign investors. The major Finnish companies have thus come under the constant scrutiny of global investors and financial analysts. This has made them transparent and comparable with other companies around the world.

Foreign ownership has made many Finnish companies more actively owned and more owner-driven than ever before (Tainio 1999; Veranen 1996). On one hand, managers of Finnish companies with substantial foreign ownership feel the increased yield expectations of these new owners, and related pressures for corporate restructuring. On the other hand, managers of companies with little or no, foreign ownership feel increasing pressures to be noticed by foreign investors. In this case, managers tend to restructure their companies in order to catch the attention and to increase the attractiveness of their companies in the eyes of investors (Huolman et al. 1999).

Under these circumstances, the growth of companies is increasingly dependent on their success in the international capital markets. It is no longer enough to outperform competitors in the product/service markets. Companies which are most capable of creating value for their shareholders are also able to obtain the most abundant financial resources on the most favourable terms. Companies can nowadays raise their stock market values with ideas, expectations, or images, often without a significant business substance. From this position, they can later acquire leading companies, break value chains, and restructure their own competitive positions. In this way, financially strong companies are able to define the rules of the game for those whose competitive advantage lies mainly in the product market arena.

In the short run, the effects of growing foreign ownership in Finnish companies look obvious: Finnish companies are being Americanized. This can be seen in the changes of goal-setting, performance criteria, and dividend policies. Similar kinds of change can also be noticed in managerial incentive schemes, governance structures, and the mix of companies' business portfolios. So far, these restructurings have occurred in Finland without substantial clashes or conflicts with local stakeholders. This is mainly due to the fact that the short-term economic outcomes of foreign ownership have been predominantly positive in the Finnish context. First, the entry of foreign capital to Finland occurred at a time when the country was in the deepest recession of all the OECD countries. At that time foreign capital was more than welcome in Finland, and was widely regarded as a major catalyst for the turnaround of Finnish firms, and the economy as a whole. Secondly, foreign-owned companies actually performed better than domestically-owned companies during the 1990s. They have been significantly more efficient in capital formation, value creation, and even in providing employment (Ali-Yrkkö and Ylä-Anttila, forthcoming).

In the long run, the effects of foreign ownership seem, however, more ambiguous. Long-term results will depend on what kind of side-effects will occur from the operations that have produced the short-term economic efficiencies and profound structural changes. It can be expected that the more the key characteristics and strategic priorities of Finnish companies are changed towards Anglo-Saxon models and principles, the more debate and controversies will eventually emerge (see Whitley's contribution in Chapter 2). It seems quite unlikely that the Americanization of Finnish companies will be a smooth process in the long run.

The purpose of this chapter is to examine how these distant and dispersed foreign investors restructure Finnish companies. First, we explore the channels of their influence. Secondly, we describe some of the major recent outcomes of these changes. Thirdly, we outline the ongoing dynamics between foreign shareholders and local managers in Finnish companies.

This is accomplished through an analysis of the thirty largest Finnish companies. Special attention was paid to the development of their foreign stock ownership, corporate restructuring, and the channels of foreign investors' influence. The data were gathered from the annual reports of the companies and interviews with their investor relations managers. These data were enriched by interviews with ten financial analysts, who were each monitoring at least one of the studied companies.

6.2. **How Does Foreign Ownership Influence Finnish Companies?**

The foreign portfolio ownership of Finnish companies started to increase after the full liberalization of foreign share ownership in 1993. Low stock prices due to the economic recession, and the related high-growth potential of Finnish companies, made them attractive investment targets right away. As the recovery of the companies progressed, investors' expectations were fulfilled and the demand for the stocks remained high.

The most significant foreign shareholders of Finnish companies are major American investment funds like Franklin Research, Fidelity Management & Research, Capital Research Management, Alliance Capital Management, Morgan Stanley, and Merill Lynch. Also, the two largest public pension funds, CalPERS and TIAA-CREF, have significant ownership stakes in major Finnish companies. Individually, the funds in a single investment fund group own rather small stakes (ranging from 0.1 to 4.0 per cent), but together they represent significant proportions of ownership in different companies.

In Finland, managers have, in general, found foreign owners more demanding than local owners. Foreigners are more concerned to get prompt returns on their investments. They do not intervene in operational matters, but they expect the value of their Finnish shares to increase. Therefore, foreign owners are active in creating conditions to ensure that this actually happens. Under these demands Finnish companies are currently experiencing a managerial revolution, which has not been witnessed before. They have started to operate in a similar way to American and British firms. Foreign investors have brought an Anglo-Saxon shareholder view and a whole new owner-driven management culture into Finnish companies (Moen and Lilja, Chapter 4 in this volume; Veranen 1996).

It is not, however, obvious how the pressures from international investors become a part of the local reality. Foreign investors still operate at arm's length from the Finnish companies they have invested in. They are distant, dispersed, and often 'faceless', yet they influence firms through multiple channels. Two of them, an indirect market-channel (exit-influence) and direct personal-channel (voice-influence), which have previously received most of the attention (see Hirschman 1970), were not the most utilized channels in the studied companies.

'Exit-influence' means that shareholders affect management by the actual sales, or the threat of sales, of their shares in the stock market. Foreign institutional investors have been relatively stable owners of Finnish stocks in these first few years. The level of their investments has, of course, varied through the passage of time, but the major investors have stayed relatively patient and retained the holdings in Finnish companies that they invested in the very beginning (Veranen 1996). So far, their investments cannot be labelled 'short-term', but nor are they yet 'long-term'.

Foreign investors rarely regarded their exit-influence as influence. Their stock trading was not talked about in terms of 'intentionally influencing management or companies'. Rather, their moves were justified by their own business objectives and logics of action. Finnish managers, however, felt strongly that the outcomes of these stock market operations, i.e. changes in the share prices, meant concrete 'punishments' or 'rewards'. This rare use of 'exit-influence' by foreign investors can be explained by quite a 'thin' market in the Helsinki Stock Exchange, where extensive sales easily hurt investors themselves. In addition, frequent changes between investment targets are also expensive, and risky, especially in an unfamiliar context and market.

The use of a direct voice-influence means that an owner/investor affects companies by giving personal instructions and advice to management in shareholder or supervisory board meetings, or in the boards of directors. In Finland, foreign investors have only rarely raised their voice in shareholder meetings. It is also uncommon for them to sit on either the supervisory boards or the boards of directors of Finnish companies. In the studied companies there were annually altogether approximately 210 directors of boards. Out of these there were only 3 foreigners in 1993, 10 in 1995, and 18 in 1998. The formal meetings, especially annual shareholder meetings and supervisory board meetings, were not regarded as the most appropriate or efficient places to intervene in corporate affairs. As one of the interviewed investors put it: 'I do not want to say in public how to manage the company well, I just want a well-managed company.'

In Figure 6.1 we summarize the major ways in which foreign investors were found to channel their influence to the studied companies. In general, the evidence suggests that although foreign owners produce market effects and apply personal influence through formal meetings, the major ways in which they influence Finnish companies are 'relational investing' and 'board reforms'. These channels comprise the lower and middle part of the figure. Relational investing means informal, but often regularly structured, meetings between foreign owners and local managers. These meetings consist of a continuous two-way exchange of information, and the exercise of influence (Useem 1996). Financial analysts and investor relation specialists are central in these meetings.

Board reforms, on the other hand, indicate the growing significance of the board of directors as a channel of influence for foreign investors. Institutional investors who do not want to sit on boards have become especially active in pressuring boards to challenge management (Lorsch 1995). Therefore, boards need to be empowered and redesigned to be able to do that.

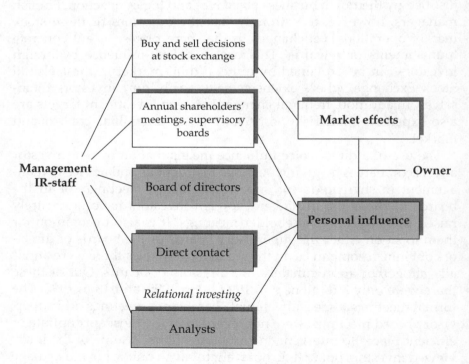

Figure 6.1. *Foreign owners' channels of influence*

6.2.1. *Relational investing*

Relational investing is a significant, but often neglected, channel of owners' influence. The informal meetings and discussions between shareholders and managers are typically surrounded by secrecy, and the ways in which the actual influence is created are seldom shared with outsiders. Anecdotal evidence (Useem 1996) and some case studies point out that most of the initiatives, especially those of institutional investors, raised in these private discussions are in fact implemented (Carleton et al. 1998).

In the Finnish context, foreign owners participate in relational investing mainly through financial analysts and portfolio managers. These financial professionals play a significant mediating role between foreign owners and local managers. To the foreign owners they provide information about various companies and their future prospects. They evaluate, rate, and compare companies as investment targets. To the management they provide information about shareholders' interests and preferences, and give suggestions and recommendations from that particular perspective. Three levels of analysts' influence on management could be identified from our data. At the weakest level, financial analysts give only recommendations and advice to sell or buy the shares. This way they mainly facilitate stock-trading (sell-side analysts). Financial analysts may also specialize in serving long-term investors in their decision-making. In this buy-side role, the main task of the analysts is to search and rate companies by their future prospects and value potential. It is possible that if sell-side and buy-side analysts serve the same investment house, their recommendations may end up being contradictory. In these kinds of situations financial analysts often created their own vision about the company, and gave their own personal suggestions to the management. This way, financial professionals also exercised their own independent influence on corporate restructuring.

The strongest influence of the analysts was implemented in their 'venture capitalist' role. There, their instructions were backed by their substantial stakes in the company. Their suggestions were often in the form of orders, which management was forced to fulfil. In addition, financial analysts turned out to be particularly important mediators for companies that were still unknown to foreign investors. These financial analysts were central in the processes by which managers tried to raise a company's attraction and visibility. Analysts are experts in giving advice on how to improve companies' investor relations practices and how to get their messages through in the international capital markets.

There exists a number of contexts or arenas where relational investing occurs and which determines how influential it is. These arenas can vary from an analyst's telephone call to check the news from a CEO to the official presentation of a company in 'Road Shows'. In between there exists a wide range of meetings and negotiations where management meets analysts, gives information about the company, and answers questions. The most common forums for this kind of informal exchange for information are one-on-one meetings, informal group gatherings, company visits, capital market days in companies, and conference calls. They differ in whether they occur in private or public, whether they are led and organized by company managements or by analysts, and whether they are based on a one-way flow of information or a dialogue/debate. The exercise of influence is dependent on the confidentiality of meetings. These arenas differ as to the intensity of influence and information-sharing. In their weakest form they are the arenas of routinized information exchange, and in their strongest form the major investors work closely with the management and implement their reform programme.

Our evidence indicates that analysts regard one-on-one meetings and company visits as the most important sources of information. It is, however, difficult to estimate how influential these meetings are in practice. Our evidence points out that the questions and hints management receives are usually listened to and taken seriously. For the preparation of these meetings, management needs a 'good story', which is clear, sensible, and interesting. It includes the business idea, strategy, and the future prospects of the company. It serves as a good sounding board for management to consider suggestions the analysts tend to make.

6.2.2. *Board reform*

The board of directors is another channel of influence, which is growing in significance among foreign owners of Finnish companies. Foreign owners have actively encouraged managers to start reforming the structure and process of boards and their decision-making. They have made suggestions to redesign the composition of boards, to develop more efficient work procedures, and to create more active and independent profiles for the boards. A board is the body that has the main responsibility for monitoring company performance. It has the formal authority to hire, fire, and compensate top management, and to provide advice and counsel for it. In the Anglo-Saxon corporate governance system it is the board of directors that represents the interest of shareholders. It meets usually a 6–10 times a year, includes outsiders, and works, in effect, on a part-time basis. Therefore, the members of a board usually represent diverse businesses and leadership experiences. A board's ability to govern depends on two main sources: knowledge about the company, and their cohesion as a group (Lorsch 1995).

So far, foreign investors themselves have not been particularly active on the boards of Finnish companies, but they have been active in underlining the principles that make a good board. Its most important components are: the quality of directors, their independence from top management, and their commitment to the company. This means that foreign owners want to redesign boards to be composed of active, critical directors, who are significant stock-owners in the companies they oversee. A good board includes a minimum of insiders and no interlocking directorships. In the Finnish context these demands mean a radical change in the composition of boards, which have traditionally been CEO-driven, passively owned, and tightly interlocked. The purpose of foreign owners is to increase the accountability of board members to shareholders, and in this way to strengthen the role of boards at the expense of top management and supervisory boards. This has started to happen in the studied companies. The number of supervisory boards is decreasing and the role of their boards of directors is increasing. This can be seen in Figure 6.2. This trend was even stronger than the figure demonstrates, since the five state-owned companies in the data are obliged to have supervisory boards, according to Finnish law. In addition, the size of the supervisory boards in the studied companies has been steadily decreasing. In 1989 there were on average fourteen members in the supervisory boards; by 1998 the average size was only five. It was in the companies where foreign ownership was low that supervisory boards were left untouched more often than in the companies with high or fast-growing foreign ownership.

Foreign investors have not hidden their critical stand towards supervisory boards. They have publicly claimed that supervisory boards are inefficient at adding value to the companies, and they do not provide an effective channel to enhance shareholders' interests. The evidence from the interviews with both financial professionals and company executives strongly supports the view that foreign

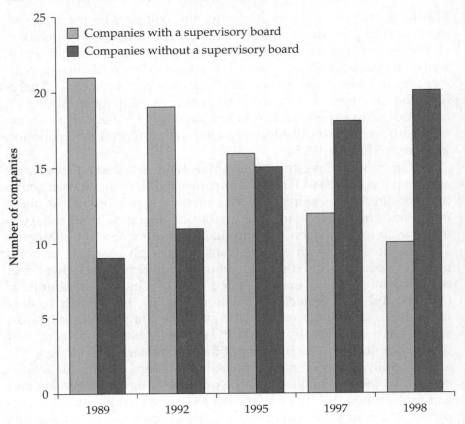

Figure 6.2. *The decrease in the number of supervisory boards in Finnish companies*

owners have played a central role in the process of changing the relative power of supervisory boards and boards of directors. At the same time, this has meant pressures to abandon the whole two-tier governance system, which has been typical in large Finnish companies. At the most general level, critics of supervisory boards have also been critical of the whole stakeholder approach it represents.

Our evidence suggests that foreign owners increasingly question the relevance and efficiency of the exit- and voice-channels in the Finnish context (this same observation has currently been made in the USA: see Carleton et al. 1998). Their major efforts to oversee and affect Finnish companies have been occurring through informal networks of personal influence, where financial professionals have played a visible role, and through structural reorganization of the board of directors building an efficient channel of influence.

6.3. **What has Changed in Finnish Companies?**

The most striking changes, which have occurred in the studied companies, have been in the areas of, first, managerial incentive schemes and, secondly, business portfolios. These are the distinct areas of restructuring, where foreign owners have been most open about the need for change. The outcomes of the changes in these areas have also catalyzed other tendencies that have increased the penetration of the shareholder view.

6.3.1. *Managerial incentive schemes*

One of the strongest effects of growing foreign ownership has been observed in managerial incentive systems. The outcome-based contracts have been seen to result directly from owner-driven governance structures (Eisenhardt 1989). The most typical forms of outcome-based compensations are stock options and equity holdings, which are regarded as means of bonding management to shareholders' interests.

Between 1988 and 1998 there occurred 90 stock option arrangements in Finnish companies listed on the Helsinki Stock Exchange. Especially since 1994, as can be seen in Figure 6.3, option schemes have become more common (Ikäheimo 1998). The first options were introduced in Finnish companies in the late 1980s. Although they were at that time favourably taxed they did not spread widely in companies. Until 1997 the new incentive schemes were designed mainly for top management. Thereafter, the key personnel, or even all employees, have been included in the option programmes. Foreign owners are not particularly enthusiastic about the broad coverage of option schemes, but they accept them in the companies, the success of which is, to a large extent, dependent on the qualified workforce and their loyalty.

6.3.2. *Business portfolios*

It is well known that foreign investors like clarity, which means specialized and focused business portfolios in the companies. Since they themselves can diversify their risks directly through their investment portfolios, they prefer 'focused and compact' individual investment targets (Amihud and Lev 1981).

This overall development was present in one form or another in all studied companies during the 1990s. In Finland, Nokia is a classical

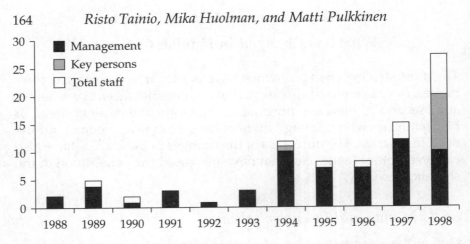

Figure 6.3. *The increase of stock option arrangements in Finland, 1988–98*

example of this development. As Jorma Ollila, chairman of Nokia, states: 'Nokia has transformed into a 100 per cent focused telecommunication company very fast.' At the end of the 1980s over 50 per cent of its revenues came from businesses such as cable, rubber, and paper, while telecommunications generated only 17 per cent of its sales. In less than ten years the company has focused its operations entirely on telecommunications, which today consists of businesses such as mobile phones (63 per cent of turnover in 1998, compared to 8 per cent in 1989), telecom networks, and other communications products.

The evidence suggests that the influence of international financial markets and the power of institutional investors have been one of the major catalysts in this development. According to the current trends in global capital markets, investors prefer companies that are highly focused around one major core business. According to this view, it is the investor, not the company, which makes the diversification. Financial professionals regard Nokia as a highly investor-oriented company. The restructuring of its business portfolio fits well with the preferences of the investors in the global financial markets.

Although Nokia's transformation was widely regarded as an extreme case during the 1990s in Finland, our evidence from the other companies points in the same direction. The most specialized companies in our database are those with the highest level of foreign share ownership. But we can also observe that some of the well-focused companies have relatively little foreign ownership. This indicates that some of the companies either anticipate the demands of foreign investors, or that other factors have also favoured specialized business portfolios. The most frequently mentioned factor has been the increase in foreign competition.

There is no doubt that foreign institutional investors like stock options to reconcile the interests of local managers to their own. It is also clear that investors do not like conglomerates. They can also get these messages across to local companies. Most of the managers confide that they still have options to choose from. Whether they say 'yes' or 'no' to these suggestions will be reflected in the share price. It is the major indication of investors' will and influence. If the local managers approve and implement the changes, they at the same time create cumulative processes for positive developments. If they disagree, there is a risk that the opposite will happen and foreign investors will react in other ways. Thus foreign investors are able to create mutual interdependencies, which are reflected in rising and falling share prices.

The outcomes of foreign owners' influence can, in this light, be seen in the form of virtuous or vicious circles rather than isolated changes in companies. Foreign owners tend to initiate or maintain chain reactions, where purposeful actions are followed by unintentional side-effects, which often create expanding or contracting dynamics. A change in the share prices typically sets off, or accelerates, such cumulative processes in corporate restructuring.

In the case of a virtuous circle a company has succeeded in making itself, or one of its new ideas, interesting to investors. They provide initial stakes, which raise growth expectations and, consequently, share prices. This expands positive publicity, which further lifts the demand for the stocks. The increased share price makes it possible for management to raise capital for acquisitions and/or R&D investments. These operations help management to restructure the company and raise it to a higher 'league'. From there it is easy to dominate the old players in the product market arena, or to break existing competitive barriers and positions . This boosts again the image of a leading company, which makes it increasingly attractive in the labour market and helps to recruit high-quality managers and expertise. The commitment of these new people is strengthened by linking payment incentives to share prices. This new human and social capital opens up further prospects for profitable businesses, which will lift the share prices even higher, which further motivates—and so on.

Falling share prices, on the other hand, tend to launch an opposite type of vicious circle in company development. When the strategies or structures of local companies do not create or maintain the interests of investors, share prices tend to stay low, or fall. This restricts management's possibilities for growth and renewal of the company. Falling share prices reinforce the unattractive image of the company. Businesses stagnate or decline, which makes outcome-based incentive systems problematic. The best people tend to leave, and recruitment of new ones becomes difficult. Decreasing quality of personnel increases production and efficiency problems, which slows down a search for new innovations or business ideas. The market value of the company falls further, and makes it vulnerable. It becomes a potential takeover target.

In the companies which we studied, both types of cycles could be identified and, through these, the outcomes from foreign institutional investments could be observed in the whole Finnish business system. Foreign owners have promoted the emergence of a new economic engine in Finland. Today's fastest growing industries are telecommunications, information technologies, and biotechnology. On the other hand, more traditional industries, like the paper industry and other process industries representing the old core of Finnish economy, struggle with their attractiveness in the capital markets. In these industries, foreign investors seem to favour more maintenance rather than capacity expansion investments (Huolman et al. 1999).

6.4. The Changing Influence of Foreign Investors in Finland

The strength of the influence of foreign investors is dependent especially on two factors: the performance of a company and the distribution of share ownership. A common observation is that the owners of companies with poor or worsening performance are more actively involved in changing strategies and structures than the owners of high-performing companies (Lorsch 1995). This indicates that owners are more influential in declining and crisis situations than the internal management is. Managers, on the other hand, are strong in times of prosperity and growth. The stronger the company is financially, the wider are the discretion and strength of its top management.

In addition, the influence of foreign investors seems to be stronger the more cohesive they are as a group. If foreign shareholders are relatively fragmented, or if they have only small stakes compared to domestic shareholders, they are likely to be less influential than if they comprise a large and unified bloc of owners (Whitley 1999). Both of these factors, the performance of a company and the distribution of share ownership, point to the same explanatory dynamics: the changing power balance between foreign owners and local management. By a simple typology, based on the relative power of foreign owners and local managers, four different situations can be identified (see Figure 6.4; cf. Pearce and Zahra 1991).

In a 'ceremonial' situation, both foreign owners and local management have a relatively weak power position. Decision-making on both sides is passive, reactive, and, at most, focused on information exchange. Owners are mostly passive and distant. They base their opinions mainly on formal financial analyses and public statements about the company. Managers are inactive in corporate development. This might be due to interests other than work in their lives or to the small stakes they own in the company. In the companies that we studied, there were very few indications that this kind of a situation was present. Some comments about the 1980s, however, indicated that there had been examples in that period. This was the time

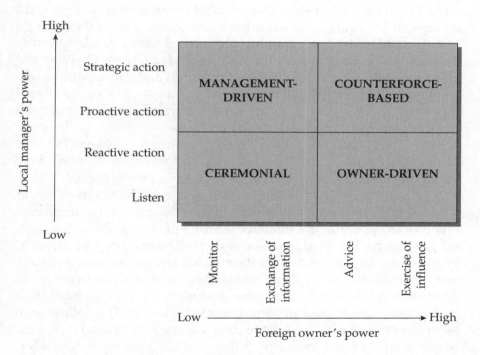

Figure 6.4. *Relative power of foreign owners and local managers*

when foreigners as industrial investors first approached Finland. Their analyses about Finnish companies were mostly superficial and mechanistic. Finnish managers, on the other hand, still worked in a sheltered and regulated business environment. Under those circumstances, foreign owners evidently had only weak influence on the performance and development of Finnish companies.

In a 'management-driven' situation, local management becomes a central player in corporate development. The strong power position of management is often backed up by the high performance of the company. Finnish companies were economically strong at the end of 1980s. This strengthened the managers' position in relation to owners. From that period stems the traditional view of Finnish companies as 'passively owned' and 'CEO-driven'. In this situation owners were mostly receivers of managerial information, and their powers were limited to the approval, or rubber stamping of managerial choices and strategies.

An 'owner-driven' situation occurs, when owners' interests dominate a company. This is typical in declining or deeply troubled companies. In Finland this situation was widely experienced during the recession in the early 1990s. Management became rapidly dependent on foreign investors, who expected managers to follow their advice and demands. Managers humbly provided detailed inside information about the company to the owners and analysts. Owners and managers held regular and frequent meetings and conversations that were typically initiated and organized by analysts. Before the annual meetings, CEOs spent a lot of time lobbying actual or potential owners. Analysts appeared mostly as 'reform experts' in the companies. They had their own theory about the reasons for the company's troubles, and their analyses and recommendations were based on careful studies and various sources of information.

A 'counterforce-based' situation is characterized by high owner as well as high management power. The existence of counterforces involves the potential for effective steering of companies and a fruitful ground for knowledge creation there. The meetings or informal negotiations are full of debate, discussion, and controversies. Extensive negotiations take place on building and reaching consensus between foreign owners and local managers. Both sides have their own active roles to play in corporate restructuring. They allow each other the opportunity to reshape their visions and strategies. Hence, two powerful parties may enrich their mutual learning by considering more alternatives, understanding a wider range of options, and expanding their conceptions about organizational reality. The expertise on both sides makes it possible critically to read plural signs of performance and to respect diversity and multiple logics in developing the company.

This situation may provide an alternative to owner-driven structures in the future. The situation in Nokia seems to involve features which qualify as a counterforce-driven situation. There, the management has more power and discretion over foreign investors than in the other studied Finnish companies, but management still carefully follows and underlines the priorities of a shareholder view.

The internationalization of capital market is by no means complete, nor are its impacts on local companies clear. Our evidence, however, suggests that foreign owners, as the key actors of international capital markets, are changing the face of corporate Finland, at least in a short-term frame. Words such as 'cause' and 'effect' are still to be used with caution, since foreign owners are only able to have a direct and strong influence on local management under specific circumstances (c.f. Kristensen and Zeitlin, Chapter 7, as well as Lane, Chapter 3, in this volume).

6.5. Conclusion

Recent shareholder activism and the rapid spread of the shareholder view around the world have generated new relationships between foreign investors and local managers, which resemble neither markets nor hierarchies. While extant literature still emphasizes 'exit' and 'voice' as the major ways for the investors to influence company affairs, our findings point to the importance of relational investing. In these informal interactions and meetings, local managers learn what actually are the demands of shareholder value. Foreign investors and their representatives, on the other hand, learn what is possible in the local product market and its social and economic context. In addition, they learn how local managers articulate their possibilities and limits.

Especially important in the process of relational investing is the mediating role of the financial professionals between investors and management. The extensive competition between analysts and their investment houses keeps constant pressures on economic efficacy also in Finnish companies. In the short run, there exist clear tendencies towards convergence, i.e. the Americanization of Finnish companies. Especially obvious in this respect are recent changes in the role of a board of directors, restructuring of business portfolios, and managerial incentive systems.

At the same time as foreign investors have pressed Finnish managers to restructure their companies, they have created turbulence in the institutional arrangements, and in the whole Finnish business system (Laurila 1999). The old industrial engine of Finland, which for over a century had been based on large-scale, capital-intensive forest sector companies, experienced a fast and profound transformation during the 1990s. New growth industries, based on advanced information and telecommunication technology, biotechnology, and other R&D intensive business areas, became the newly emerging core of the Finnish economy (Lilja and Tainio 1996).

The straightforward application of the American model to Finnish companies has already raised substantial debate and controversies. The outcome of these conflicts will depend on the relative power of various interest groups and the strength of the Finnish institutional structures. It is quite likely that they will produce locally and nationally distinct ways to govern and structure Finnish companies. A short-term convergence between Finnish and American companies is thus bound to lead to their divergence in the long run.

REFERENCES

Ali-Yrkkö, J. and Ylä-Anttila, P. (forthcoming), 'Globalisation of Business in a Small Country—Implications for Corporate Governance', *Management International Review*.

Amihud, Y. and Lev, B. (1981), 'Risk Reduction as a Managerial Motive for Conglomerate Mergers', *Bell Journal of Economics*, 12: 605–17.

Bowman, E. and Singh, H. (1993), 'Corporate Restructuring: Reconfiguring the Firm', *Strategic Management Journal*, 14: 5–14.

Carleton, W. T., Nelson, J. M. and Weisbach, M. S. (1998), 'The Influence of Institutions on Corporate Governance through Private Negotiations: Evidence from TIAA-CREF', *The Journal of Finance*, 53: 1335–62.

David, P., Kochhar, R. and Levitas, E. (1998), 'The Effect of Institutional Investors on the Level and Mix of CEO Compensation', *Academy of Management Journal*, 41: 200–8.

Eisenhardt, K. (1989), 'Agency Theory: An Assessment and Review', *Academy of Management Review* 14: 57–74.

Hirschman, A. (1970), *Exit, Voice, and Loyalty*, Cambridge, MA: Harvard University Press.

Huolman, M., Pulkkinen, M., Rissanen, M., Tainio, R. and Tukiainen, S. (1999), *Ulkomaisen omistuksen vaikutus yrityksen johtamiseen ja innovaatioihin (The Impact of Foreign Ownership on Management and Innovations)*. Helsinki: LTT-Researh Ltd.

Ikäheimo, S. (1998), 'Optiojärjestelyt Suomessa: teoria ja empiiriset havainnot' (Option Schemes in Finland: Theory and Empirical Observations), in K. Lukka (ed.), *Pekka Pihlanto-individuaali laskentatoimen tutkija*. Turku: Turku School of Economics and Business Administration, Publications, 65–94.

Laurila, J. (1999), 'Management in Finland', in M. Warner (ed.), *Management in Europe*. London: International Thomson Business Press, 211–17.

Lilja, K. and Tainio, R. (1996), 'The Nature of the Typical Finnish Firm', in R. Whitley and P. H. Kristensen (eds.), *The Changing European Firm: Limits to Convergence*. London: Routledge, 159–91.

Lorsch, J. (1995), 'Empowering the Board', *Harvard Business Review*, 73: 107–17.

Pearce II, J. and Zahra, S. (1991), 'The Relative Power of CEOs and Boards of Directors: Associations with Corporate Performance', *Strategic Management Journal*, 12: 135–53.

Tainio, R. (1999), *Ulkomaalaisomistuksen vaikutus suomalaisten yritysten johtamiseen ja rakenteeseen. (The Impact of Foreign Ownership on Management and Structure of Finnish Companies)*, Suomalaisen Tiedeakatemian vuosikirja 1998 (Academia Scientiarum Fennica, Year Book 1998), Vammala: Vammalan Kirjapaino.

Useem, M. (1996), *Investor Capitalism*, New York: Basic Books.

Veranen, J. (1996), *Tuottoa vaativat omistajat (Yield Demanding Owners)*. Porvoo: WSOY.

Whitley, R. (1999), *Divergent Capitalisms. The Social Structuring and Change of Business Systems*. Oxford: Oxford University Press.

7

The Making of a Global Firm: Local Pathways to Multinational Enterprise

PEER HULL KRISTENSEN AND JONATHAN ZEITLIN

7.1. Introduction

The putative lead agent of globalization, the multinational company (MNC) is traditionally seen as a coherent entity that will change the competitive selection process and make firms extinct that do not adapt to its new reality. The comparative advantage of the multi-national, transnational, and global firm is believed to be its ability first to exploit, then to coordinate, and finally to optimize activities across countries with different comparative advantages at any given moment. Firms that do not possess such comparative advantages will suffer. It is the very essence of the concept of the emerging global firm that it should eventually acquire control over, and consequently inscribe into its own logic and internal hierarchy the local comparative advantages of non-global firms (Dunning 1993: xv, Exhibit 0.1.). Pushed by this lead agent, globalization unfolds according to a given logic that structures the world for all other agents.

In researching whether and how the global hierarchy of one MNC might also serve the development of its local entities, the subsidiaries, and their regional or national contexts, we made a number of highly surprising observations. These observations, though based on a single case study, served to complicate the received image of multi-nationals and raised larger questions about how to conceive of globalization.

Three 'drill samples' from our observations may illustrate these complications and the urgent need for re-conceptualization.

7.1.1. *The local outlook of a headquarters versus the global outlook of local subsidiaries*

In conducting interviews at all staff levels in both the headquarters (HQ) and the subsidiaries of a British-owned multinational engineering group,[1] we found that the terminology used to describe progress and development differs sharply. In subsidiaries progress and development are spoken of in terms of technological innovations and improvements, being told as narratives that also integrate the biographies of significant persons. The language at the HQ, on the contrary, draws on the generalizing idioms of MBA programmes for global and financial managers, focusing on current topics in management journals. Attention is directed towards general objectives concerning subsidiaries, and only becomes specific when dealing with the predicted behaviour of major investors in relation to the conjectures of the stock market.

A first interpretation of this difference in languages and in the conceptualization of the history of the MNC reinforces the expected view that the HQ is pursuing a global vision of global issues, whereas subsidiaries rather focus on local or narrow technical concerns. This interpretation may, however, be misleading. A closer look at the points of reference for the London-based HQ shows that these are all typically located less than an hour away. The managerial staff is using the terminology of the nearby business schools and other similar institutions scattered around the metropolis, where most of them have received some training. These business schools, together with proximate international consulting firms, furnish the managerial staff with the general perspectives and strategies that they pursue in relation to the subsidiaries which they think they control. The sentiments of major investors and the stock market are easily monitored through everyday relations and gossip, as the City of London is part of the neighbourhood. Most significantly, however, the attention of the managerial staff is basically focused inwards, as the HQ resembles the scene that Machiavelli portrayed with virtuosity in *The Prince*. Each manager must be careful of each step he takes (and it is

---

[1] This group specialized in the design and manufacture of automated systems and equipment for the food-processing, beverage, personal care product, pharmaceutical, and related industries. Having doubled in size through a series of acquisitions during the 1980s, the group had worldwide sales of $1.5 billion in 1993 and employed 14,000 people on five continents, mainly in Europe and North America. In 1997, it was acquired in turn by a larger UK-based multinational group.

still usually he rather than she in this world), as everyone else will be prepared to take advantage of any kind of weakness, being mutually aware of the fact that probably none of them possesses much valuable knowledge about the concrete global activities of the MNC. Furthermore, they are equally unable to assess the value of this improbable knowledge, should anyone possess it. Consequently, managers play a coalition-building game in which they take for granted that anyone can easily be replaced by a multiplicity of substitutes employed or seeking work elsewhere in the local 'corporate HQ district'. The individual manager is basically following a strategy aimed at improving his prospects in the local labour market.

Compared to the HQ, the knowledge and the language deployed at the subsidiary carry strikingly international connotations. When employees in the subsidiaries recount the firm's victories, these are always measured against the rival technologies of leading competitors, wherever they may be located in the world. And when individual biographies are incorporated into these tales, they involve persons from many continents. The detailed knowledge about which persons around the world are described as being most qualified for a certain job in a project is thought-provoking. It demonstrates that the geographical scope of assessment and possible cooperation is indeed global. The sense of rivalry and competition is also high in subsidiaries, but the focus is upon other subsidiaries of the same MNC or on competitors belonging to other MNCs. To our surprise, both ordinary employees and managers were highly informed about how well they performed compared to production entities belonging to a similar category, whether these were located nearby or far away. While none of the top managers really dared to leave HQ except for official missions, we found among certain subsidiaries a high global mobility extending down to skilled blue-collar workers, who took part in a shifting array of projects across multiple continents. For that reason, many employees in the subsidiaries had highly elaborated and detailed proposals about how synergies could be created across different national constituent firms of the MNC. But they lacked the social and organizational space for communicating this information. It was their experience that such detailed concrete knowledge could not be conveyed and understood within the language of the HQ.

7.1.2. *Unintended local consequences of the headquarters' global strategies*

The HQ's local ties to carriers of universalized globalization theory and issues make it responsive to emerging rationalized myths (Meyer and Rowan 1991), stemming mainly from worldwide academic discourses, which become the primary stimulus for coordinating and controlling acts towards subsidiaries. But obviously acts of control and coordination may only accidentally have an intelligent relation to *what* is controlled and coordinated, at least from the perspective of the staff at subsidiaries. In consequence, the evolution of MNCs may be dominated by a stream of not-very-rational unintended consequences, which make the ideal-typical, well-coordinated agent of a supposedly irresistible globalization process appear a highly improbable configuration. One example will suffice for illustrative purposes.

Inspired by the fashionable trend in strategic management towards downsizing of non-core activities, the London HQ instructed one of its American subsidiaries, a plant developed around the ideal of vertical integration, to lay off some 25 per cent of its blue-collar employees, who had been designated surplus to requirements by an external consultancy report. A chain reaction of unintended consequences was set in motion when the managers distributed lay-off notices. Since the American subsidiary was a unionized shop with strong seniority rules in its collective bargaining agreement, a high seniority worker whose job was eliminated by the reorganization could 'bump' any worker with lower seniority, and so on down the line. A veritable chain reaction was triggered, until the lay-offs reached the youngest workers whose low seniority left them no one else to bump. In this way, the lay-offs fell effectively on the ranks of a group of recently recruited young machinists for whom the US subsidiary had incurred high costs to train as operators of programmable CNC machinery, a key element of its modernization programme. In short, the lay-offs reached exactly the holders of those competencies that the Americans considered vital for core activities in the future. Only by 'farming out' a large part of its production to external suppliers at premium prices could the plant fulfil urgent orders for key parts from internal customers elsewhere within the MNC. In effect, the subsidiary lost, at least temporarily, the ability to carry out its core manufacturing processes, while simultaneously providing neighbouring subcontractors with the skills and labour that enabled them to take on their new and highly expanded role.

7.1.3. *Unintended global consequences of local strategies*

Painful experience has made the London HQ aware of the possible opportunistic behaviour of foreign subsidiaries. From the conviction that trust is good but control is better, it had positioned a recently acquired Danish subsidiary under double control. Financially, it was controlled by a Danish holding company, also fully owned by London, while its product portfolio was placed under the control of a German subsidiary producing a competitive range of pumps and valves, distributed mainly within the MNC. The German subsidiary immediately launched a sales campaign in which it told its sister companies within the MNC that the Danish subsidiary's products would gradually be eliminated until production would come to a standstill. However, these plans met with no support from the Danish subsidiary's domestic financial controllers—quite the contrary. The Danish subsidiary responded by launching an alternative sales campaign in which it promised the sister companies to deliver customer-specified pumps and valves within a month, or one-third of the delivery time offered by the German subsidiary. This approach turned the Danish pumps and valves into a high-value industrial service. Since one of the specialties of the London-based MNC was building tailor-made turnkey food-processing plants within a given contractual period, one of the major technical problems was to meet the specifications without incurring penalty fees for late delivery. Technically, engineers designing such plants can 'fix' design failures if they can change the specifications for pumps and valves for the process after they have installed all the other tubing and equipment. However, waiting until the last moment to specify and order pumps and valves will usually involve the risk of penalties for late delivery. This dilemma the Danish subsidiary could help resolve. In so doing, it was not only considered a highly valued partner, thereby ousting its German 'controllers', but it simultaneously allowed the London-based MNC to take on jobs with shorter lead times than most of its multinational competitors. But no one in the London HQ had ever envisaged such a comparative advantage as a strategic goal. It was a gift that they had never dreamed of achieving and which they hardly appreciated, as it fell outside the language they spoke.

These three surprising tales from our field study may be very dependent on the case studied. But if they reflect stories of a similar type that can be found in most other MNCs, it immediately calls into question whether multinationals and their more advanced emergent successors do or indeed can possess the detailed intelligence that would enable them to become coherent entities—the new mutations among the species of firms—which makes all the other species extinct. As we have demonstrated, neither their points of departure nor their approaches to control, coordination, and optimization make them look more advantageous than smaller firms living in closer contact with the details of specific human beings, distinct technologies, and markets. But if this is the case, very different forces may be driving the process of constructing global firms and globalization itself than normally suggested by current theories. Therefore, the whole project of globalization may be heading towards a very different future state of the world economy than is conventionally imagined.

In this chapter we will focus on how the agents are constructed who are believed to construct globalization. We will do this by referring to a set of diverse historical narratives and by analysing the interacting web of strategies pursued by actors within a contemporary MNC. Thus the chapter is based on a narrative case study of a single 'actually existing' MNC. We do not believe that from a single case we can generalize a new theory of multinationals, but it will enable us to raise a series of general questions. What we will question are the overarching generalizations that underpin the current conventional wisdom. By demonstrating the complexity of the processes taking place at the micro-level, we believe our study to have far-reaching implications for perceptions and conceptualizations of the larger, macro-process of globalization. We can highlight the complexity of micro- and macro-processes by studying a single MNC in greater detail, and we would expect any in-depth study of another MNC to uncover further complications that will challenge the taken-for-granted assumptions underlying current approaches to economic life.

Our study has evolved from the conviction that what matters is to get the details right and to find coherent ways of recounting these details that do not violate the actors' own efforts to make sense of what is going on. In order to do so, field researchers must engage in a long-term contact with their subjects, so that the understanding of the actors can gain sufficient weight compared to the theoretical prejudices of the scholar. We have in one way or another been engaged with the actors in this field since 1984.

7.2. The Construction of MNCs in the Current Globalization Debate

Stephen Hymer's 1960 PhD thesis is taken to be the very break-through of modern theorizing about MNCs. Until then, MNCs were seen simply as 'arbitrageurs of capital, moving equity from countries where returns were low to those where it was higher' (Jones 1996: 7). Hymer 'asserted that FDI involved the transfer of a whole package of resources and not simply finance' (ibid.). The package involved technology, management skills, entrepreneurship, etc., and firms were 'motivated to produce abroad by the expectation of earning an economic rent on the totality of their resources, including the way in which they were organized' (Dunning 1993: 69). Hymer's basic view of the international firm, thus, is that it internalizes or supersedes the market, thereby allowing for the cross-border transfer of knowledge, business techniques, and skilled personnel (Hymer 1960: 48, 60; Dunning 1993: 69). By transferring this package of resources to a foreign country, the MNC gains a comparative advantage over local firms. Especially firms that have gained a monopoly position in their home market—for instance through exploiting a technological, cost, financial, or marketing advantage—may use territorial expansion to extend the range of their operation. The MNC thus becomes a means of advancing monopoly power but also a means of solving market failure problems on an international scale, the role which Coase (1937) has argued firms perform in a market economy more gener-ally (Hymer 1968; Dunning 1993: 70).

As is already evident in Hymer's theory, a firm becomes a MNC by exploiting some kind of superiority not only in its home country but also in a number of host countries. The basic idea therefore is that it spreads from a single national centre to operate in a basically similar manner in new countries. A closely related idea underlies the product-cycle theory proposed by Vernon (1966). Vernon explained how the US competitive environment created comparative advan-tages with respect to technological innovation, which allowed domes-tic firms continuously to upgrade their assets. But to protect their competitive technological advantage from becoming eroded or elim-inated by foreign firms in later phases of the product cycle, US com-panies were forced first to export, and then, as products and production processes became standardized, to engage in overseas manufacture to reduce costs. This dialectic of the competitive process may even continue to the point where US-based firms export from foreign countries back to the domestic market, thereby gaining a new comparative advantage in the oligopolistic competitive game at home. Whereas in Hymer's theory it is the offensive expansion of monopoly power to foreign countries that makes the oligopolist go multinational, this is instead a defensive strategy in Vernon's theory. In both cases, however, it is important that the firms are large, as this strategy is dependent on their ability to take big risks and to pay the high costs of information, search, negotiation, and learning, which smaller companies usually cannot afford (Aharoni 1966; Dunning 1993: 73.). Consequently, only firms that may benefit from considerable ownership advantages and can afford the costs wind up going multinational.

On the other hand, if a firm initiates such a process, it is generally expected to derive additional ownership advantages from the very process of becoming multinational.

These advantages of common governance derive from the ability to co-ordinate separate value-added activities across national boundaries. Multinationality can enhance operational flexibility by offering wider opportunities for global sources of input. It can provide more favored access to international markets. It can provide the ability to diversify or reduce risk. (Jones 1996: 9)

Adding to this picture, Bartlett and Ghoshal (1989, 1990) have argued that MNCs operating in a variety of environments are exposed to external stimuli that enable them to develop competencies and learning opportunities not open to domestic firms. With these advantages, then, it is no surprise that the formation of MNCs is cumulative and that globalization is seen as an irresistible process.

One common feature, however, runs through both the older and more recent attempts to understand the initial determinants and ongoing dynamics of multinationalization. It is the firm's calculating managerial apex, which autocratically decides to go multinational, and when it does, the MNC's comparative advantage in turn derives from exploiting initial ownership advantages developed in and by this centre. Such multinationalization may then engage this centre in a learning process by which it gains new ownership and internalization advantages, partly by benefiting from the learning opportunities that access to a multiplicity of different environments in turn makes possible. The gradual character of the learning process implies that internationalization is expected to unfold through a number of phases in which a firm starts to export typically through agents, then sets up sales and marketing facilities, and finally establishes production facilities in foreign host countries. With this in place, the MNC starts to integrate its regional and global activities (Dunning 1993: 193–204).

It is remarkable that the literature envisages no substantial difficulties for managers in making these calculations. Nor does it offer any close investigations of the possible problems of actually learning from the experience of going global. The results of learning opportunities in diverse environments are simply transported by assumption into the learning curves of the centrally located managers, who are unquestionably able to govern (coordinate and control) many diverse value chains as a single coherent whole, which can then be optimized. How these complicated organizational problems are in fact solved is discussed less with reference to empirical enquiry than to abstract theorizing about the design of principal-agent relations (see, e.g., Jones 1996: 20) or by reference to Bartlett and Ghoshal's (1989) term: 'the administrative heritage'.

But it is widely believed that this administrative heritage of the multinational is precisely becoming its 'core competence' for the future. MNCs may reduce their ownership of assets, but their roles as centres of integration will increase. Dunning sees this competence as three-pronged:

First, it involves taking full advantage of the economies of scale and scope arising from global integration. Second, it involves a proper appreciation of differences in the supply capabilities and consumer needs in different countries. Third, it involves using the experience gained in global and national markets to strengthen the resource base of the firm as a whole. (Dunning 1993: 602)

The organization and management of MNCs have been the focus of numerous studies (for an overview, see Hedlund 1993) and yet it has normally been assumed that they could be analysed as hierarchical pyramids, managed through 'general managers' (see Hedlund and Kogut (1993), for a critique). Building on Perlmutter's (1965, 1969) typology of multinationals, Hedlund (1986) argues that organizational and managerial complexities emerge when MNCs develop past the first 'missionary phase', as described by Hymer and Vernon, and enter into polycentrism:

As time goes by, foreign business may become dominant rather than marginal, the subsidiaries get more activities and become more self-sufficient, management becomes more host-country oriented and consisting of host-country nationals. The MNC becomes an assemblage of semi-independent units. . . . The tendency in terms of control mode is to move toward looser coupling between units and from the hierarchy (in this case also somewhat in the etymological sense) of ethnocentrism to market solutions. Transfer pricing based on market prices rather than internal costs, freedom to choose external suppliers, rewards and punishment in monetary terms, and elaborate bonus payment systems accompany greater turnover rates of personnel and organizational units being sold and bought. Internationalization is more and more conducted through acquisitions than green-field ventures. (Hedlund 1986: 13–14)

The third phase of 'geocentrism', which follows ethnocentrism and polycentrism in Perlmutter's typology, is seen as the one in which the MNC 'internalizes the exploitation of (country) comparative advantages'. In this phase:

The subsidiaries have to implement strategies formulated according to a global logic, they have to be able to act quickly in response to competitive conditions, they must be encouraged to look at a wider picture. Most writers on global strategy give the subsidiaries a less independent role than that implied in a polycentric MNC. A re-centralization of authority to HQ often follows . . . the trend towards markets in the polycentric MNC is reversed. Also reversed is the tendency to duplicate activities in various subsidiaries. (Hedlund 1986: 16)

What is striking in this evolutionary pattern are the breaks and seeming inconsistencies involved. Hierarchy transforms into market and then, finally, back to hierarchy again. In this evolution it is difficult to see administrative heritage as a process of accumulating experience. Rather, it suggests that the organization of 'mature' MNCs is an experimental phase, where a number of normative templates compete. Thus Hedlund himself suggests that 'hierarchy' should be replaced by 'heterarchy' in the third—and final—evolutionary stage, to help improve the mutual learning ability of the MNC. But this transformation to a flexible network of 'many centres, of different kinds' is nonetheless thought to be implemented deliberately by the central apex of the HQ as 'a meta-institution, whose unique role is the effective design, on the basis of experience, of institutional arrangements for specific tasks' (Hedlund and Rolander 1990: 25).

As soon as the MNC evolves beyond the initial missionary phase, it thus becomes highly unclear what type of logic is unfolding. Perhaps the contradictions between the polycentric and the geocentric phase are a signal that many, partly contradictory, logics are at play simultaneously? Might the MNC be in a state of schizophrenia? Or is it our theoretical discourse that generates these paradoxes?

7.3. **The Construction of a Multinational from Our Field Studies**

Paradoxes and schizophrenia are resolved and cured if one adopts a polycentric perspective to describe a polycentric situation. In that case an MNC is not only constituted as a narration of the evolution of the core firm's gradual extension from local, through a national, to an international phase. Rather, a number of narratives that focus on a variety of firms in different countries may be told to account for why and how formerly independent firms have now become part of the MNC: how they perceive of being members of this new 'association', what they expect from the membership and how they mutually struggle over the division of labour to decide which social space they each shall occupy within the multinational.

In our view it is misleading to see the evolutionary construction of a multinational as a singular evolutionary path, once the MNC has been constituted through mergers of formerly independent firms. In such cases, which may be frequent (Wortmann and Dörrenbacher 2000), organizational learning, the evolution of successful routines and competencies have followed multiple paths and concepts of rationality, while the allocation of attention among the actors involved gives strong impetus for following distinct strategies. In Porter's terminology, the MNC is a firm with multiple home bases (Porter 1990). The evolution of the MNC then becomes dependent on the pattern of interacting strategies among formerly independent strategic actors and their abilities to associate and mutually create a division of labour. Whether and how this association can be controlled from the HQ depends on whether the firm has been able to internalize the art of control and coordination as routines in the past, or will be able gradually to obtain this authority through the unfolding of current actions. Other parts of the MNC, however, may either by chance or design achieve these functions, leaving the formal HQ with quite different tasks, as is obviously the case in our narrative.

It is actually by telling the story of a multinational as a set of first independent and later interwoven narratives that the process of constructing a multinational appears in a new and clear perspective.[2] From the construction of four such narratives about three subsidiaries

---

[2] In an earlier version of this chapter, we constructed four such narratives about three subsidiaries (in Denmark, Britain, and the USA) and the British firm that happened to become the carrier of the name and HQ of the MNC. Unfortunately, in a short chapter such lengthy

(located in Denmark, Britain and the USA) and the British firm that evolved to become the carrier of the HQ we can summarize a number of findings.

Each of the three subsidiaries became part of the MNC partly as a result of its own strategic efforts. The local strategists were looking for a new owner because the old one wanted to sell (the British subsidiary). They might have considered being acquired by the British MNC, as a low-cost method of expanding their presence in foreign markets (the US subsidiary). Or they might have provoked their sale to the British MNC after carefully contemplating how they, as a subsidiary, would fit into the portfolios of factories and markets of different MNCs (as in the Danish case). This suggests that rather than simply being propelled by sharks, which eat the small fishes, globalization is also propelled by small birds seeking protection under the eagle's wings. Consequently, an MNC happens to associate actors that reflect in very different ways on their own situation and for that reason become part of the MNC, partly as a result of their own strategic choices. The British subsidiary made its choice from the conviction that in exchange for ownership-stabilization it would have to surrender independence to a new feudal lord and prepare itself to receive orders. In contrast, the American subsidiary regarded what for more than a decade appeared to be a merger of equals or strategic alliance as an opportunity to enhance penetration into European markets so that it could continue to expand as a vertically integrated organization. It wanted to continue old routines under the new order.[3] Finally, in entering the MNC, the Danish subsidiary celebrated gaining a foothold on a new continent, which it planned to conquer. Thus subsidiaries enter into a MNC and into mutual competition carrying along a variety of aspirations and goals that make them a highly ambiguous and heterogeneous group of actors. The continuous success of this association, however, depends on how well they interact, compete, and cooperate—despite their differences.

narratives are impossible and the reader of this version must rely on what we learned by constructing such multiple narratives. In the Danish case the narrative was constructed through retrospective interviews with participants, while in the British and US cases, we could also rely on published company histories and internal documents. In a later book we plan to publish the full story.

[3] At the end of the 1950s, managers of the American subsidiary had already engineered its voluntary acquisition by a larger US conglomerate in order to protect the firm's autonomy from the potential threat of a hostile takeover motivated by an unanticipated appreciation of the book value of its stock above the current market price.

Stated this way, there is no single standpoint from which to deduce what constitutes the MNC. It is widely taken for granted that firms that become MNCs are successes, whereas firms that are acquired as subsidiaries in this way prove their failure. Our four narratives tell a much finer-grained story. Each of our four firms has proven to be a successful strategist capable of surviving in the world market for more than a hundred years. The British subsidiary struggled for many years to remain the leading producer of rotary lobe pumps and became a fountainhead of many local imitators. The American firm took the lead to become a large, functionally integrated producer and marketing firm in the oligopolistic game of the American market. The Danish subsidiary earned a very high reputation, even among its domestic competitors, as a skilled supplier of competent and flexible tailor-made technical solutions for advanced customers. Consequently, the subsidiary had no problems in recruiting the best workers and technicians. For each of these firms, their strategizing led to incorporation into a MNC as the best possible alternative in a given situation during the 1970s or 1980s. Even their transformation into subsidiaries may be considered a success, measured against their local aspirations. One may say that they tried to be bought by the MNC precisely in order to continue pursuing the evolutionary logic of their localities, technologies, and organizations.

The story of the fourth firm—which happened to become the formal owner of the others—is not very different. What is peculiar about this firm is that from the beginning it was linked up through family relations to the international banking community. This offered the firm the opportunity to expand and grow more than the average firm without such connections. However, this opportunity in a way also made the firm fail. Stimulated by high engineering aspirations, it engaged in large-scale investments that led to over-capacity; over-capacity led to losses; and losses reinforced its ties to and dependence on the family bank. With the weakening of the family presence in both the firm and the banking community, this virtuous circle gradually evolved into a vicious one. The firm resolved this crisis during the late 1950s and the early 1960s by institutionalizing modern accounting routines and professional rather than family ties to the financial community. In this way, it not only acquired the core competence that would enable it to continue its original fast growth track but also to function as a sort of consultant to other firms which found it difficult to obtain financial capital to solve emergency crises. Often, formal ownership relations by and to its 'clients' reciprocated this service. As long as engineering dominated over accounting aspirations, such ties often built on collegial community among engineers, but as the accounting and financial professions gained a larger say over its strategies, such situations were increasingly considered strategically important in their own terms. During the period when engineering and financial concerns struggled over the control of the firm, the heterogeneous reflections by which different clients anticipated their incorporation could each be reinforced by the heterogeneous and ambiguous reactions from the emergent HQ. Subsidiaries would simply receive the signals they wanted to hear. Obviously, such an HQ may be considered very favourable to join. The firm that considers becoming a member may indulge in receptive conversations about engineering projects with understanding colleagues who have access to people in positions, which can connect ideas with money. It is difficult to see who is the most successful in such conversations.

Whereas the MNC HQ may be approached through the engineering network, it is the intangible assets of financial experience in the MNC that are brought into action, when a new firm is considered for membership. How cheaply can controlling equity be transferred to the new owner and what are the resources necessary to bail the entering firm out of its current troubles in order for it to remain a going concern? This price depends on how the assets of the entering firm can be used to finance its own entrance, how the merger is considered by the financial community, and how creatively the financial markets may be induced to provide the required capital. Thus, instead of the mutual exchange of engineering ideas, the stage is set by the financial and accounting departments and the discourse between the HQ and the new 'subsidiary' changes. The paradox is that the more the engineers are attracting colleagues in other firms for conversations over membership, the more the engineers become dependent on financial and accounting competence. This competence grows by giving further training at business schools to engineers and by hiring new people trained at business schools and with experience from financial and consultancy firms or the finance department of other MNCs. Through this hybridization process, the HQ becomes a serious player in the London corporate HQ and financial district. Concepts of strategy and organizational concerns change from the possible synergies of cross-national engineering and production to focus on managing internal financial flows in order to smooth relations with institutional investors, stock markets, and banks. The latter game is highly competitive, as the audience in the local London

district is continuously comparing the finance departments of different MNCs. With this pressure the scene is set for an ongoing battle
between engineering and financial concerns, a battle that may go on
within individual persons, among professional groups, and across
subsidiaries, making it very unclear which strategic lines are dominant and which principles shall govern administrative control and
coordination and the division of labour within the MNC. This battle
may never be settled, and therefore the MNC oscillates between polycentric and geocentric principles for a considerable period.

In this confusing play around the HQ, how much room the individual subsidiary has for manoeuvre may well be determined by its
indigenous reflections on its own situation. If it decides only to move
on orders from the HQ, it may gradually lose all chances. If it enjoys
its new stability as a subsidiary and concentrates on defending its
entrant position against the international division of labour in the
MNC, it may experience stagnation. If instead it approaches its new
membership as a world of endless possibilities, the MNC may
become exactly this for the subsidiary.

The subsidiary's disposition towards reflective activity is not solely
determined by the managers that happen to be in charge at the
moment the firm is admitted into the MNC. Rather, this reflection is
inscribed in and represents the underlying logic of its own narrative
by which it has historically made sense of and coded its practices, its
ability to defend and change these practices, and the skills that continuously are brought to bear when a new situation asks for definition. Thus, whether the ambiguous situation of the entire MNC is
objectively to be described as a hierarchy, a market, or a heterarchy
need not affect how each of the subsidiaries anticipates the situation.
By continuing their patterned historical strategic reflections, some
will continue to live in a hierarchy, others in a market, and still others
in a heterarchy. For that reason, an objective description must include
the distribution of types of strategic reflection on top of the underlying logic of the narratives among the subsidiaries, rather than stick-
ing to the formal design of the organization as seen from the top
executives at the HQ.

The British subsidiary had learned to live with idiosyncratic
owners, for whom their ownership role was more important than
growth and profitability. In this scenario, luck comes and goes
depending on the current mood of the owners, and when luck came
the workshop and engineering department would spend time on
improving the product in which the entire pride of the factory rested:

the rotary lobe pump. This existence as a 'sleeping beauty' was possible because the owners never initiated a systematic Taylorization of work. For that reason it was easy for the firm to recruit or train highly skilled workers who could work on the rotary lobe pump when improvements could be afforded. As the firm had given birth to several spin-offs among imitating firms, owners and managers lived in hostility with their neighbouring colleagues, but workers in the local labour market were related to one another through family ties spanning company boundaries. The 'sleeping beauty' thus became a meeting place for individualistic (the firm was not unionized), highly skilled workers, especially when times were good. These workers could always return to other firms in the region when times turned less promising, because of the subsidiary's reputation for employing excellent workers and for the technical superiority of its products. In this way, the 'sleeping beauty' always helped to re-establish the old equilibrium among firms in the rotary lobe pump district, in which she was recognized as the source of many technical improvements from which the other firms could profit. During the 1970s and the 1980s these colleague firms had been taken over by other multinationals. By preparing itself to take orders from a new owner after being acquired by the London-based MNC, the 'sleeping beauty' in fact prepared herself to live exactly the life to which she had gradually become accustomed since the Second World War.

In the same manner, the American subsidiary had seen its own potential being gradually improved by including more and more differentiated capabilities through dedicated functions, departments, manufacturing units, and machinery within its own organization. To continue this type of growth was not only the essence of what it considered success, but was where it actually had invested in routines for creating new routines. For that reason any attempt to circumscribe its functional role from the larger perspective of the global MNC would seem harmful and destructive in the eyes of local beholders, and betray the very joint venture into which they thought they had entered by selling off their formal independence.

The Danish subsidiary approached the MNC as a new arena within which it could expand and improve its superior technical reputation, as it had been accustomed to do in the past with Danish owners, customers, colleagues, sub-suppliers, and the labour market for skilled technicians and machinists. Now the staff had all the employees and customers of the MNC as an audience before which to demonstrate their skills. Ends and means turned out to be especially favourable for the Danish firm. It could mobilize resources from the Danish labour market, vocational institutions, traditional customers, sub-suppliers, and, especially, its own workers in pursuing a strategy that was formally opposed to London's plans but which would help it gain a high reputation in the global engineering circles of the MNC. The Danish subsidiary soon learned to keep London happy by pro-viding the flow of funds and earnings that it had promised in the bud-getary negotiations. It seemed to have realized a continuation of past strategic patterns within the new 'association', which were formally in conflict and yet became even more highly reputed for that reason, because they worked.

One important phenomenon that runs through this summary of the narrative of the initial association of old independent firms into a MNC is that the 'administrative heritage' continues to be diverse and rooted in the experience that local actors had gained from their involvement in the games of diverse regional or national business systems. None—or so it seems—of our actors, including the HQ, have managed to gain experience in coordinating a multitude of local players, whereas the latter has gained experience in dealing with the capital market through the City of London.

When, however, the HQ begins to coordinate activities among and between its subsidiaries, this leads to a range of unintended conse-quences. Even though such initiatives are most often seen by the sub-sidiaries as the owner's legitimate role, our three drill samples explain how the HQ in many instances loses this formal authority, precisely by exercising it. Such actions simply look stupid and wrong when measured by the local rationality according to which each of the firms governs its individual strategies. Thus, in exercising its formal authority, the HQ loses its legitimacy vis-à-vis its subsidiaries. This makes it very difficult to create an administrative heritage for the multinational HQ. Coordinating efforts that lead to failures often have the effect of indicating deficient competencies among HQ man-agers. Managerial responsibility implies that incompetent managers should be fired. The managerial team of the HQ therefore becomes very unstable. In effect, deals negotiated between HQ and local sub-sidiaries are often violated in the eyes of the latter. Therefore, even attempts at mutual coordination become still weaker, until a game that looks like situational cheating, freeriding, and local opportunism to all participants has spread to every corner of the 'association'. In other words, it becomes a 'Groucho Marx' club to which its own members would not like to belong. We will investigate this game more closely in a later article and only anticipate some expected results from our analysis here. We think that this shared interpretation by the actors in the game is mistaken. Instead, the game is one in which the players each try to follow the rationality of their local legacy, but because their acts seem foolish or cannot be understood by the other players, the result is accumulated shared misinterpretations. Nothing indicates that this game should be more transaction cost-effective than the market. Many MNC headquarters discover this and are ready to sell off their assets to the highest bidder, while in response subsidiaries are always looking for potential new owners and associations, which they would consider worth joining, and where they might—rightly or wrongly—expect to meet greater mutual understanding.

7.4. Reconstructing the Process of Globalization

Our field study observations both confirm and contradict the observations and ideas of recent literature on globalization. We think that Ghoshal and Nohria's (1989) term, 'differentiated networks' and Hedlund's term 'heterarchy' capture the situation of current MNCs much more precisely than previous interpretations of MNCs as highly centralized hierarchies. However, our case studies suggest that these authors are wrong in seeing the development as the outcome of a deliberate HQ strategy of organizational design for the MNC.

It is, rather, an unintended consequence of the very process of globalization, that instead of being controlled and authored by the central apex of HQs, the MNCs' structures become caught up in games of strategic interaction among many agents, each following distinct local logics of action. The emergence of such conflictual interactions among many partly contradictory strategists implies that we can neither speak about MNCs as theoretically given entities, nor think of globalization as the unfolding of a unitary logic. Both are pursued by agents who want to impose very different strategies on each other so that the evolution of the individual MNC depends on whether this interaction coheres towards a virtuous or vicious pattern, and globalization as such depends on the competition among these far from optimized organizations.

Critics may rightly say that we draw too many general lessons from our case study, which is rather untypical as it reflects the perspective of a multinational created through the acquisition of long-established independent firms with strong individual narratives. We agree that caution should be exercised. But we think that subsidiaries created by acquiring formerly independent firms, or firms owned by other large multidivisional or holding companies, are increasingly becoming a component of MNCs' subsidiary portfolios (Wortmann and Dörrenbacher 2000). This is not only because MNC HQs operate as sharks in international waters, but also, as we have shown, because firms without skills in managing global capital markets try to shelter themselves from greater dangers by making themselves attractive targets for takeovers by these HQs.

Even if this claim is wrong, and future MNCs will still be dominated by green-field investments in fully dependent subsidiaries created and designed according to HQ logics, there is strong evidence that the existence of diverse subsidiary logics is nonetheless a quite general phenomenon in the maturing phase of global expansion. A growing number of studies focusing on subsidiary–HQ relations in Canada, Ireland, and Scotland (see Birkinshaw and Hood 1998) show that over time a rather large fraction of subsidiaries develop strategies for expanding their 'mandate' (Delany 1998). This they primarily do by taking steps to broaden the scope of their activities compared to the initial assignment received from the HQ. If these entrepreneurial subsidiaries succeed in earning more money for the HQ than the more passive subsidiaries, which stick to the logic of their assigned mandate, they will in general be given greater autonomy. As far as we can see, the unintended consequences of such an evolution within MNCs could easily be that those who pursue subversive strategies and break with the logic of their original mandate will grow quickly, while the 'boy scouts' who stick to a given mandate will stagnate. Thus, even within multinationals that base growth primarily on green-field investments, this literature suggests that an increasing diversity of evolutionary logics will emerge from the unintended consequences of their global expansion.

This literature has so far focused on studies of subsidiaries owned by different MNCs in a single country at a time. Within each of the countries studied, there has been a distribution of diverse strategies among subsidiaries vis-à-vis the parent firm. The focus of explanation has fallen on individual managers and the room for manoeuvre that they have detected and managed to exploit. Sölvell and Zander (1998), however, come to a similar conclusion regarding the gradual disintegration of MNCs through a deduction based on two theoretical premises. Against the traditional view that MNCs have special advantages in the development and diffusion of new technologies, they reinterpret the literature on innovation. They suggest that subsidiaries engaged in technological innovation will be able to achieve greater cost-effectiveness in R&D investments (through which they gain independence in the short term from the HQ) by communicating with external actors in their local context rather than using the international network of the MNC. This in turn will have long-term consequences:

As foreign units over time become more firmly established in their local innovation system, they gain to an increasing extent unique and insider access to local knowledge exchange. This unique access to the local innovation system will create independence and simultaneously make the foreign unit more difficult to control from headquarters. Thus, while increasing commitments to operations in foreign countries provides the MNE with one of the prerequisites for assimilating knowledge on an international scale, integrating activities and exercising control becomes more difficult. Put somewhat differently, as the MNE becomes an insider in local innovation systems, it will at the same time become an outsider within itself. (Sölvell and Zander 1998: 411)

This process is reinforced by the HQ–subsidiary power struggles within the MNC.

Our case study suggests that both the logic of a given subsidiary and the contextual conditions for pursuing this logic are dependent on the institutions, culture, and history that constitute this actor. Certain regions or nations may empower agents acting on behalf of such subsidiaries differently and create highly different conditions for success from those in other countries. This does not mean that individuals do not play a role. Certain individuals are skilled in reflecting on and discovering possibilities in new situations and can assemble the local context of stakeholders in support when implementing intelligent strategies. Others are less experienced in exploiting similar situations. So skilful and intelligent people are needed even in favourable regional or national contexts. However, some contexts may be favourable for generating potential strategists, because the institutional, cultural, and historical contexts provide many tools for strategic experimentation, while other national and regional contexts are deserts in this respect. For that reason, subversive strategists and independence-seeking R&D projects may be much more frequent in some countries than in others, which then gain 'comparative advantages' in constructing 'boy scouts'. In some countries, subversive strategists may even think of themselves as 'boy scouts' when they develop their subversive strategies (do they not serve the multi-national owner best by pursuing a strategy, which they consider rational?). In other cultures, 'boy scouts' may consider their behaviour precisely as the most subversive of all towards the parent multi-national (are they not severely harming the multinational owner by refraining from following strategies that they themselves consider rational?). If this is the case, the preconditions for mutual misunder-standings are legion, and no one will be able to discriminate between good and bad behaviour.

In any case, the multinational corporation, rather than imposing an ethnocentric logic on subsidiaries from other cultures and communities, as suggested by Whitley in Chapter 2, becomes instead a battle-field among subsidiaries representing and mobilizing their own regional capabilities and national institutional means against the rest. Our case, however, illustrates how this battle is framed by the financial and accounting coordination methods characteristic of Anglo-Saxon MNCs, and it is hardly to be doubted that both battles and negotiations would have taken a quite different path had the HQ dealt with its subsidiaries following the logic of the German business system.

In our view, the central issue is that a competitive battle is going on and seems not to be heading towards a balance. This tendency is reinforced because the 'project' of the individual MNC has become very unclear. In the initial thinking about multinationals, it was assumed that they were the carriers of superior technology, and it was this that made them so competitive against other firms around the world. Often, multinationals were seen as the most efficient agencies for technology transfer and in effect the development agency for the less developed part of the world. This image of transnational cooperation as fostered by engineers with great ideas of worldwide modernization projects is supported by Henrik Glimstedt's analysis (see Chapter 5) of the prewar period when transnational cooperation took place between national companies, which joined forces to mobil-ize capital, pool patents, and stabilize demand. But the leading idea uniting the actors was their engineering image of a possible modernization project. Today, there seems seldom to be a very clear technological logic, which can unify diverse regional and national business logics into a common project. We have suggested that this lack of clarity emerges when engineering and financial matters compete with concerns for the dominance of the firm. On the one hand, as Taino et al. argue in Chapter 6, it is, increasingly, firms that have gained the capacity to deal with global capital markets that are capable of mobilizing enough cheap finance to undertake large-scale projects. On the other hand, however, when the power balance between engineering and financial concerns becomes unclear, MNCs seem to lose the means of unifying multiple business logics into a coherent exploration. Therefore, many subsidiaries seem to see the multinational corporation as a mechanism, within which others may exploit you if you are incapable of exploiting them for the benefit of your own local explorative aspirations.

Hedlund's concept of heterarchy tries to resolve many of the paradoxes and contradictions we have mentioned by creating a common unitary corporate culture, securing long-term employment for its members, building up experience in and among employees of the organization, shaping interlocking directorates, and fostering global project teams and meetings across subsidiaries and different HQs. The intention is to build up an MNC that functions rather 'as one integrated brain' than as a system, in which 'one brain' controls and coordinates globally dispersed organs (Sölvell and Zander 1995: Table 3; Hedlund and Rolander 1990: 25–6). This proposition rests on the premise that a corporate culture can be constructed which overshadows the effects of the national cultures or regional contexts from which subsidiaries act. We have indicated that attempts to create such a culture may run up against exactly the processes that are at play among different parts and pieces of an MNC. In other words, they are moving towards increasing mutual misunderstandings in their mutual game. If that is the case, we need far more detailed studies of the games going on within multinationals before anything can be said about whether, in what sense, and through which interventions such a common culture can be constructed. Without such a common culture, or some alternative set of mechanisms for orchestrating cooperation among partially autonomous subsidiaries and functional units, the remaining elements of the heterarchy would simply provide further battlefields for the games such as those we have analysed in this case study.

REFERENCES

Aharoni, Y. (1966), *The Foreign Investment Decision Process*. Boston: Harvard Graduate School of Business Administration, Division of Research.

Bartlett, C. A. and Ghoshal, S. (1989), *Managing Across Borders—The Transnational Solution*. Boston: Harvard Business School Press.

—— (1990), 'Managing Innovations in the Transnational Corporations', in C. A. Barlett, Y. Doz and G. Hedlund (eds.), *Research on Multinational Management*. London: Addison-Wesley.

Birkinshaw, J. and Hood, N. (eds.) (1998), *Multinational Corporate Evolution and Subsidiary Development*. London: Macmillan.

Chandler, A. D., Hagström, P. and Sölvell, Ö. (eds.) (1998), *The Dynamic Firm. The Role of Technology, Strategy, Organization, and Regions*. Oxford: Oxford University Press.

Coase, R. H. (1937), 'The Nature of the Firm', *Economica*, 4, November: 386–405.

Delany, E. (1998), 'Strategic Development of Multinational Subsidiaries in Ireland', in J. Birkinshaw and N. Hood (eds.), *Multinational Corporate Evolution and Subsidiary Development*. London: Macmillan.

Dunning, J. H. (1993), *Multinational Enterprises and the Global Economy*. Wokingham, UK: Addison-Wesley Publishing Company.

Ghoshal, S. and Nohria, N. (1989), 'Internal Differentiation Within Multinational Corporations', *Strategic Management Journal*, 10: 323–37.

Hedlund, G. (1986), 'The Hypermodern MNC—A Heterarchy?', *Human Resource Management*, 25(1): 9–35.

—— (1993), 'Introduction: Organization and Management of Transnational Corporations in Practice and Research', in G. Hedlund (ed.), *Organization of Transnational Corporations*. United Nations Library on Transnational Corporations, vol. 6. London: Routledge.

Hedlund, G. and Kogut, B. (1993), 'Managing the MNC: The End of the Missionary Era', in G. Hedlund (ed.), *Organization of Transnational Corporations*. United Nations Library on Transnational Corporations, vol. 6. London: Routledge, 343–58.

Hedlund, G. and Rolander, D. (1990), 'Action in Heterarchies—New Approaches to Managing the MNC', in C. A. Bartlett, Y. Doz, and G. Hedlund (eds.), *Managing the Global Firm*. London: Routledge, 15–46.

Hymer, S. H. (1960), *The International Operations of National Firms: A Study of Direct Investment*. PhD thesis, published in 1976 by MIT Press, Cambridge, MA.

—— (1968), 'La Grande Firme multinationale', *Revue Economique* 14(b): 949–73.

Jones, G. (1996), *The Evolution of International Business*. London: Routledge.

Machiavelli, N. (1961), *The Prince*. Harmondsworth: Penguin Books.

Meyer, J. W. and Rowan, B. (1991), 'Institutionalized Organizations: Formal Structure as Myth and Ceremony', in W. W. Powell and P. J. DiMaggio (eds.), *The New Institutionalism in Organizational Analysis*. Chicago: The University of Chicago Press.

Perlmutter, H. V (1965), 'L'enterprise internationale—trois conceptions', *Revue Economique et Sociale*, 23.

—— (1969), 'The Tortuous Evolution of the Multinational Corporation', *Columbia Journal of World Business*, January–February: 9–18.

Porter, M. E. (1990), *The Competitive Advantage of Nations*. New York: The Free Press.

Sölvell, Ö. and Zander, I. (1995), 'Organization of the Dynamic Multinational Enterprise', *International Studies of Management and Organization*, 25(1–2): 17–39.

—— (1998), 'International Diffusion of Knowledge: Isolating Mechanisms and the Role of the MNE', in A. D. Chandler et al. (eds.), *The Dynamic Firm: The Role of Technology, Strategy, Organization, and Regions*. Oxford: Oxford University Press.

Vernon, R. (1966), 'International Investment and International Trade in the Product Cycle', *Quarterly Journal of Economics*, 80: 190–207.

Wortmann, M. and Dörrenbacher, C. (2000), 'Multinational Companies and National Systems', Paper presented to ESRI workshop, *Forms of Transnational Governance and Paths of Economic Development*, Lisbon, 16–20 September.

8

Globalization and Change: Organizational Continuity and Change within a Japanese Multinational in the UK

DIANA ROSEMARY SHARPE

8.1. Introduction

Recent debates on changing forms of managerial control and work organization have often neglected the ways in which management systems and work practices are implemented and sustained in different contexts. This chapter presents a contribution based on an in-depth comparative study of how one internationalizing manufacturing organization from Japan has sought to introduce management systems and work organization at two UK sites. This provides an interesting context in which to examine if, and how, parent company systems are transferred, adapted, and sustained in an overseas subsidiary and to examine multinational organizations as potential sites of negotiation and conflict within which the influence of different business systems and actors is confronted and contested in the day-to-day management practices and processes of the foreign subsidiary.

The cultural and institutional specificity of management practices found in Japanese organizations has received much interest in the literature (see for example Abo 1994; Sorge 1996; Whitley 1997). Whilst within multinationals pressures for 'isomorphism' may occur through attempts to transfer 'best practices' (Mueller 1994), the local context including national political, financial, labour, and cultural systems influence how multinationals' management practices transfer across business systems and with what outcomes (see also Kristensen and Zeitlin, Chapter 7, and Whitley, Chapter 2, for further coverage of this).

This chapter examines the importance of the local context and the influence of home business context in influencing management initiatives and outcomes at subsidiary level. The findings illustrate how the change processes that took place across the sites were significantly influenced by the local context, the characteristics of the workers and the socio-technical system in which the changes took place.

8.2. Management Practices within Multinationals and across Business Systems

There has been a recent interest in the literature in the ways in which contextual influences and contingencies may influence the extent to which alternative production and control systems can be successfully maintained. In the early stages of this debate Monden (1983) argued that there was, in principle, no problem in foreign companies outside of Japan adopting a just-in-time (JIT) system, which he had identified in Japanese organizations, except for the possibility of union problems. Increasingly, however, the cultural and institutional specificity of management practices found in Japanese organizations has been given attention by those examining the degree to which Japanese organizations may be able to transfer, or consider transferring, practices used in operations at home to overseas contexts (for example, Abo 1994; Cool and Lengnick-Hall 1985; Dore 1973; Hibino 1997; Kenney and Florida 1993; Kenney et al. 1999; Lincoln and Kalleberg 1985; Streeck 1996; Trevor 1988). The specific features of Japanese business systems and societal structures which support a certain configuration of management practices have been identified and discussed. For example, Dore (1973) and Clark (1979) argued that an important feature of larger Japanese companies was the degree to which a number of characteristics linked together into a cohesive whole. A low level of self-sufficiency is encouraged by risk-sharing with subcontractors and other members of business groups. A high degree of homogeneity of markets and skills, together with distinctive employment practices, traditionally have linked together to facilitate high commitment to the enterprises as a whole (Streeck 1996). This commitment in turn facilitates some decentralization of decision-making and flexible control systems (Whitley 1990). Further studies of the internationalization of Japanese industry (for example, Abo 1994, 1995; Ozawa 1979) have indicated how 'fundamental factors of production differ in terms of how they react to identical economic stimuli depending on the societies of which they are part'

(Abo 1994: 9). It is therefore of interest to consider *why* distinctive patterns of work organization and control have become established in different capitalist societies and the roles of various groups in these institutionalization processes.

In such an analysis it is difficult to isolate the work process and control practices from more general employment and labour management strategies, as these are often mutually implicative. How tasks are structured and task performance controlled are usually quite closely interlinked with recruitment, training, and reward and bargaining strategies. These in turn are often associated with an organization's product and market strategies (Whitley 1997: 229).

The societally specific features influencing work organization and control systems (see also Maurice et al. 1986; Rubery 1994; Sorge 1996; Sorge and Warner 1986; Tayeb 1994) are thus seen to help explain changes in work organization and control systems across capitalist economies. In this way societally specific features work against the establishment of a single standard pattern of work organization throughout a sector across institutional boundaries, with local conditions mediating the adoption of production systems from elsewhere. As Whitley (1997: 255) notes, the 'wholesale transfer' of managerial practices without alteration from one context to another appears impracticable.

Whilst national institutions and societal factors need to be considered, the analysis of the transfer of management practices also has to consider the influence of 'organizational effect' and 'globalization effect' as potentially mediating the influence of cultural-societal effects (Mueller 1994). Supranational institutions, for example, may influence organizational practices, through processes of adaptation, differentiation, or hybridity (see Chapters 9, 10, and 11 by Morgan, Djelic and Bensedrine, and Plehwe, for further analysis of the influence of supranational institutions).

Secondly, there may be pressures within multinationals for a form of 'isomorphism' through efforts to transfer 'best practices' and the diffusion of technologies and knowledge. Therefore the nature and influence of societal, globalization, and organizational effect on processes of homogenization, differentiation, and hybridity (see Morgan's contribution in Chapter 9) should be examined by detailed case studies of specific cases. Smith argues that companies selectively transfer value and operational capacities to fit local labour and product markets, hence reinforcing existing patterns of diversity rather than leading to a homogenization effect (1995: 3). Such an argument is supported by research in America by Milkman (1991) of Japanese manufacturing investment in the USA, in which she argues that 'managements' will select from among a repertoire of employment policies in the light of political and economic circumstances, and especially labour market conditions.

It is being increasingly recognized that some of the literature in this area has worked with an 'idealized' concept of a 'Japanese management system' which may not actually exist in many Japanese organizations operating in Japan (Elger and Smith 1994). Smith and Elger, for example, note that international companies are important media for the transmission of innovations in the organization of production and the regulation of labour, but that the very character of such 'model practices', as embedded, evolving, and incomplete recipes, means that they are never simply reproduced at any specific production site, at home or overseas. Corporate managers and local managers are seen as drawing on different cultural repertoires of organization practice and are engaged in the more or less skilful selection, adaptation, and development of these practices. This takes place in the specific and evolving role of the plant within the wider company, distinctive configurations of suppliers, customers, and sister plants, and the environmental institutions, for example of state regulation, labour supply, and industrial relations (1996: 27). From their research, the substantial variations in the ways in which Japanese subsidiaries in Telford, UK, implemented total quality management (TQM) and JIT systems were related to the distinctive features of the local labour force, and also to the production exigencies experienced by different sorts of branch plant (Elger and Smith 1997).

Looking at Japanese investment in the USA, Cutcher-Gershenfeld et al. (1994) identify two distinct waves of investment. The first pre-1980 investment, involving Japanese organizations with little experience working overseas, selected what they considered to be the most successful work system at that time but struggled to implement it. This supports the view that work organization is more than a series of separate techniques, and is an interweaving of factors including technology, management techniques, and people's knowledge. In post-1980 Japanese investment in the USA, managers became part of a global process of diffusion that involved both planned learning and unintended learning through the choices they made and sought to implement in the transfer of work practices. For example, Toyota's joint venture with General Motors was seen as a planned experiment for Toyota to learn about a US workforce and for General

Motors to learn about Toyota's manufacturing system (Cutcher-Gershenfeld et al. 1994; see also Kristensen and Zeitlin's discussion in Chapter 7 of unintended consequences in subsidiary evolution within multinationals).

Research on Japanese manufacturing organizations with overseas operations has noted the significant role of the expatriate manager as the visible hand (Chandler 1977) in the coordination and control of activities. Also noted has been the relationship between the presence of expatriates and the effective implementation of a lean production system, even though this may leave host country managers in a marginalized position. For example, Rodgers and Wong (1996) examined human resources management (HRM) practices, work organization, and lean operations in Japanese organizations in Singapore and found that HRM practices identified with Japanese home countries were not always present. However, the high relative proportion of expatriates found in companies which adopted the softer dimensions of lean production practices, such as teamwork and group orientation, was related to the important role they play and the idea that expatriates are still being managed by the HRM policies and practices of the parent company. Following White and Trevor (1983), Rodger and Wong argue that it is possible that expatriates may transmit the internalized norms and values underlying the form of work organization characterized by group orientation and teamwork through multiple channels, including formal organization structure, informal reporting relationships, formal and informal communications, instructions, training, and advice, and their own example. In this process the 'visible hand of management' may become internalized into the culture and routines of the organization.

The importance of the wider environmental context of relatively high unemployment and weakening trade-union strength in facilitating the implementation of new work practices in Japanese subsidiaries in the USA and the UK has been noted in other research (Wilkinson and Oliver 1992). Abo argues that the underlying source of strength of the management and production system found in Japanese manufacturing firms is the human factor, which is

intimately related to the historical and cultural characteristics of the Japanese society. As a result, through a pure application of the Japanese management and production technology, no Japanese enterprise would be able to recreate efficiency properties of its technological system in the foreign country—the countries whose socio-cultural backgrounds differ to varying degrees from that of Japan. (1995: 1)

He argued that Japanese companies abroad attempt to apply their indigenous management and production systems, but their efforts are often limited by the local cultural and institutional environment leading to a number of strategic options. These include, first, active adaptation—which could be due to managers' willingness to duplicate the local system or to the significant influence of the local context. Secondly, passive adaptation—when managers realize that parts of the system, e.g. industrial relations, must be replaced with local practice, and adaptation therefore takes place to the extent that the 'Japanese system fails'. Thirdly, revised application—the parent company decides to export certain core elements and to adopt some local practices as a vehicle for facilitating the implementation of the management practices. Through empirical studies at US subsidiaries of Japanese plants, Abo examines the extent of application of the Japanese form of each of these criteria.

8.3. The Implementation of Management Practice as Ongoing Social Processes—Moving from Structures to Processes

Abo's work calls attention to the variety of strategies that may be adopted by Japanese organizations overseas in the transfer of management practices, but says little about the social relations and social processes surrounding implementation processes. As Botti (1995a) outlines, Abo's model is too static to examine ongoing processes, and, as Bonazzi (1996: 305) notes, Abo's base assumptions must be recognized in interpreting the model. The first is the description of an ideal-typical Japanese model. The second is the unidimensionality of the continuum along which, according to Abo, the Japanese ideal type and its opposite, represented by the traditional Fordist American company, can be plotted. As Botti notes (1995b: 79), there is little to be gained by 'precisely defining the term [referring to 'transplant'] and thereby implicitly referring back to some ideal typical clonable model whose characteristics might eventually be measured'; it can be heuristically more productive to recognize that part and parcel of the logic which drives 'globalization' is the fact that there can be an uneven distribution worldwide of the policies and methods which are characteristic of the model as practised 'at home'. In this way, Botti argues that transplants may be considered as sites where organizational knowledge is translated and negotiated (see

202 *Diana Rosemary Sharpe*

also Kristensen and Zeitlin, Chapter 7). As Elger and Smith (1994) note, not even in Japan does there exist a single monolithic model of management and it is also important to look at *how* organizations are influenced by such contextual factors as government policies and market opportunities.

Similarly, it was not the intention in the research presented in this chapter to map 'hybrid' forms of organization, or to work with the assumption that there can be a range of practices from an ideal Japanese to an ideal American which could be identified within one plant. The comparative ethnography carried out aimed to study social processes and be sensitive to contextual factors in explaining outcomes (Burawoy 2000). As noted in the research of Oliver et al. (1994), quantitative studies of performance and its relationship to work organization and HRM practices need to look at underlying processes, not only structures, if they are to help in the understanding of outcomes. In their study they found organizations adopting similar structures having different outcomes, which they discussed as requiring an *understanding of process* as well as context. Measurements of structure are a snapshot at one period in time. As Oliver et al. note 'Japanese and UK plants may exhibit similar structures, but cultural differences may mean that the outcomes are quite different' (1994: 62).

8.4. Deconstructing the Visible Hand: The Importance of Context in Analysing Processes of Consent and Resistance to New Management Practices

Differences in social relations and industrial relations across contexts (Maurice et al. 1980; Sorge and Warner 1986) could influence worker responses to lean production systems. In Japan, the predominance of factory-based labour unions implies the absence of common standards and regulations concerning wage levels, working conditions, etc. on an industry basis (Skorstad 1994). In such a context, conditions of work easily become firm-specific and in the long term may not be subject to negotiation at all (Kumazawa and Yamada 1989).

The internal labour market, combined with firm-specific skills in large Japanese organizations, has tended in the past to lead to careers and conditions of work circumscribed by the opportunities and restrictions within a single firm. In the absence of common rules and regulations negotiated by representatives at a national level, management is free to make preferences of its own. In the case of promotion, for example, formal skill levels or seniority may become less important than cooperativeness, diligence, and high performance (Kumazawa and Yamada 1989). The nature of industrial relations thus shifts the balance of power in favour of management (Skorstad 1994).

In contrast, seniority systems, industry-wide standards of conditions of work, and strong labour unions in many Western contexts provide a different context in which collective action is legitimized as part of the system. In Western contexts, Skorstad argues that lean production systems will lead to worker resistance. However, in situations of high unemployment, for example, consent may be easier to achieve. In this way consent to lean production systems by workers is not because of any experienced improvement in conditions or quality of working life, but because of economic conditions and the wider context, which may lead to consent or acquiescence. Delbridge et al. (1992) note how in Japan JIT/TQM have often tended to have been underpinned by a well-established system of HRM, which bonds core workers to the company. Often in larger companies the practices of lifetime employment, seniority-based wages, and company 'welfarism' tended to heighten the dependency of workers on their companies (Oliver and Wilkinson 1992) being supported by enterprise unionism. Supported by favourable economic and political conditions in the UK in the 1980s and into the 1990s, inward investors have established on green-field sites, often in areas of high unemployment. Such companies have been able to be highly selective of their workforces and to institute systems of direct communications, flexible working practices, supportive pay and appraisal systems, and strict discipline on time and attendance. As the case study below illustrates, however, the visible hand of management does not remain unchallenged, and the process of sustaining and developing managerial control systems is ongoing. Skill structures required of teamworking within a lean production environment demand broad company-specific skills rather than specialized, portable skills, which are often developed within Western training environments (Streeck 1996). Under the flat functional hierarchies characteristic of lean production there are fewer opportunities for individual advancement, which, whilst acceptable in a Japanese work culture where there is a separation of role from status, may not be so to Western employees with different expectations of career paths: 'skill structures, work organization and employment practices are closely interrelated, with a range of larger institutional, political and cultural arrangements and understandings that extend far beyond the individual firm and deep into the fabric of society' (Streeck 1996: 144). This emphasizes the importance of the wider context in influencing how alternative production and control systems may be received. The research work briefly reviewed above and supported by my own research (Sharpe 1997, 1998a, 1998b) provides examples of the increased recognition of the influence of context on the introduction of managerial control systems, including the difficulties of change on brown-field sites.

8.5. The Evolution of a Japanese Subsidiary in the UK

The findings reviewed in this section are taken from a larger ethnographic study of a Japanese manufacturing subsidiary operating in the car industry in the UK. The subsidiary is 75 per cent owned by the Japanese parent company but has a minority shareholding by an Italian manufacturer which is explored in later sections on board-level processes. The case provides an interesting context in which to examine the evolution of an overseas subsidiary, including if, and how, parent company systems were transferred, adapted, and sustained within both a greenfield and a brownfield location. Through comparative analysis within and across cases of management initiatives on the greenfield and brownfield sites in the UK, it has been possible to examine the influence of context and contingencies on how management systems were implemented and sustained, and their outcomes.

8.5.1. *The influence of context on the evolution of the subsidiary*

The change processes that took place across the two sites were significantly influenced by, first, the local context in which they took place; secondly, the characteristics of the employees at shop floor and higher levels, including their orientation to work; and, thirdly, the socio-technical system in which the changes took place. The two sites studied displayed significant differences in the ways that change initiatives were managed and their outcomes. A contributing factor to this was the difference in the context of the sites studied. As summarized in Table 8.1, the greenfield factory (newly built) was located in a new town which had a strong Japanese investment. The local

Table 8.1 *Comparative analysis across sites—history and context*

	Greenfield factory	Brownfield factory
Social environment	Informal network to communicate information on work across factories Homogeneous skill levels Young and ethnically homogeneous labour force	Job opportunities not so clearly communicated across the labour market—heterogeneous skill levels Ethnically diverse work-force
Relationship of company with other companies in the region	Japanese companies maintain close contact and cooperation on salaries and recruitment	Awareness of the major companies wages' practices—some communication by local directors
Position of company in local labour market	One of approx. 14 large employers requiring similar unskilled workers	One of largest manufacturing employers in the region
Local institutional context	New town, many greenfield sites, high overseas (including Japanese) investment, non-unionized environment	Traditional declining manufacturing region, low inward investment, unionized environment
Availability of unskilled work in the region	Comparatively high	Comparatively low
Availability of skilled workers in labour market	Low compared to other regions of the UK	Low compared to other regions of the UK

labour market was non-unionized and composed of comparatively young and unskilled workers. In contrast, the brownfield site in the North of England was located in a traditional unionized manufacturing area that had little foreign direct investment. Therefore, the local institutional context at the greenfield site provided a supportive context for the implementation of management practices, having a large presence of Japanese foreign direct investment (FDI) in the region, the absence of a strong union presence, the availability of a young, unskilled workforce, and the absence of a traditional UK manufacturing industry in the area.

The findings from this research emphasize the importance of the local context at the greenfield site in facilitating the introduction of new forms of management systems and work organization through the comparative study with a brownfield site in a different local labour market context. The comparative study emphasized the difficulty of introducing change in a traditional UK manufacturing area with a union presence and an experienced workforce. The comparative study also helped to identify features of the social context at the greenfield site which were conducive to change and were absent at the brownfield sites. As summarized in Table 8.2, these included the presence of a homogeneous workforce (along the dimensions of background, work experience, and lifestyle) with a local orientation. This 'New Town' was a very 'closed community', where workers often lived on the same housing estates and shared the same community activities and lifestyle, factors that were conducive to the development of a sense of shared purpose and team spirit within the factory. These findings build on the work of Streeck (1996), who notes that features of the local labour market in Japan, including the homogeneity of skills and markets, are supportive to the high commitment management practices introduced within the organizations. The local labour market, in a planned New Town, has developed features supported by government initiatives and FDI, which are conducive to the introduction of new management practices.

The local institutional context at the greenfield site provided a supportive context for the implementation of management practices. Having a large presence of Japanese FDI in the region led to a situation where workers were aware of new work practices and shared their experiences with informal networks of workers in the town. The closed community of relatively young inexperienced non-unionized workers at the greenfield site provided a context in which change could be implemented without significant resistance. Industrial relations in the local labour market were excellent, with few examples of stoppages and strikes. Few firms had a union and workers were used to a non-unionized work environment. The labour market surrounding the greenfield site was therefore quite homogeneous, with many new manufacturing organizations operating in a non-unionized environment, having similar wage rates, and employing mainly unskilled manual workers. Some examples of coercive isomorphism (DiMaggio and Powell 1983) took place, with local pressures for conformity in payment systems from other Japanese investors. The workers in the local labour market had comparatively little experience in traditional UK manufacturing.

In contrast, the brownfield site researched was in a labour market of unionized manufacturing industry with little inward investment.

Table 8.2 *A comparative analysis of work context and change practices*

Labour market and work context	Greenfield site	Practices facilitated/resisted	Brownfield site	Practices facilitated/resisted
Trade-union presence	Non-unionized labour market. No history of union activity	Facilitated introduction of associate meetings as an alternative to worker representative councils or union presence	Traditional union presence. History of union activity and antagonistic relations of shop floor with management	Not conducive to attempts to develop a 'unitary culture'
FDI including Japanese	High, including Japanese greenfield sites	Workers familiar with practices to be introduced, 'grapevine' effect from friends in other factories. Local Japanese companies provide support and advice on practices/wage rates and labour	Very low. No other major Japanese investment in the area	Resistance to new methods of work and shop floor practices
Background, experience, and orientation of workforce	Large supply of unskilled workers in close homogeneous community with local orientation	Facilitated efforts to create a sense of shared, unified work culture in the factory	Workforce heterogeneous in backgrounds, previous factory experiences, place of residence/social background	More difficult to develop a sense of shared, unified work culture
Local labour market wage rates, availability of unskilled workers/work contracts	Low labour rates in market, availability of a pool of unskilled workers willing to work on base rates	Facilitated employment of a large unskilled workforce which could be trained on the job	Low labour rates but some pressure from local unions. Unemployment and poor job opportunities weakening bargaining power of workers	Facilitated use of 'temporary contracts' and the acceptance by the workers of the removal of demarcation lines and compression of the grade system

Workers maintained a network of social relations outside of work which enabled them to know about working conditions and availability of work in other factories. The local labour force was also comparatively heterogeneous at the brownfield site in terms of skill levels, experience, and cultural background. However, whilst the greenfield local context was more conducive to the introduction of management systems than the brownfield context, there were still significant challenges to the introduction of work practices and systems on the greenfield site, which came from the expectations and orientation of the workers.

The location of the greenfield site in a non-unionized environment provided an opportunity to implement key HRM practices that would facilitate the shaping of the organization culture and practices and in doing so played an important role in management control.

Both the greenfield and brownfield sites worked in the automotive supply industry with the same key customers. The major customer was particularly influential across both companies in laying down expectations concerning supplier management and production practices in order to meet standards required. Quality control standards were tightly monitored by this customer. The JIT system operated by customers demanded reliability of quantity and quality.

Competition in the industry was also a driver of change and influenced the shaping of practices. With competitors seeking increasingly to raise productivity with low profit margins to stay ahead, companies were constantly seeking ways to improve productivity and reduce costs. Similarly, relationships with their own supplier network were important in influencing their ability to implement a JIT system and maintain quality and productivity standards. The greenfield factory invested extensively in the training and development of its chosen suppliers so that it would be reliable and be able to work within the demands of a JIT system. Over time, the influence of the major customers in the industry has been felt down the supply chain, influencing, in turn, the systems of work organization, coordination, and control of these firms.

8.5.2. *Board-level processes and the evolution of the subsidiaries*

At both sites of the joint venture the Japanese parent company held a majority 75 per cent shareholding. The composition of the board and management team and processes of board-level communication and decision-making were, however, very different across the two sites, although in both cases the Japanese presence and involvement in directing subsidiary operations were significantly higher. At the greenfield site the two parent company representatives, the Japanese managing director and the Italian general manager, worked closely together in implementing management initiatives in the organization. They were supported by thirty managers, fifteen of whom were Japanese expatriates, some working as coordinators in a guiding role to the local managers (Rodgers and Wong 1996).

The comparatively larger board at the brownfield site (at the time of the research this included five Japanese expatriates, five local nationals, and one Italian director) made communication more complex. Changes at board level following the Japanese purchase also led to some difficulties in establishing communication and shared understanding between the local nationals and the Japanese expatriates. The differences in approach to management between the locals and the Japanese were not resolved at board level, leading to inconsistencies in practices implemented at shop-floor level. The board was fragmented culturally between the local managers and the Japanese expatriates, and functionally amongst local managers heading different departments (Sharpe 1998a).

On the greenfield site the Japanese director was able to develop systems from scratch and, with the insight of the Italian representative on the board, a clearly defined set of policies and practices was developed. In contrast, board decision-making and influence on the brownfield site were more complex, with a mix of expatriate and local managers often in disagreement about short-term and longer-term goals and practices (see Kristensen and Zeitlin's discussion in Chapter 7 of the significance of board-level processes at subsidiary level), challenging the notion often held in the literature about a monolithic management.

Whilst the Japanese parent was hesitant to become involved on the brownfield site and began with a minority presence on the board of directors, over time it changed its approach to managing the operation. Recognizing that performance was not meeting targets, there was a decision to increase its presence on the board and direct involvement in management of the shop floor, in order to achieve its targets and satisfy Japanese customers. Planned and actual change programmes initiated by the directors in the two organizations were influenced by a range of factors, including the parent companies' expectations from the joint venture and the degree of control they maintained over management practices in the organizations (Sharpe 1998b). An example here is the requirement from the parent company in Japan for performance feedback along continuous improvement targets for safety, absenteeism, quality, productivity, and scrap levels across all sections of all sites.

Whilst these control measures were required, the *way* that these performance measures were acted upon, in terms of processes for recording, monitoring, and directing shop-floor activity varied across the sites and across sections. The composition of the board was important in influencing responses to the Japanese parent's require-ments. The mix of local directors and Japanese board members on the brownfield site created a heterogeneous board in terms of back-grounds, expectations, and understandings of what was required. The Japanese expatriate board members tended to have little aware-ness of the local industrial relations context and the orientation to work of workers. Their ideas for continuous improvement activities did not consider the potential resistance from workers accustomed to traditional ways of working and relating to management. The hetero-geneity of management thinking at board level led to inconsistencies in management practices on the shop floor, and the unintended con-sequence of workers becoming cynical of management initiatives.

The parent organizations' strategy for the two sites was important in influencing the number of expatriates sent to direct the organiza-tion, and the attention to management practices within the organiza-tion. On the brownfield site, the Japanese parent kept at arm's length in managing the venture, until performance results were considered unsatisfactory and new business with Japanese customers was devel-oped. The Japanese parent company was particularly concerned that the organizations should meet the standards required to serve their Japanese customers. This meant management systems and proced-ures that were expected by the customers, such as Statistical Process Control (SPC) and quality control. On the greenfield, site the consid-erable investment by both parents was supported by a team of one representative from each working together on the board. The two rep-resentatives on the greenfield site would discuss their views, and the management systems that resulted were often 'hybrids' of their own viewpoints and what they believed would work in the local context (Abo 1995).

On the brownfield site the composition of the board was also very significant in influencing shop-floor practices. The board had an equal number of Japanese and local directors—five each. The local directors mainly had a long history in the organization prior to the joint venture and had established ways of working that were now being challenged. The local and Japanese directors had different assessments of the capacity for change in the local workforce and different understandings of the local culture, industrial relations, and workers' orientation to work. The local directors often sought to explain to the Japanese directors that the changes they were suggesting in some areas would not go down well, or as intended with the local workforce. Some of the impetus for change came from local customers and global competition in the industry which was recognized by the local directors. However, the board remained a scene of negotiations and fragmentation, the outcomes of which were reflected in a lack of integration and consistency, and contradictions in management practices at shop-floor level. These findings are based on the evolution of the subsidiary over the first six years of its operations. At the time of the research it was recognized by directors that building a cohesive board was an important task in the process of managing change in the organization. Central to the change process had been the intention to introduce a continuous improvement culture within the context of teamworking and lean production. Such a change initiative requires consistency of approach and thinking at all levels if it is to be sustained effectively. An unintended consequence of the evolution of the subsidiary through the incremental introduction of expatriates at board level was that practices at board level remained fragmented. Planned change in the organization was the outcome of a process where parent company expectations and control over activities were translated, interpreted, and adjusted by the board of directors who were also influenced and constrained by their own knowledge, experience, and understanding of the local context. These findings build on the work of Kristensen and Zeitlin, as given in Chapter 7, on the influence of competing business logics within the subsidiaries of multinational organizations.

8.5.3. *The evolution of change in the subsidiaries*

The shop-floor workers' orientation to work varied considerably across sections and sites and influenced the way that management sought to introduce control systems on the shop floor as well as the consequences of the management systems introduced. At the greenfield site there was a clear strategy of recruiting young, inexperienced, unskilled workers, who would have few prior experiences or

expectations of shop-floor work. Over time, however, it was realized
that the younger workers showed little commitment to staying with
one organization and tended to follow their friends to other factory
vacancies. In contrast, middle-aged women were seen to be more
dependable and also willing to work with the impromptu overtime
hours required of a JIT system, and so the company adapted its
recruitment strategy to take on more middle-aged women. The vast
majority of women, however, remained at non-managerial level on
the shop floor and at the time of the research appeared to have
reached a glass ceiling above which local male managers and expatriates operated, and through which only male team-leaders tended
to pass.

The influence of the local labour market at the brownfield site was
mitigated significantly in the newer section of the factory through
recruitment and selection strategies which sought workers with little
prior experience in traditional manufacturing environments. The
workers in the older sections, however, had experience from within
the company of a unionized factory environment. This was a significant difference, as it influenced the way that management practices
were perceived and responded to by the workers. The older men in
the press shop had a very different approach to work from the
younger men and women in the new section of the factory, based on
their different experiences and thus expectations of factory work. As
the subsidiary evolved, the older press shop and the newer manufacturing section of the plant continued to maintain significantly different types of worker who had different orientations to work. Across
these sections, the technical and normative managerial control
systems that were developing and being sustained also reflected the
different cultures and orientations of the workers. For example,
across the new section of the brownfield factory team-leaders
appeared to have an increased role in normative control, adopting a
disciplinary role, encouraging their team to be disciplined in their
work, have good time-keeping, follow the rules, and have a positive
attitude. They were in this way much more involved in social as well
as technical dimensions of control on the shop floor than in the press
shop, holding daily meetings with their team and identifying poor
performances.

A comparison of one of the greenfield assembly lines with the
brownfield press shop brings out the most striking contrasts in
gender, age, and orientation. On the assembly line it was possible to
implement a system of normative control with less resistance than in

the press shop. For example, there were daily meetings, where individual defects were pointed out, and reference was made to team commitment, letting the team down, and motivation to be the best line in the factory. Such practices and attitudes would have appeared almost childlike to the press shop workers who held a basic relationship to work of antagonism against the demands of the job and the management. Over time, however, it could be anticipated that recruitment and selection strategies, combined with the turnover and retirement of employees in the press shop would provide an opportunity to introduce a new pool of workers in the press shop, who could be developed from scratch, thereby reducing the legacy of history and inertia in the older parts of the brownfield site.

The team-leader role was of central importance in the implementation of management initiatives for change on the shop floor. The choice of team-leader was therefore crucial, and they tended to be selected from the group they were to manage. In the press shop the team-leader's strengths were also his weaknesses. In identifying with the press shop workers' concerns, he also saw many things through their way of thinking and did not fully take on board the continuous improvement, safety first, positive attitude ideals that the Japanese managers were seeking to spread through the company. Given the composition of the workers in the press shop, however, experienced and hardened in traditional ways of working, it would have been difficult to have an outsider step in and take over the leadership role during this early period in the change programme.

Relationships between levels in the manufacturing hierarchy were important in developing a coherent approach to the content and process of change. Where the team-leaders and section leaders/supervisors were inconsistent in the values they espoused, this led to contradictions on the shop floor in the way that work was managed and the expectations of the shop-floor workers. The section leaders across all sections of the brownfield site displayed a significantly different style of leadership than the team-leaders, the majority of them having been recruited from the union representatives who used to be on the shop floor. They were very directive and authoritarian in their style and were wholly task-orientated. They tended to lack the social facilitator skills of the team-leaders and also did not appear to have internalized the wider philosophy, for example, of teamwork and continuous improvement. They remained aloof from the shop-floor workers and would sometimes appear aggressive in challenging workers who did not pull their weight. An important feature of the section leaders' behaviour, which significantly disturbed attempts by the team-leader to develop new values in the workforce, was the section leaders' reliance on tried and tested ways of getting results. Output came first, even when safety or quality was threatened. Thus the section leaders appeared less committed to supporting a change in organizational culture than with short-term output targets for which they were responsible. This often led to frustration by team-leaders and shop-floor workers who could see the inconsistencies between the espoused values of the company and the behaviour of the section leaders.

At the greenfield site inconsistencies between levels in the hierarchy were not so clearly noticeable, although there were some 'weak' links in the management of culture and normative control, for example a team-leader or supervisor who was not communicating the Kaizen philosophy and team spirit. The greenfield assembly line studied provided a good example of a comparatively strong link of shared values between team-leader, supervisor, and manufacturing manager, which facilitated the implementation of new initiatives. The importance of a strong link of shared values down the organizational hierarchy in the implementation of planned change builds on previous research (see, for example, Delbridge and Lowe 1997; Lowe et al. 1996) on the changing role of the supervisory system with the move from mass production to 'lean production'. The findings also illustrate how, on the brownfield site, the unintended consequences of this 'hybrid control system' in the older parts of the factory were worker disillusionment with new management systems and an unwillingness to buy into new social relations built on the values of teamwork and mutual respect.

8.6. Discussion

The above analysis has addressed the importance of context and the characteristics of the workers in influencing the nature of evolving management practices in the subsidiary of a Japanese multinational in the UK. Across sections and sites the 'template' of management and work practices as held by the Japanese parent company expatriates was translated, mediated, refined, and sometimes ignored in the process of implementation of management initiatives. Important factors influencing the evolution of practices in the subsidiaries included the power balance between directors and the outcome of negotiation and attempts to influence the nature and direction of change by the local and expatriate directors and managers, the local workers on the works committee (on the brownfield site), and shop-floor workers. In this way the multinational became a site of negotiation and conflict in which the underlying mechanisms of different business systems and actors came into confrontation and contest.

8.6.1. *Control and deconstructing the visible hand of management*

Whilst the Japanese expatriates were usually very familiar with the practices they were interested in implementing, other directors and managers were often less familiar with the practices (for example, 5S (a system of shop-floor practices, including preventative maintenance), TQM and continuous improvement). This influenced the way that change was managed at managerial level and led to variations in practices across sections. This was particularly significant considering the attempts by the parent organization to introduce a company-wide continuous improvement culture, through normative as well as technical control systems. An unintended consequence of the fracture at managerial level was that a coherent system of normative control was not sustainable throughout the brownfield subsidiary and was only superficially introduced in the older sections of the site.

Resource constraints in terms of technology, time, labour, and skills were also factors influencing how the visible hand of management was applied. For example, in the press shop the Japanese directors had little knowledge of the technology used, and did not want to invest immediately in new technology. In this way they had to work around the existing technology in considering management practices and managerial control systems. Customer expectations and competitors' practices were important pressures encouraging changes in work practices and a realization of the need to change by local managers.

The research found that whilst across both sites the Japanese parent organization was seeking to adopt similar structures and control systems (for example, the introduction of the team-leader role, a grading structure which compressed the traditional craft-related hierarchy on the brownfield site, and monitoring of performance along the dimensions of productivity, quality, and safety), the outcomes were influenced by the context in which they were introduced. Therefore, as noted in the work of Oliver et al. (1994), whilst organizations may on the surface appear to have adopted the same formal structures, this says little about the underlying processes at work.

The study makes a contribution to the debate by indicating that despite the pressures of isomorphic pulls towards 'best practice' within the car component industry, driven by 'organizational' and 'globalization effects' (Mueller 1994), the cultural and institutional specificity of management practices and the influence of organizational inertia in the management of change (Sorge and Warner 1986; Streeck 1996; Whitley 1997) should also be analysed. To understand how multinational organizations seek to transfer practices across their operations, it is necessary to move away from the view of the organization as a black box and to examine through in-depth case studies the linkages and relations between institutional structures such as national and supranational cultural, political, and economic structures (see Chapters 2 and 9 by Whitley and by Morgan, respectively) and the internal relations and processes within and between organizations. Analysis should therefore look at the linkages across a number of levels of analysis which cut across the organization/environment boundary and include micro- and macro-levels of analysis (see also Burawoy 2000).

8.6.2. *Continuity and change and the role of expatriates*

Expatriates had an important role to play in the visible hand of international management in this case study through board-level influence and direct hands on influence on the shop floor. On the brownfield site, during the first few years of ownership, attempts to manage from a distance by the Japanese parent company proved problematic, and performance indicators were unsatisfactory. The increased presence of expatriates on the brownfield site, however, did not provide an easy and immediate opportunity to manage change, especially in the older sections of the plant where there was a legacy of custom and practice that persisted despite management initiatives to change shop-floor practices and routines. The study uncovers how, despite the introduction of management practices across sections that appear to be similar, e.g. based on HRM policies and control procedures for continuous improvement activities, *in practice* across departments there were significant differences in control processes and worker responses. By deconstructing the visible hand of management in one organization, it is possible to examine actual processes and practices that have evolved. The research found that the Total Industrial

Engineering (TIE) department managed by expatriates played an important role at the greenfield site in the introduction and management of control systems on the shop floor through managing the introduction of Kaizen activities. The expatriate TIE manager acted as a guide and teacher to the local TIE associates as part of the process of transfer of work practices and procedures from the Japanese manager to the shop-floor workers encouraging the introduction of new practices. This was carried out through the transmission of internalized norms and values underlying the form of work organization characterized by group orientation and teamwork through multiple channels, including formal organizational structures, informal reporting relationships, formal and informal communications, instructions, training and advice, and their own example (see also Rodgers and Wong 1996).

Such a process also took place to some degree in the new section of the brownfield site where the Japanese expatriates were most heavily involved in management at shop-floor level. In the other sections of the brownfield site, however, the formal communications in terms of performance standards and commitment to Kaizen were not supported through a shop-floor presence by the Japanese expatriates. This placed the responsibility on the local employees down the managerial hierarchy to implement new practices. The research highlighted how the lack of consistency in approach amongst the local employees, including the sharp difference in management approach and attitude between the section leaders and team-leaders, created significant barriers to the internalization of new norms and values of teamwork and group orientation.

The findings from the brownfield site provide an interesting case study in which traditional UK management practices have been questioned by increasing customer and industry pressure for change, a change in the climate of industrial relations in the UK, and by a change in ownership with the introduction of a Japanese influence at board level. The research highlights the difficulty of introducing a 'new industrial relations' and restructuring subsidiary operations of mature organizations. Adversarial relations which had traditionally existed between the unionized shop floor and management on the brownfield site proved difficult to change following the Japanese purchase of the subsidiary. Local managers continued in a relationship of tension with the shop floor with traditional structures and reporting relations embedded in the local institutional context (DiMaggio and Powell 1983).

Recruitment, selection, training, and promotion systems worked together across the greenfield site, to encourage workers with the 'right attitude' to come through the system. The strategy on the greenfield site of selecting comparatively inexperienced younger workers for the assembly lines, rather than the process sections, facilitated the introduction of work practices and social control systems (for example, the use of peer pressure) which would have been, and were, considered less favourably by more experienced workers who had become cynical of management in UK manufacturing organizations. However, even under these supportive conditions, on the greenfield site there was a continued tension in the control system. Resistance was still present although it had been channelled and diluted with the management practices discussed in this chapter. On the greenfield site workers did express resistance by quitting the job, but up to the time of the research, six years following the set-up of the greenfield site, there had been no significant collective resistance that threatened production or management authority on the shop floor.

In summary, by looking at processes of change and inertia, the focus of this chapter has been on *how* the visible hand of management has been implemented, sustained, and resisted across different contexts of a multinational's subsidiaries and the unintended consequences of management action on the shop floor.

REFERENCES

Abo, T. (1994), *Hybrid Factory: The Japanese Production System in the United States*. Oxford: Oxford University Press.

—— (1995), 'Technology Transfer of Japanese Corporation. "Application-Adaptation" of Japanese Production Systems in North America, NIES, ASEAN and Europe'. Paper presented at the International Conference on Chinese and Japanese Management, School of Management, Zhongshan University.

Bonazzi, G. (1996), 'New Developments in the Debate on the Japanese Model', *Organization*, 3(2): 311–12.

Botti, H. F. (1995a), 'Going Local: The Hybridization Process as Organizational Learning'. Paper presented at the workshop sponsored by the European Science Foundation, European Management and Organisations in Transition Programme, on 'The Production, Diffusion and Consumption of Management Knowledge in Europe', Barcelona, Spain.

—— (1995b), 'Misunderstandings: A Japanese Transplant in Italy Strives for Lean Production', *Organization*, 2(1): 55–86.

Burawoy, M. (2000), 'Introduction: Reaching for the Global', in M. Burawoy, J. A. Blum, S. George, Z. Gille, T. Gowan, L. Haney, M. Klawiter, S. H. Lopez, S. O. Riain, and M. Thayer, *Global Ethnography*. London: University of California Press.

Chandler, A. D. (1977), *The Visible Hand: The Managerial Revolution in American Business*. London: Harvard University Press.

Clark, R. (1979), *The Japanese Company*. New Haven: Yale University Press.

Cool, K. O. and Lengnick-Hall, C. A. (1985), 'Second Thoughts on the Transferability of the Japanese Management Style', *Organisation Studies*, 6(1): 1–22.

Cutcher-Gershenfeld, J., Nitta, M., Barrett, B., Belhedi, N., Bullard, J., Coutchie, C., Inabe, T., Ishino, I., Lee, S., Lin, W., Mothersell, W., Rabine, S., Ramanand, S., Strolle, M., and Wheaton, A. (1994), 'Japanese Team-Based Work Systems in North America: Explaining the Diversity', *California Management Review*, 37(1): 42–64.

Delbridge, R. and Lowe, J. (1997), 'Manufacturing Control: Supervisory Systems on the "New" Shop Floor', *Sociology*, 31(3): 409–26.

Delbridge, R., Turnbull, P. and Wilkinson, B. (1992), 'Pushing Back the Frontiers: Management Control and Work Intensification under JIT/TQM Factory Regimes', *New Technology, Work and Employment*, 7(2): 97–106.

DiMaggio P. J. and Powell, W. (1983), 'Institutional Isomorphism—The Iron Cage Revisited', *American Sociological Review*, 48: 147–60.

Dore, R. (1973), *British Factory—Japanese Factory: The Origins of National Diversity in Industrial Relations*. Oxford: University of California Press.

Elger, T. and Smith, C. (eds.) (1994), *Global Japanization? The Transnational Transformation of the Labour Process*. London: Routledge.

—— (1997), *Exit, Voice and Mandate: Labour Strategies and Management Practices of Japanese Firms in Britain*. Working paper RP9715. Aston Business School, Birmingham, England.

Hibino, B. (1997), 'The Transmission of Work Systems: A Comparison of US and Japan Auto's Human Resource Management Practices in Mexico', in R. Whitley and P. H. Kristensen (eds.), *Governance at Work: The Social Regulation of Economic Relations*. Oxford: Oxford University Press, 158–70.

Kenney, M. and Florida, R. (1993), *Beyond Mass Production: The Japanese System and its Transfer to the United States*. Oxford: Oxford University Press.

Kenney, M., Romero, J., Contrera, O., and Bustos, M. (1999), 'Labor–Management Relations in the Japanese Consumer Electronics Maquila-doras', in S. C. Beechler and A. Bird (eds.), *Japanese Multinationals Abroad: Individual and Organisational Learning*. Oxford: Oxford University Press, 151–68.

Kumazawa, M. and Yamada, J. (1989), 'Jobs and Skills Under the Lifelong Nenko Employment Practice', in S. Wood (ed.), *The Transformation of Work?* London: Hyman, 102–26.

Lincoln, J. R. and Kalleberg, A. L. (1985), 'Work Organization and Workforce Commitment: A study of Plants and Employees in the US and Japan', *American Sociological Review*, 50, December: 738–60.

Lowe, J., Morris, J., and Wilkinson, B. (1996), 'British Factory, Japanese Factory, Mexican Factory: Supervisory Systems in Global Context'. Paper presented at Globalisation of Production and the Regulation of Labour International Conference, Warwick Business School, England, September.

Maurice, M., Sellier, F., and Silvestra, J. J. (1986), *The Social Bases of Industrial Power*. Cambridge, Mass: MIT Press.

Maurice, M., Sorge, A., and Warner, M. (1980), 'Societal Differences in Organizing Manufacturing Units', *Organization Studies*, 1: 59–86.

Milkman, R. (1991), *Japan's California Factories: Labour Relations and Economic Globalization*. Los Angeles: University of California Press.

Monden, Y. (1983), *Toyota Production System: Practical Approach to Production Management*. New York: Industrial Engineering and Management Press.

Mueller, F. (1994), 'Societal Effect, Organizational Effect and Globalization', *Organization Studies*, 15(3): 407–28.

Oliver, N., Delbridge, R., Jones, D., and Lowe, J. (1994), 'World Class Manufacturing: Further Evidence in the Lean Production Debate', *British Journal of Management*, 5, June: 53–63.

Oliver, N. and Wilkinson, B. (1992), *The Japanization of British Industry: New Developments in the 1990s*. Oxford: Blackwell Publishers.

Ozawa, T. (1979), *Multinationalism, Japanese Style*. Princeton: Princeton University Press.

Rodgers, R. A. and Wong, J. (1996), 'Human Factors in the Transfer of the "Japanese Best Practice" Manufacturing System to Singapore', *The International Journal of Human Resource Management*, 7(2): 455–88.

Rubery, J. (1994), 'The British Production Regime: A Societal-Specific System?', *Economy and Society*, 23(3): 335–54.

Sharpe, D. R. (1997), 'Compromise Solutions: A Japanese Multinational Comes to the UK', in R. Whitley and P. H. Kristensen (eds.), *Governance at Work: The Social Regulation of Economic Relations*. Oxford. Oxford University Press.

—— (1998a), 'Working with Organisational Complexity and Diversity: An Empirical Study of the Formation and Evolution of a European-Japanese International Joint Venture', in G. Hooley, R. Loveridge and D. Wilson (eds.), *Internationalization: Process, Contexts and Markets*. London: Macmillan, 78–95.

—— (1998b), 'Shop Floor Practices Under Changing Forms of Managerial Control: A Comparative Ethnographic Study', PhD thesis, Manchester Business School, Manchester.

Skorstad, E. (1994), 'Lean Production, Conditions of Work and Worker Commitment', *Economic and Industrial Democracy*, 15: 429–55.

Smith, C. (1995), *Japan, The Hybrid Factory and Cross-National Organisational Theory*. Working Paper Series, RP9502. Aston Business School, UK.

Smith, C. and Elger, T. (1996), 'The Global in the Local: Transplant Localisation as a Conditional and Contested Process'. Paper presented at the Globalisation of Production and the Regulation of Labour International Conference, Warwick Business School, England. September.

Sorge, A. (1996), 'Societal Effects in Cross-National Organization Studies', in R. Whitley and P. H. Kristensen (eds.), *The Changing European Firm*. London: Routledge, 67–86.

Sorge, A. and Warner, M. (1986), *Comparative Factory Organization*. Aldershot: Gower.

Streeck, W. (1996), 'Lean Production in the German Automobile Industry: A Test Case for Convergence Theory', in S. Berger and R. Dore (eds.), *National Diversity and Global Capitalism*. London: Cornell University Press, 138–70.

Tayeb, M. (1994), 'Japanese Managers and British Culture: A Comparative Case Study', *International Journal of Human Resource Management*, 5(1): 145–66.

Trevor, M. (1988), *Toshiba's New British Company*. London: Policy Studies Institute.

White, M. R. and Trevor, M. (1983), *Under Japanese Management*. London: Heinemann.

Whitley, R. D. (1990), 'East Asian Enterprise Structures and the Comparative Analysis of Forms of Business Organisation', *Organisation Studies*, 11(1): 47–74.

—— (1997), 'The Social Regulation of Work Systems: Institutions, Interest Groups, and Varieties of Work Organization in Capitalist Societies', in R. Whitley and P. H. Kristensen (eds.), *Governance at Work: The Social Regulations of Economic Relations*. Oxford: Oxford University Press.

Wilkinson, B. and Oliver, N. (1992), 'Human Resource Management in Japanese Manufacturing Companies in the UK and USA', in B. Towers, *The Handbook of Human Resource Management*. Oxford: Blackwell, 49–66.

PART III

CHANGING NATIONAL AND INTERNATIONAL ECONOMIC ORDERS: CONSTRUCTING AND RECONSTRUCTING SYSTEMS OF ECONOMIC ORGANIZATION AND REGULATION

9

The Development of Transnational Standards and Regulations and their Impacts on Firms

GLENN MORGAN

9.1. Introduction

Economic transactions require an element of shared values and norms which are enforceable within and beyond the transaction itself. Without these shared standards, it is difficult to build and sustain economic relationships. These shared standards are embedded in formal and informal institutions which govern transactions and act as the rules of the game. Within national contexts, these standards are part of a broader process of building and maintaining institutions in conditions of transactional uncertainty and complexity. Outside these national contexts, however, the existence of shared standards is much more precarious. If such standards are important at an international as well as a national level, where do they come from and what is their impact? In this particular chapter, the focus is on how certain sorts of transactional uncertainty and complexity provide the basis for firms and other economic agents to construct systems of standardization that operate beyond the national level to give actors an institutional basis for their economic relationships. It is clearly the case that, at this level, certain actors are more powerful than others. Some states or groups of states are able to influence standard setting more strongly than others. Certain firms are in powerful positions to influence particular forms of standard setting. Even 'civil society' groups and global social movements can have some influence on these processes (see O'Brien et al. 2000). Emerging international institutions that seek to provide standards for economic activity are complex arenas in which many different groups may engage. This engagement may give rise to 'epistemic communities', i.e. forms of transnational communities built around particular issues and sectors (see, e.g., Djelic and Bensedrine in Chapter 10 on the development of such a community around CCF regulation). These communities link particular departments and interests from within governments to firms and their associations (whose interests may be affected by international regulation) as well as to non-governmental organizations and civil society bodies that articulate specific local, regional, and global interests (Rosenau 1997; Braithwaite and Drahos 2000). In this chapter, the huge complexity of international regulation is addressed through focusing in particular on the link between transactional uncertainties and standard setting. Multinational corporations have an interest in establishing transnational standards as this particularly affects their ability to do business across national boundaries. However, the standards, which they are used to within their own national contexts are only one of a series of possible sets of standards. Therefore, the standards which emerge arise out of processes of power, conflict, and negotiation and embed the interests of certain firms and national contexts more than others.

9.2. **Transactional Uncertainties and the Creation of Standards**

Trade and economic activity have always crossed political, cultural, and religious borders (see, e.g., Curtin 1984). Before the advent of nation-states and the creation of a single jurisdictional authority, backed up with military force, over carefully demarcated areas of land, trade relationships relied on a variety of techniques from religious and kinship networks through to forms of diplomatic treaties or 'safe-passes' negotiated on a bilateral basis under the imprimatur of various emperors, kings, dukes, and other forms of political and religious authority. Backed up by the acceptance of the value of gold and silver as well as a willingness to barter, a certain *lex mercatoria* took root in most of European 'Christendom' with some forms of extension into Asia and Africa in the premodern period (see, e.g., the discussions in Tracy 1991).

This system gradually declined, however, as certain parts of Europe and elsewhere established themselves as nation-states in the eighteenth and nineteenth centuries. Social and economic life became increasingly coordinated within the borders of nation-states. It was out of this process of ordering that distinctive national business systems emerged based on institution-building within the key spheres of politics, education, culture, and finance. This in turn led to the establishment of particular types of firms with their own specialisms, leading each national system to have its own distinctive patterning of firms and sectors (see Quack et al. 2000). The creation of formality and order within the state meant that the previous system of informality, disorder, and uncertainty outside the boundaries of the state became a source of potential instability in the international system as a whole. As Whitley describes in Chapter 2, these sorts of market uncertainty *within* national contexts are dealt with by the extension of existing social institutions of law, contract, and trust (see also Lane and Bachmann 1998). At the international level, the institutional bases of such ways of managing and mitigating uncertainty are not present, leading Whitley to refer to its 'anomic' nature. Within the Westphalian model that has governed relationships between states from the early modern period onwards, international law has a precarious and limited significance, since 'the fundamental norm of Westphalian sovereignty is that states exist in specific territories within which domestic political authorities are the sole arbiters of legitimate behavior' (Krasner 1999: 20). Therefore, the orderliness of international economic activity in the era of nation-states has not arisen from the creation of a set of laws and enforcement mechanisms which stand above the national level; rather, it has derived from the formal and informal pressures to conform to certain standards of behaviour in order to be able to engage in transnational economic activity. These pressures themselves reflect the interests of those actors (both governmental and private) who wish to extend international economic activity and in order to do so recognize the necessity of establishing certain standards. The standards which emerge may be embedded in formal institutions of international regulation or in private mechanisms (such as credit rating). If a nation or a firm does not indicate at the very least a willingness to abide by these standards (whether it does so or not in practice), then it will find it difficult to engage in the forms of international trade which the standards are designed to facilitate.

In summary, within a national context, business systems develop characteristic institutional mechanisms for dealing with varieties of non-performance in economic contracts. Actors learn to predict the relative ability of others to perform as required and adjust price and contractual mechanisms accordingly. There is predictability of performance and of the mechanisms for sanctioning non-performance.

Moving across borders, this element of predictability reduces. This may not be a serious problem where cross-border activity is either limited or is between systems that approximately share certain standards and approaches or is in contexts which are dominated by a single powerful actor setting standards. However, when these conditions are not met, then it becomes likely that new mechanisms will emerge on an experimental basis to resolve the problems. These mechanisms can make being able to engage in certain sorts of international economic relationships conditional on meeting particular standards agreed at an international level (whether this 'international level' is global, regional/triadic, or non-regional).

In this chapter, I distinguish three main types of standard which are becoming increasingly important mechanisms in managing the transactional uncertainties and complexities that arise from these processes of international economic activity. These standards relate to three key areas. The first area is the product or service itself; what is being bought and what sanctions are available in cases where products fall below expected standards? The second type relates to the actors involved; are they fit and proper persons to engage in specific types of transactions? The third type refers to the nature of the market context within which the transaction takes place; is this market functioning in an appropriate manner? The basic framework and issues to be discussed are summarized in Table 9.1. In what follows, I pursue each of these issues of transactional complexity and uncertainty in order to reveal what international institutions are arising to manage these processes (for more comprehensive surveys see Braithwaite and Drahos 2000; also Murphy 1994).

9.3. **Product Standards**

Product standards are ways of overcoming uncertainty because they provide a transparent template for the parties in a transaction. They come in two main forms (for a summary of the argument see Table 9.2), which will be discussed separately.

The first type of product standard derives from firm-based attempts to standardize their production systems. In Fordist production systems, the standardization of specifications for parts allowed for competitive and multiple sourcing. It therefore encouraged a limited form of innovation amongst suppliers as they sought to compete for contracts. In a more dynamic framework, firms set stand-

Table 9.1 *Types of international standard setting*

Types of standard	Dominant types of sanctions	Types of standard setting institution
Product standards	Market mechanisms: unwillingness to trade	Mainly private bodies
Fit and proper persons standards	Not allowed to conduct business in certain areas	Mix of public and private bodies
Fair dealing standards	Punitive sanctions including fines	Public: inter-governmental

Table 9.2 *Product standards*

Types of standard	Sanctions against failure to meet standards	Standard setters
Technology derived	Loss of connectivity, leading to loss of markets	Private firms sustained by patents and intellectual property rights; also standard setting bodies (public/private)
Standards of performance; badges of 'quality'	Possible loss of 'reputation' leading to loss of markets	Standard setting bodies (mainly private)

ards for their suppliers by creating a platform on which firms can then develop their own versions of products, e.g. the recent establishment of the WAP (Wireless Applications Protocols) for standards in providing internet access from mobile phones. Such standards can be enforced by dominant firms using monopoly power and creating in customers and suppliers huge sunk costs that make switching to new and different standards highly expensive, e.g. as with Microsoft and its Windows applications (see Langlois and Robertson 1995 for a discussion of these processes). Standard setting then may be termed a 'near-market' form of regulation. It is something which firms continuously engage in, seeking to enforce certain terms on those with whom they do business. In the case of very large and powerful firms with some proprietary knowledge, this can work without the intervention of any further body. It can be carried over national boundaries to reduce transactional uncertainty by ensuring that all products share broadly the same standards.

However, in international contexts, the issue of standards can become highly intense and political where firms from different contexts compete in global markets on the basis of different standards, e.g. in mobile phone technology. In these contexts, international standard setting bodies come to the fore as private means of resolving uncertainties. Once a technological standard is set either by a regulatory body or a monopoly provider, it enforces a certain pattern on firms. If they wish to connect themselves and their products to a standardized system, they are forced to conform to the norms.

By contrast, there are other standards that are more in the nature of 'badges' than forces which impact profoundly on the internal workings of the organization. For example, take the case of standards derived from the development of programmes to check quality such as International Standard Organization (ISO) 9000. This involves a standardized methodology for assessing the quality of procedures and processes within organizations. ISO standards become markers that firms have conformed to these processes. However, as authors such as Hancke and Casper (2000) make clear in their study of ISO 9000 in the French and German automobile industries, the impact of these processes of certification within firms can vary enormously depending on the institutional context. Their coercive effect on the firm is strongly mediated by the competences and skills of the managers and workers implementing the standards. Therefore, as Hancke and Casper show, the result is not homogenization and a convergence in practices based on the ISO 9000 standards, but a deepening of existing differences between firms in different institutional contexts. However, the 'badging' process itself remains important even though there is a great deal of scepticism about its real meaning in terms of 'quality'. It becomes a signal across borders of conformity to certain international standards and creates what DiMaggio and Powell labelled as a mimetic process of institutional isomorphism. As they note, 'these developments also have a ritual aspect'. It is not so much that the badging guarantees a certain level of quality and standards but that it provides a reassurance in a context when 'organizational technologies are poorly understood, when goals are ambiguous or when the environment creates symbolic uncertainty' (1983: 151).

Quality standards also tend to work within a market framework. They provide a badge across borders that companies have participated in the standard setting process. In some cases, firms will let it be known that they will not deal with other firms that have not met particular standards. In these cases, there is a market compulsion on companies to participate. However, as the badging does not guarantee that the standards are met in reality, firms may still find poor performance by badged firms and will therefore withdraw their business and take it elsewhere. Conversely, firms that do not display the badges are unlikely to have 'failed' to meet the standard and more likely not to have bothered. If a firm decides seriously to seek the standard, it is difficult to fail to do so as long as sufficient time and resources are put into the process internally (in setting up an appropriate team) and externally (in employing specialist consultants, etc.).

This arena of standard setting is essentially concerned with reducing transaction costs in markets and is therefore supplementary and possibly complementary to other mechanisms for achieving this goal, e.g. the price mechanism itself. It is closely associated with the making of contracts and transactions between business partners. As Lane (1997) has shown in her study of Britain and Germany, standard setting bodies vary in their nature across different institutional contexts, as do the mechanisms of market, contract, and trust. Whilst there may be a degree of integration of government within these mechanisms, they are essentially concerned with encouraging firms as market contractors to reach certain standards of performance. In the UK, the British Standards Institute (BSI) is a private company which basically deals in the business of creating and selling standards (as revealed in Table 9.3). As Lane notes in her comparison between the BSI and the equivalent German body:

In Britain, standards have been devised both by individual large firms (particularly but not solely in the nationalised industries) and by national standard-setting institutions. At the national level, the British Standards Institute (BSI) founded in its present form in 1931, has long been the most important institution for the preparation and promulgation of standards. It is an independent, non-governmental organisation but it receives a significant portion of its income from the state—the government matches the income derived from membership fees. (1997: 205)

At the international level, the ISO plays a central role in coordinating the various specialist standards bodies from different countries. The ISO is constructed as a world federation of national standards bodies from 130 countries, one from each country. In 1999, the ISO had registered a total of 12,524 international standards, 961 of which had been registered that year. Many of these standards reflect the ISO's commitment to free trade and the notion that establishing global standards, particularly in materials and technology,

Table 9.3 *The British Standards Institute*

Subscribing members	18,416
Committee members	19,103
Current British Standards	18,155
British Standards sold	660,922
Kitemark, Safety Mark and other product certification licences	2,046
Registered business locations	33,216
Number of BSI staff	3,477
Countries with BSI operational centres	90

Source: British Standards Institute website (accessed 20/02/2000): *http://www.bsi.org.uk/bsi/cor-porate/stakeholder/index.xhtml*

will contribute to the disappearance of so-called 'technical barriers to trade'. They are therefore primarily technology-based. The largest number of new registrations was in the category of engineering technologies (253, making a total of 2,867 standards in this sector) followed by materials technologies (236, making a total of 3,652), and electronics, information technology, and telecommunications (203 making a total of 1,852) (source: ISO web-pages accessed 10/02/2000: *http://www.iso.ch/infoe/iso_in_figures.pdf*).

Standardization of the type described is taking place at all sorts of level and through all sorts of mechanisms. As well as standards that have implications for all firms working in global markets (either managed through a public body such as the ISO or enforced by a virtual technological monopoly), there are regionally set standards, e.g. within the European Union (some of which may be negotiated through the institutions of the EU and some of which may be agreed across industry associations in different member states) or standards privately negotiated between firms (within the same country or in the same region or different regions).

9.4. Fit and Proper Persons Standards

In economic transactions within states, there are institutional constraints on the forms of business organizations. I refer to this as standards concerned with 'fit and proper persons'. The term 'person' in this context refers both to the individuals involved and to the 'corporate entity'. In other words, states may proscribe who can and cannot be directors of companies; states also prescribe the nature of the corporate entity itself and the system of governance that must be followed. For example, in the UK firms have to follow certain rules if they wish to conduct their business as a limited liability company. In Germany, there is a much wider variety of legal statuses which firms can adopt and which affect the governance structures that are adopted, e.g. in terms of supervisory boards and works councils. However, it is not just states that exercise this power of standard setting. It can also be exercised in different ways by other types of organization. In the international arena, it may be argued that it is these other types of organization that are the most significant, since failure to abide by these standards means that one cannot enter the market in the first place. The 'fit and proper person' standard can therefore be exercised to deny market access to companies. In this sense, it is a highly coercive instrument, which, as it develops, cannot be ignored by companies seeking an international presence.

For firms working in international environments, what guarantee is there that those with whom they are doing business are 'fit and proper persons'? One solution to this is to assume that standards, although not the same in each country, are roughly equivalent. Within the European Union, this was the route that was taken in the development of the single market up to 1992. Companies were not required to register in every member of the EEC (as it was then); it was assumed that registration in their home base was sufficient to provide for rough equivalency, a not unreasonable premise given the limited numbers of members in the EEC and their long-term shared history. However, as this example illustrates, such a system tends only to work within a set of relationships that are already highly interdependent. Even here, however, this notion was highly problematic within certain sectors (such as financial services: see Morgan and Murray 1991).

As an example of the issues involved both in agreeing within a fixed regional space such as the EU and more widely, one can take the example of financial institutions. In the Keynesian era, the national peculiarities of banks, which derived from their distinctive social and historical origins (for an analysis of these in the case of the UK, see Morgan and Sturdy 2000), were sustained and reproduced (see Morgan 1997 and the other contributions in Morgan and Knights 1997). What was a 'fit and proper person'/bank in one context was different from that in another. In particular, this related to the risks that banks were willing and able to undertake and how these were to be insured against. Countries differed on the rules which they operated about how banks' liabilities were to be covered. How much capital was it necessary for the bank to have quick access to in order to ensure that badly performing loans did not undermine the strength of the bank as a whole? As banks were released from quantitative governmental constraints on their lending abilities and deregulated capital markets opened up to allow access to funds purely on the basis of market rates, banks were able to take on higher risks without necessarily having to build internal risk management systems to match their new-found freedoms. Differences in regulation across national boundaries meant that even though banks in one environment did not directly make risky loans (e.g. to developing countries in the late 1970s and early 1980s, to leveraged buy-outs in the mid-1980s, to property speculators in the late 1980s and early 1990s, to vulnerable East Asian newly industrializing countries (NICs) in the mid-1990s), they might be drawn into any crisis because they had lent to 'respectable' banks in other countries which had not shown such caution. In other words, it was becoming increasingly difficult to tell who was a 'fit and proper *corporate* person' in the banking field.

In order to overcome these difficulties, central bank officials from the main industrialized countries began to meet in Basle to draw up a set of standards to which all banks that wanted to conduct business outside their own borders had to commit. The accounts of these meetings reveal the role of both national differences in banking standards and the necessity to reach an agreement to which all parties could subscribe (see, e.g., Kapstein 1994; Underhill 1997). It was the central banks that were monitoring the systems with the highest levels of lending exposure and the least regulated conditions of lending, i.e. the Bank of England and the US Federal Reserve, which moved earliest to establish international standards. Reaching a bilateral accord on capital requirements, they persuaded Japan to join them in placing pressure on the Europeans to come into line. However, as Kapstein notes, 'it was obviously in the interest of the Bank of England and the Federal Reserve to shape a standard which every G-10 member could agree upon and, just as important, live up to by domestic enforcement' (1994: 115). The proposal called for banks operating in international markets to have a capital base that would be 8 per cent of total risk assets. The capital required was, in turn, differentiated, as were the risks built in to the banks' assets. What the proposal meant was that banks would have to shape their international lending activity according to the standards of what became known as the Basle Accord. In some cases, this has had drastic effects. In the 1980s, for example, Japanese banks were borrowing in international markets and lending on with very narrow spreads on the basis of their huge assets in Japan. However, as subsequent events in the 1990s showed, this asset base was illusory, primarily derived from the pumped-up value of property in what was known as the Japanese 'bubble economy' (see, e.g., Murphy 2000). Under the more rigorous capital adequacy rules of the Basle Accord, the Japanese could no longer borrow and lend with such ease. They had drastically to improve their balance sheets by cutting loans to correspond to the proportions allowable under Basle, given the nature of their free capital. The result was a credit squeeze in Japan, contributing to the downward spiral of the economy in the 1990s. Kapstein argues:

The Basle Accord represents the most significant step taken to date by bank supervisors in advancing policy convergence and creating an international banking regime, with formal principles, norms, rules and decision making procedures. To be sure, supervisors had already accepted the general principle that no international bank should escape supervision and that banking regulation should rest on home country control ... But the Basle Accord went beyond these prior agreements in demanding complete convergence with respect to one of the most crucial areas of banking supervision: banking adequacy. With the Basle Accord, central bankers had demonstrated their ability to structure agreements that met the demands of safety and soundness, as well as international competitiveness. (1994: 118–19)

The Basle Accord was an attempt to ensure that banks operating in the international arena could be trusted to be 'fit and proper persons'. It was developed primarily by central bankers who took into account the interests of their own financial institutions but created a framework which was distinctive from any particular national context. In this sense, the Basle Accord is an example of an international public body setting new rules of the game for financial institutions. The Accord, in Kapstein's words, left 'many commercial banks with no choice but to raise equity and shed assets' (ibid.: 124). The public nature of the Accord should not, however, be overemphasized. Discussions took place in secret and decisions were reached behind closed doors, influenced primarily by the interests of the financial institutions themselves.

The idea of a 'fit and proper corporate person' extends beyond merely the commercial banking sector. A similar analysis could be made of the emergence of systems for managing financial firms dealing in securities. Again, the same issues arise about the interdependence of institutions from different national contexts as they become increasingly interdependent through cross-national dealings.

Here, the problems can be described as arising from market risk, i.e. that one of the two parties to a deal cannot carry it out and therefore 'contaminates' the other. For example, in the case of Barings, the 'rogue trader' entered into contracts which he could not deliver, resulting in potential losses to the counterparties to the trades, and threatening the financial viability of the counterparties. International standard setting becomes a means of reassuring counterparties to trades that they will be able to resolve their deals. The International Organization of Securities Commissions (IOSCO) was founded in 1984 with this purpose in mind. It has a membership of securities regulators from different countries, whose goal is to exchange information and enforce a common standard of supervision within diverse national traditions. In terms of its institutional form, Underhill describes it as follows:

IOSCO considers itself a non-governmental international organization. It requires legitimacy in the eyes of market actors . . . and so its proposals are developed in consultation with self-regulatory organizations and their corporate membership . . . This closed policy community constitutes a case of . . . *esoteric politics*, wherein an elite group works out the management of its own vital interests without wider public involvement. (1997: 31)

IOSCO is central to a web of activities that are emerging in order to set standards for 'fit and proper persons' in the arena of international finance. This involves two aspects. The first is ensuring that home and host supervisors coordinate their activities and ensure that the entire risk profile of a financial institution dealing through subsidiaries and branches in many centres around the world is assessed as a total package. Following some years of discussions and negotiations, this has led to the model of the 'lead regulator', where one particular national regulatory body (which may be in the home or the host jurisdiction) takes the main responsibility for a consolidated analysis of the firm's risk position.

Secondly, however, IOSCO has become increasingly involved in a broader standard setting role. The members of IOSCO are often stock exchanges or bodies engaged in similar regulatory activity. Stock exchanges invariably have rules about the conditions under which corporate entities can be quoted and traded. In the past, these rules have been different, meaning that purchasing shares on one stock market involves the purchaser and dealer in a different information and knowledge matrix than in another. Rules, for example, on the provision of company accounts, on transparency of the various parts of the organization, on 'hidden reserves', on the publication of results quarterly, and on the rules regulating insider trading, have differed across national exchanges. In a period when fund managers and investors are looking to invest globally, these differences become significant. Whilst actors can proclaim the economic rationale behind what is termed 'regulatory arbitrage', the reality is that these differences make it complex for multinational and other firms to raise funds outside their home base. When firms are seeking to raise capital outside their home base, what may be fit and proper (in terms of disclosure and other aspects of corporate governance) in one context may not be deemed to be so in another. IOSCO, as the collective body for stock exchanges (the main gatekeepers to equity capital), has played an important role in sponsoring research and policy formation designed to define, agree, and enforce certain standards of 'fit and proper persons'. Underhill summarizes these:

Many issues which are important to IOSCO's efforts are outrightly delegated to private-sector associations and think-tanks. The harmonisation of accounting standards, central to facilitating the globalisation of securities trading and the levelling of the playing field for major market players is the province of the International Accounting Standards Committee, an offshoot of the accounting profession. Clearance and Settlement issues were handed to the Group of 30 (G-30), a private sector think-tank whose membership reads like the *Who's Who* of global corporations, central banking and other autonomous agencies. The Group of Thirty also did the first major report on derivatives regulation. (1997: 32; see also Coleman and Underhill 1998)

The impact of these decisions goes very wide. Sassen gives the example of the emergence of international accounting standards developed by the International Accounting Standards Committee (IASC). She states that:

Japan resisted changing its national accounting system, one lacking the standards of 'transparency' that have become the norm in international transactions. It was indeed Japan's reluctance to implement such standards of transparency in a wide range of business activities in conjunction with its reluctance to continue deregulating its financial sector which, it seems to me, aborted Tokyo's rise as a major international financial centre. Tokyo remained too Japanese. (1999: 156)

These developments have encouraged an environment in which US-based rules on transparency and reporting requirements, developed in Wall Street, are becoming an international standard. Sassen comments that 'Japanese companies had already begun to implement accounting standards that are closer to Anglo-American standards' (ibid.: 156). Certainly, companies seeking to raise funds in the US have to change their systems in order to show that they are fit and proper corporate persons, a situation that now requires not just adherence to IASC financial reporting rules but also to the GAAP (General Accounting and Auditing Principles) rules which are the Wall Street standard. For example, Deutsche Bank has been unable to get a New York Stock Exchange listing because it has so far only reported according to IASC rules and not GAAP conventions.

The idea of a 'fit and proper corporate person' goes deeper still into a terrain that is increasingly private- and business-dominated, outside the scrutiny of public or quasi-public bodies. It is a standard, that can be constructed by private entities to determine with whom they are willing to trade. As Glimstedt illustrates in Chapter 5 (see also Strange 1996: ch. 11), large international firms have often developed cartels and systems of agreements about their relative share of particular overseas markets and the appropriate pricing systems for geographically diverse markets. They have decided for themselves who should be in or out of this cartel arrangement, as well as how these standards should be operated and enforced. In the contemporary period, these private systems are developing in a new direction away from cartels (which are generally seen as anti-trust and therefore not acceptable; see Djelic and Bensedrine's discussion in Chapter 10 of the development of anti-trust regulation) and towards more specifically specialist agencies which monitor 'fitness' primarily as a financial matter and give companies credit ratings. Sassen, in particular, has explored how these private systems intersect with internationalization. She writes:

The importance of private oversight institutions has increased with the deregulation and globalisation of financial services. These agencies are now key institutions in the creation of order and transparency in the global capital market and have considerable power over sovereign states through their authority in rating government debt. Also the rise of international commercial arbitration as the main mechanism for resolving cross-border business disputes entails a declining importance of national courts in these matters ... All of these begin to amount to a privatised system of governance ensuring order, respect for contracts, transparency and accountability in the world of cross-border business transactions. (Sassen 1999: 155; see also Sassen 1996)

Sassen points to two distinct types of 'private oversight institutions', which, in the terms used in this chapter, construct standards as to who is a fit and proper corporate person and how they are expected to behave. First, there are the credit rating agencies. These have developed a system of ranking the credit worthiness of states and companies. In this respect, they do not so much decide *who* is fit and proper but *how* fit and proper particular entities are. They are still therefore operating a set of standards, but a more variegated set than in some other cases. Clearly, these organizations are entirely private and yet their ratings have a global impact. They act as a means of indicating to the providers of capital and other potential business partners across borders the 'quality' of firms (and states); they act, in effect, in a way that regulates both the flow of capital and its price (see Germain 1997; Sinclair 1994).

The second type of institution consists of private law-making on an international scale. The rules out of which these systems develop are increasingly shaped by US law (see Braithwaite and Drahos 2000). Sassen describes the changes and their consequences as follows:

Over the past twenty years, international commercial arbitration has been transformed and institutionalized as the leading contractual method for the resolution of transnational commercial disputes. . . . The globalization of law through private corporate lawmaking has assumed the Americanization of commercial law . . . it is now possible to argue that American business law has become a kind of global *jus commune* incorporated explicitly or implicitly into the case law and even the statutes of many nations. (1996: 14–20)

This is reinforced through the role of the largest UK and US law firms in advising on cross-border deals and how to construct 'fit and proper corporate persons' out of the competing legislation of different national authorities. In turn, this also appears to come down to an increasing Americanization of law and its practice (see Dezalay and Garth 1996). An article in *The Economist* stated:

For the biggest and richest law firms the growth of world capital markets and the globalisation in other industries mean that advising on cross-border deals is becoming the fastest-growing and most lucrative aspect of their business. . . . [The top tier New York and London firms] are the firms that already advise the world's biggest companies and banks. They cream off the best business in two of the world's three biggest capital markets which generate the most lucrative legal work. They work in English, the language of international business. More significantly, for historical reasons and because companies everywhere want to tap the London and New York capital markets, a growing proportion of international business is conducted under English or American law, even where the firms involved are continental European or Asian . . . New York [legal] firms . . . have close ties to the three largest investment banks—Morgan Stanley, Goldman Sachs and Merrill Lynch. This gives them a prime advantage in winning an advisory role in big deals. (26 February 2000: 115)

The legal firms provide the framework within which companies involved in international dealing can work. Representation by global legal firms becomes a marker of a commitment to these shared values and practices (similar to the situation which Podolny (1993) describes in relation to the self-reinforcing reputational effects which come from linkages between high-prestige investment banks and their 'blue-chip' clients). As *The Economist* stated: 'When billions are at stake, nobody is sacked for hiring the best lawyers. . . . For these reasons, the world's biggest companies have traditionally played safe and reached for one of the top New York or London firms' (26 February 2000: 119).

In conclusion, there has emerged an infrastructure of international institutions at various levels of the national, regional, and global which have developed mechanisms for identifying fit and proper persons. These mechanisms range over the financial position of the firm, its governance structure and accountability to investors, and its willingness to abide by international dispute settlement procedures managed in the Anglo-American model and through the major law firms. Failures to meet these standards lead to a number of sanctions—loss of market share, restrictions on entry to certain national markets and business sectors, unwillingness of other firms to trade, etc. They constitute a complex set of relationships with an impact on how firms evolve within national settings.

9.5. Standards of 'Fair Dealing'

Within national systems, firms within particular sectors share similar market conditions. Where this is not the case and there is a lack of what is termed a 'level playing field', then governments may intervene to regulate the sector. The lack of a level playing field inside a particular national context can arise in a number of ways, e.g. unfair subsidy, monopolistic power in the marketplace, lack of knowledge on the part of customers, etc. Sanctions against these processes can occur through the withdrawal of business licences, the imposition of fines, the enforced restructuring of the company, and an increase in the required information disclosure. In international dealings, not only is there a lack of a single jurisdictional power capable of

monitoring and imposing sanctions, there are also potential dis-
agreements about the nature of the 'unfairness'. In this section, I want
to consider two elements to the notion of unfairness in trading. The
first refers to the idea that firms from different countries are receiv-
ing differential advantages not from the relative efficiency of their
organizational processes, but from the overt and covert actions of
governments in reducing the cost of inputs (through direct subsidies
to the companies or through indirect subsidies, which have the effect,
for example, of reducing the costs of energy, labour, land, or technology). Therefore, the question arises as to how these issues can be
identified, monitored, and acted upon in an international context. The
second stretches the notion of 'fairness' rather more by considering
it from the point of view of access to markets—is it fair to keep
markets closed? How can states be persuaded to open them and with
what consequences? From this perspective, it could be claimed that
it is 'unfair' of one state to close its borders to companies from another
state where the borders are more open. Fairness, then, becomes
defined in terms of keeping borders open and reducing 'artificial'
barriers to trade (in goods and services) as well as to foreign direct
investment (FDI). Therefore, the restructuring of social institutions
can be justified on the basis that this is necessary in order to allow
'fair competition'. In other words, within this discourse, 'fair trade'
becomes a matter of creating and sustaining the conditions for
'free trade'.

The primary instruments of regulating for 'fair competition' on an
international scale have come in the form of the GATT (General
Agreement on Tariff and Trade) agreements followed by the formation of the World Trade Organization. Sell states:

> The GATT's success in cutting tariffs and reducing border impediments over
> successive rounds has led negotiators to address inside-the-border, or struc-
> tural, impediments and non-tariff measures that distort free trade. These
> measures implicate domestic regulatory policy, fundamentally challenging
> states' policy-making discretion. Issues such as market access, rights of
> establishment for foreign enterprises, trade related investment measures
> (e.g. performance requirements) and the protection of intellectual property
> rights reach much deeper into state policies than previous GATT issues.
> (2000: 175)

The GATT system generally built on the idea that nation-states were
free to control their own borders. In principle, this meant that states
could set their own rules for entry on labour, capital, and goods. For
example, in the area of financial services, many states had rules which

protected their home market by prohibiting entry of foreign companies except on a very limited and circumscribed basis. This principle was, however, tempered by the general expectation within GATT that there would be a reduction of tariffs and a gradual reduction of barriers. More specifically, it was expected that a state would not set differential tariffs between goods coming from different countries—the Most Favoured Nation principle—except where there were formal regional economic entities such as the EU, NAFTA etc. However, once firms entered, there was to be in principle no discrimination between foreign investors and products on the one hand and home investors and products on the other (the National Treatment principle). This applied generally to formal barriers, but there were a host of informal barriers in terms of particular sorts of regulation which had the effect of making it difficult for external competitors to enter some markets and which became increasingly objectionable to some countries, e.g. the US perceived Japan's home market to be closed to its manufacturers due to informal barriers arising from the structure of the retail trade; see the discussion in Upham (1996).

GATT's concern with a level playing field was also reflected in its anti-dumping and subsidies regulation. Hoekman and Kostecki state:

Loosely defined, dumping occurs when products are sold by a firm in an export market for less than what is charged in its home market for the same product. Dumping is also said to occur if the export price of a product is below the costs of production. GATT rules allow action to be taken against dumped imports if dumping causes or threatens material injury to a domestic import-competing industry. (1995: 171)

Anti-dumping cases tended to be taken up by the advanced industrial states such as the USA and the members of the EU, primarily against developing societies. However, the complexities involved in demonstrating the existence of dumping meant that only a few cases were taken to GATT and most of those were lost by the complainants. The tendency in the adjudication process was to treat anti-dumping claims as attempts to protect home markets unless there was very strong evidence to the contrary. In relation to subsidies, Hoekman and Kostecki state that at the Uruguay Round: 'Agreement was reached on a definition of the term "subsidy". A subsidy is deemed to exist if there is a financial contribution by a government (or public body). . . . Three categories of subsidy are distinguished: non-actionable, prohibited and actionable' (ibid.: 106–7). Prohibited subsidies are mainly those aimed at reducing the cost of exports either directly or indirectly.

Actionable subsidies are cases where provisions to domestic industry are such that it is difficult for outsiders to compete. In these cases, outsiders may take countervailing action to close their own markets to companies from the offending country. GATT rules allowed for such issues to be referred to the dispute settlement procedure.

By the 1990s and the discussions on the Uruguay Round and the setting up of the WTO, there was increasing pressure to extend the idea of the level playing field further. The major exporting nations argued that any barriers to entry (whether formal or informal) or potential subsidies should be open to question through the WTO dispute resolution system. The main discussions on implementing these principles took place around the agreements on trade-related intellectual property rights (TRIPs), trade related investment measures (TRIMs), the General Agreement on Trade and Services (GATS), and the financial services agreement. Membership of the WTO is conditional on abiding by each of these agreements and a willingness to accept the WTO system of dispute resolution system in the event of conflict. Each of these impacts on the internal regulatory structures of states. The TRIPs agreement, for example, was sponsored by major US multinationals concerned that their technological innovations were being copied cheaply. According to Sell:

[The TRIPs accord] requires signatory states to enact implementing domestic legislation, adopt enforcement measures, provide intellectual property owners with a 20-year monopoly right and face the threat of trade sanctions if they fail to comply with TRIPs provisions . . . the short-term impact of the agreement undoubtedly will be a significant transfer of resources from developing country consumers and firms to industrialized countries. In short, it represents a decisive triumph for established private sector interests. (2000: 176)

The GATS agreement arose out of US concerns to gain access to the service markets of Japan and East Asia. However, there was strong opposition from these countries as well as other large developing nations such as India and Brazil to accepting the idea of a free market in services. As a result, the WTO agreement contains 'some limited rights of market access for providers of services, based on an "opt-in" approach that allows the host state to specify which sectors of service industries will be open for foreign investors as well as non-discrimination standards for the treatment of foreign investors' (Muchlinski 1999: 52). In the financial services area, the right of establishment in other countries without discrimination was discussed and established in principle. The TRIM agreements were also reduced in their overall impact by opposition from a range of developing countries as well as countries such as France, Canada, Australia, and New Zealand. The range of issues that were of potential concern was wide. The USA wanted an end to all rules about local content, i.e. host states insisting that subsidiaries source a certain proportion of production from the local industry. It also wanted to outlaw export performance rules which insisted that foreign subsidiaries in a particular market had to export a certain proportion of their production. The eventual agreement recognized these concerns, but gave countries time to change rather than insisting on a specific timetable.

The WTO agreements were subject to the dispute settlement procedure. Developed countries made 109 of the complaints up to the end of 1999 (around two-thirds were against other developed countries); 36 complaints were by developing countries (50/50 against developed and other developing countries); and 4 were from both developed and developing countries (see Figure 9.1). These negotiations were considered by the USA in particular as partial failures. Within their own sphere of influence, NAFTA, the USA had achieved a much stronger set of mechanisms for ensuring 'free trade'. Drache states:

Under NAFTA there is no impartial third party review of non-compliance by governments to any of its provisions. Washington is entitled to review all Canadian and Mexican legislation to see whether 'offending legislation' (a) impinges on NAFTA's investment provisions and (b) whether any proposed legislation, particularly with respect to government policy, directly or indirectly fails to extend full protection to US investors . . . the consequence is that the new legal and political norms eliminate to a significant degree the discretionary authority of Canadian and Mexican authorities to favour local firms, communities, regional authorities and industries, while preserving crucial US trade restrictions. (2000: 192)

Panitch describes ironically the effect of NAFTA on Canada and Mexico as 'forced to be free'; he states that 'taken together these various provisions have the effect of redesigning the Mexican and Canadian states' relation to capital to fit the mould made in the United States by establishing and guaranteeing state defence of new private property rights that go well beyond those recognized in Canadian and Mexican law, if not that of the United States' (1999: 97).

Following the relative failure of the initial WTO agreements to meet their wider demands, and building on the example of NAFTA, private sector companies and the US government pursued these issues further through the Multilateral Investment Agreement (MAI)

	Complaints notified to the WTO	Active cases	Appellate body and panel reports adopted	Settled or inactive cases
Reporting period/date	since 1 January 1995	on reporting date	since 1 January 1995	since 1 January 1995
Number	190 (149 of which involve distinct matters)	22	32	32

Figure 9.1. *WTO dispute settlement procedure: statistical overview*

discussions held under the auspices of the OECD. The aim remained the same—enforcing an opening up of the borders of states to FDI in all industries and without conditions. According to Picciotto (1999: 87), MAI would create a right of entry for foreign direct investors; any nation-state refusal or discrimination could lead to complaints. For example, MAI would have enabled companies to challenge any restrictions which a nation-state might place over takeovers in key industries (such as defence or the media). It would have stopped states placing restrictions on land ownership by foreigners. It would have prevented states insisting on a limit to foreign share ownership in joint ventures or operating any sort of screening requirements in the case of foreign investment. Picciotto states:

Such explicit restrictions would be invalid in principle under the MAI . . . it would enable a foreign firm to object to any internal laws which could be said to be indirectly discriminatory . . . this could make it possible to challenge any administrative or legislative act which could be said to reduce the scope of an investor's expectations. (1999: 87, 90)

The fact that negotiations on MAI were abandoned in late 1998 as a result of a combined opposition from countries in both the developing and the developed world, should not be taken as other than a temporary respite in the pressure on countries to produce a particular sort of level playing field—one in which fair trade is defined by 'free trade' and the unconditional access to countries. Conflicts over this will continue within the WTO, but they provide a strong framework enforcing a particular conception of standards of 'fair trade' with consequences for states and firms involved in global competition.

The notion of a level playing field is also paradoxically enforced by the actions of organizations such as the World Bank and the International Monetary Federation (IMF). Both institutions have as one of their key objectives the development of a world market in which capital and goods flow freely and easily across borders. This is clearest in the role that these institutions have played in 'structural adjustment' programmes across the world. In general, countries that have become heavily indebted internationally as a result of various forces have had to seek out help from these institutions. Biersteker describes the general consensus as 'around the objectives of fiscal discipline, adjustment of public expenditure priorities, tax reform, financial liberalization, exchange rate adjustment, privatization, deregulation and support for property rights' (1995: 178).

Creating a level playing field means reducing the ability of the state to control economic activities both at the entry point to the society and within the internal market. As Harris states in relation to the IMF, 'conditionality is the fulcrum for the Fund's relations with the governments to which it lends' (1999: 199). In general, it is at moments of crisis that the institutions are able to exert this influence by making their loans conditional on structural change, e.g. in the Mexican peso crisis in 1982, the debt crisis of the developing countries in the 1980s and 1990s, the collapse of communism in the early 1990s, and the financial crises of the mid- to late-1990s in Mexico and Latin America, Russia, and East Asia (see also Grabel 1999; McMichael 1998).

These institutions act as means whereby a particular sort of level playing field is constructed, one in which access to markets and the reconstruction of internal systems of governance and regulation are made a condition of financial support and, through this, of involvement in the broader international economy. Whilst countries may respond differently to these conditions (e.g. during the East Asian crisis, Malaysia resisted the IMF, whilst other East Asian countries submitted; see Jomo 1998), there was strong pressure to accept the rules of the game as spelt out by the IMF and the World Bank.

The commitment to and enforcement of open markets which derive from the actions of these institutions impact on firms in two ways. First, standards of fair dealing and open markets make it increasingly difficult for national governments to sustain formal protective environments for home-based companies. Attempts to provide forms of state aid become open to challenges in various arenas, e.g. within the EU, the British government's loan package to Rover-BMW was subject to investigation; on a wider scale, the contribution of various

European governments to the development by Airbus Industries of a new generation of super-Jumbo passenger jets may be challenged by the USA in the WTO. Secondly, the more markets are opened up, the larger the economies of scale and scope which can be realized by the very largest companies. This is seen particularly within certain sectors, most obviously cars, where over the last few years a process of concentration and restructuring has gathered such pace that medium-sized producers are rapidly being swallowed up—e.g. Ford's acquisition of Jaguar, Land Rover, and Volvo, and GM's relationship with Mazda and its recent deal with Fiat—whilst other medium-sized companies are seeking to achieve larger scale through merger or takeover—e.g. the Daimler-Chrysler merger and the failed attempt by BMW to extend through acquisition of Rover.

9.6. Conclusion

Sustaining a system of international trade in goods, services, and capitals requires the development of certain minimal standards to ensure a stable framework for economic activity. These standards can emerge from various sources. In the last twenty years, as international economic activity has grown and therefore the need for agreed norms and institutions has increased, the conditions under which such standards can emerge have become more complex. The result is an environment of overlapping, interconnected and interactive standard setting regimes which work across borders, within geographical regions, self-identifying groups of states (such as the G-10), and more widely. These standard setting regimes reflect the complex institutional make-up and power resources of their various members, but they also represent attempts at structural solutions to problems of international economic coordination.

This chapter has identified three particular types of standard setting at the international level, which seek to reduce transactional uncertainty and complexity. First, there is the area of standard setting for products and services. These emerge out of firms seeking security and stability in their dealings across borders by agreeing technical standards or demonstrating standard operating procedures (such as in the case of ISO 9000). These types of standard setting activity are very close to market mechanisms. Whilst they are supported by governments, they are mainly constructed by companies and regulators working together as forms of private ordering at the international level. The emergence of entities such as the ISO is part of this process. The implications of these standards for firms vary across sectors but, in general, they contribute towards standardization pressures, particularly at the technological level. Actually how this works out in practice within the firm cannot be determined in advance. As Hancke and Casper (2000) show in relation to ISO 9000 and its impact on the French and German automobile industries, it may enhance differentiation in distinctive institutional contexts.

Standards for 'fit and proper' corporate persons impact more directly on the governance structures of firms. These standards have become increasingly important in the sphere of international financial institutions where the interdependence of markets and firms leads to the potential for system contagion in the event that a single major organization collapses. To protect against this process, international organizations such as IOSCO and agreements such as the Basle Accord are enforcing a particular model of a fit and proper corporate person onto financial institutions that seek a global presence. Manufacturing firms also find themselves subject to these sorts of pressure as they seek listings on foreign stock exchanges. These standards also operate through more private systems of accountability and governance. One aspect of this is the role taken by credit rating agencies in delivering their verdict on various companies. Another aspect is the increasing expectation that international firms will enter into agreements to deal with problems on contracts through an accepted arbitration procedure often based on Anglo-American law. To be a proper person in this context is demonstrated also by having the proper 'friends': to be represented in the legal arena by one of the major US or UK law firms, to be audited by one of the major international accounting partnerships, and to be advised in terms of capital markets by one of the major investment banks. Again, these processes pressurize towards homogeneity. Where the core of the business is affected by these regulations, as is the case in the financial sector, the pressure is towards a certain global form regulated by global standards. Where manufacturing firms move into certain types of capital markets, they face similar pressures at the level of corporate governance, though this may coexist with differentiation at the level of production sites (see the contribution by Kristensen and Zeitlin in Chapter 7).

Firms are also affected by the development of standards for open markets. The development of international institutions, which increasingly monitor openness and take action to enforce it, creates an arena within which nation-states find it even more difficult to play a protective role. This impacts on firms in two ways. By opening up home markets, it exposes firms to international competition, which may lead to the decline of certain sectors and the expansion of others. By increasing the overall size of the market, it encourages the search for global economies of scale and scope and is therefore another factor pushing firms into merger and takeover activity as they seek to achieve requisite size. The international institutions which enforce these standards constitute complex social actors in themselves, representing various national and corporate interests.

In conclusion, the argument presented here is that in order to understand the development of multinational firms, it is necessary to examine how international institutions are emerging to manage cross-border activity. These institutions are playing an increasingly important role in setting standards to which firms have to conform if they wish to participate in certain types of cross-border activity. The institutions themselves are varied in form (public/private), geographical coverage (regional, international, etc.), modes of enforcement (withdrawal of rights to trade, fines, etc.), and relative autonomy from national interests (particularly from the dominance of the USA). For firms, these processes mean a shift in aspects of standard setting from the national to the international level. Although the impact of this varies between sectors, the international standards set new constraints on the actions of firms that wish to trade internationally. Certain minimal forms of adaptation are necessary. The levels of the firm that are affected by these processes will vary, as will the degree to which this leads to adaptation, differentiation, or some form of hybridity. To understand these interactions in more detail, further research in particular sectors and focusing on particular actors is necessary (see, e.g., the contributions by Djelic and Bensedrine, and by Plehwe in Chapter 10 and 11, respectively).

REFERENCES

Biersteker, T. J. (1995), 'The "Triumph" of Liberal Economic Ideas in the Developing World', in B. Stallings (ed.), *Global Change, Regional Response: The New International Context of Development*. Cambridge: Cambridge University Press, 174–96.

Braithwaite, J. and Drahos, P. (2000), *Global Business Regulation*. Cambridge: Cambridge University Press.

Coleman, W. D. and Underhill, G. (1998), 'Globalization, Regionalism and the Regulation of Securities Markets', in W. D. Coleman and G. Underhill (eds.), *Regionalism and Global Economic Integration*. London: Routledge, 223–48.

Curtin, P. D. (1984), *Cross-Cultural Trade in World History*. Cambridge: Cambridge University Press.

Dezalay, Y. and Garth, B. G. (1996), *Dealing in Virtue: International Commercial Arbitration and the Construction of a Transnational Legal Order*. Chicago: University of Chicago Press.

DiMaggio, P. and Powell, W. W. (1983), 'The Iron Cage Revisited: Institutional Isomorphism and Collective Rationality in Organizational Fields', *American Sociological Review*, 48(2): 147–60.

Drache, D. (2000), 'Trade Blocs: The Beauty or the Beast in the Theory?', in R. Stubbs and G. Underhill (eds.), *Political Economy and the Changing Global Order*, 2nd edn. Oxford: Oxford University Press, 184–97.

Germain, R. (1997), *The International Organization of Credit*. Cambridge: Cambridge University Press.

Grabel, I. (1999), 'Rejecting Exceptionalism: Reinterpreting the Asian Financial Crisis', in J. Michie and J. Grieve Smith (eds.), *Global Instability: The Political Economy of World Economic Governance*. London: Routledge, 37–68.

Hancke, B. and Casper, S. (2000), 'Reproducing Diversity: ISO 9000 and Work Organization in the French and German Car Industry', in S. Quack, G. Morgan, and R. Whitley (eds.), *National Capitalisms, Global Competition and Economic Performance*. Amsterdam: John Benjamins Publishing, 173–88.

Harris, L. (1999), 'Will the Real IMF Please Stand Up: What Does the Fund Do and What Should It Do?', in J. Michie and J. Grieve Smith (eds.), *Global Instability: The Political Economy of World Economic Governance*. London: Routledge, 198–211.

Hoekman, B. and Kostecki, M. (1995), *The Political Economy of the World Trading System: From GATT to WTO*. Oxford: Oxford University Press.

Jomo, K. S. (ed.) (1998), *Tigers in Trouble*. London: Zed Books.

Kapstein, E. B. (1994), *Governing the Global Economy*. Cambridge, MA: Harvard University Press.

Krasner, S. D. (1999), *Sovereignty: Organized Hypocrisy*. Princeton, NJ: Princeton University Press.

Lane, C. (1997), 'The Social Regulation of Inter-Firm Relations in Britain and Germany: Market Rules, Legal Norms and Technical Standards', *Cambridge Journal of Economics*, 21(2): 197–215.

Lane, C. and Bachmann, R. (eds.) (1998), *Trust Within and Between Organizations*. Oxford: Oxford University Press.

Langlois, R. N. and Robertson, P. L. (1995), *Firms, Markets and Economic Change*. London: Routledge.

McMichael, P. (1998), 'Development and Structural Adjustment', in J. G. Carrier and D. Miller (eds.), *Virtualism*. Oxford: Berg, 95–116.

Morgan, G. (1997), 'The Global Context of Financial Services: National Systems and the International Political Economy', in G. Morgan and D. Knights (eds.), *Regulation and Deregulation in European Financial Services*. London: Macmillan, 14–41.

Morgan, G. and Knights, D. (eds.) (1997), *Regulation and Deregulation in European Financial Services*. London: Macmillan.

Morgan, G. and Murray, F. (1991), 'Strategic Changes in Personal Financial Services: The Impact of the Single European Market', in A. Rugman (ed.), *Research in Global Strategic Management: Volume 2, 1991*. London: JAI Press, 103–24.

Morgan, G. and Sturdy, A. (2000), *Beyond Organizational Change: Structure, Discourse and Power in UK Financial Services*. London: Macmillan.

Muchlinski, P. (1999), 'A Brief History of Business Regulation', in S. Picciotto and R. Mayne (eds.), *Regulating International Business: Beyond Liberalization*. London: Macmillan, in association with Oxfam, 47–59.

Murphy, C. N. (1994), *International Organization and Industrial Change: Global Governance Since 1850*. Cambridge: Polity Press.

Murphy, R. T. (2000), 'Japan's Economic Crisis', *New Left Review*, 1 (Jan–Feb 2000): 25–53.

O'Brien, R. Goetz, A. M., Scholte, J. A. and Williams, M. (2000), *Contesting Global Governance: Multilateral Economic Institutions and Global Social Movements*. Cambridge: Cambridge University Press.

Panitch, L. (1999), 'Rethinking the Role of the State', in J. H. Mittelman (ed.), *Globalization: Critical Reflections*. Boulder: Lynne Reiner Publishers, 83–113.

Picciotto, S. (1999), 'A Critical Assessment of the MAI', in S. Picciotto and R. Mayne (eds.), *Regulating International Business: Beyond Liberalization*. London: Macmillan, in association with Oxfam, 82–105.

Podolny, J. (1993), 'A Status-Based Model of Market Competition', *American Journal of Sociology* 98(4): 829–72.

Quack, S., Morgan, G., and Whitley, R. (eds.) (2000), *National Capitalisms, Global Competition and Economic Performance*. Amsterdam: John Benjamins Publishing.

Rosenau, J. R. (1997), *Along the Domestic-Foreign Frontier: Exploring Governance in a Turbulent World*. Cambridge: Cambridge University Press.

Sassen, S. (1996), *Losing Control? Sovereignty in an Age of Globalization*. New York: Columbia University Press.

—— (1999), 'Servicing the Global Economy: Reconfigured States and Private Agents', in K. Olds, P. Dicken, P. F. Kelly, L. Kong, and H. W. Yeung (eds.), *Globalisation and the Asia-Pacific: Contested Territories*. London: Routledge, 149–62.

Sell, S. K. (2000), 'Big Business and the New Trade Agreements: The Future of the WTO?' in R. Stubbs and R. D. Underhill (eds.), *Political Economy and the Changing Global Order*, 2nd edn. Oxford: Oxford University Press, 174–83.

Sinclair, T. J. (1994), 'Passing Judgement: Credit Rating Processes As Regulatory Mechanisms of Governance in the Emerging World Order', *Review of International Political Economy* 1(1): 133–59.

Strange, S. (1996), *The Retreat of the State*. Cambridge: Cambridge University Press.

Tracy, J. D. (ed.) (1991), *The Political Economy of Merchant Empires: State Power and World Trade 1350–1750*. Cambridge: Cambridge University Press.

Underhill, G. (1997), 'Private Markets and Public Responsibility in a Global System: Conflict and Co-operation in Transnational Banking and Securities Regulation', in G. Underhill (ed.), *The New World Order in International Finance*. London: Macmillan, 17–49.

Upham, F. K. (1996), 'Retail Convergence: The Structural Impediments Initiative and the Regulation of the Japanese Retail Industry', in S. Berger and R. Dore (eds.), *National Diversity and Global Capitalism*, Ithaca, NY: Cornell University Press, 263–97.

10

Globalization and its Limits: The Making of International Regulation

MARIE-LAURE DJELIC AND JABRIL BENSEDRINE

10.1. Introduction

Recent developments, particularly in Europe, make it difficult to ignore the debates around globalization. Mergers, acquisitions, and alliances are rapidly bringing about the reconstruction of many industries over and beyond national boundaries. Economic activities and transactions cross over national borders, making transnational mechanisms of governance increasingly likely and necessary. Some have argued that global pressures are leading, on a worldwide level, to the increasing convergence of governance and organizational structures and of business knowledge or practices (Alvarez 1998; Chandler 1990; Ohmae 1995; Scott et al. 1994). There is ample evidence, though, that local or national institutional arrangements still play a significant part when it comes to shaping economic structures and constraining economic behaviour (Hollingsworth and Boyer 1997; Whitley and Kristensen 1996). Whether these institutional path dependencies do really imply the increasing divergence of national business systems in spite of global competition (Whitley 1999; see also Kristensen and Zeitlin's contribution in Chapter 7) or whether they create the conditions for a hybridization of global pressures (see Lane in Chapter 3) is still a matter for debate. In any case, though, it seems that the most pressing and interesting questions do lie at the point of intersection and interaction between transnational trends on the one hand, and national or local actors and institutions on the other (Arias and Guillén 1998; Djelic 1998; see also Morgan in Chapter 1).

This chapter approaches the issue of regulation from such a perspective. Regulation—or the setting of standards, as Morgan terms it in Chapter 9—is an important mechanism for the coordination of economic activity. The definition, interpretation, and implementation of regulation have traditionally been, at least in the age of the nation-state, the sole prerogatives of local and, in particular, national state authorities (McCraw 1984; Weiss 1988). However, since the end of the Second World War, the trend has been for regulation to take on a transnational dimension. Still, little is known about the making of regulation in the international environment or about the way transnational regulatory standards are then implemented, whether in supranational, national, or subnational arenas. The objective of this chapter is to go some way towards filling this gap.

We focus in turn on competition regulation and on the regulation of chlorofluorocarbon (CFC) products as two examples of standards with a transnational, if not a global, impact. Rather than taking these regulatory standards for granted and assessing their impact on the behaviour of economic actors, we define them as our dependent variables. What we want to understand, through our empirical cases, is the way in which transnational regulation has been and is constructed, diffused, interpreted, and implemented. With this objective in mind, we engage in a double exercise in deconstruction, looking for conditions, actors, and mechanisms explaining the emergence, diffusion, and institutionalization of transnational regulatory standards with respect to competitive behaviour or CFC production. We pay particular attention to the interplay between transnational and national spheres, pointing to a highly contested process in both cases, although with quite different characteristics. In the end, the comparison allows us to draw more general conclusions about the contribution of transnational regulation to structural and behavioural convergence. It allows us to reflect, in other words, on the process of globalization and on its limits.

10.2. A Hybrid Neo-Institutional Framework

The broad claim that economic activity and interactions are embedded in wider sets of environmental or institutional constraints is a good starting point to approach the issue of regulation. Regulation as the formalized expression of standards and norms is, indeed, hard to disentangle from the context of its construction, diffusion, interpretation, and implementation. This, though, tells us little if anything at all. Important questions remain, bearing on the nature, scale, or scope of that institutional context, on the extent to which it allows action and is likely to undergo change (Djelic 1998). Existing variants of neo-institutionalism differ quite significantly, in fact, on all those dimensions (Clemens and Cook 1999). As they stand, none of these variants is able to grasp on its own the full complexity of the issue at hand, particularly with respect to the interplay between transnational and national spheres. We propose a combination or cross-breeding of two of those variants, which are labelled, respectively, 'phenomenological' and 'historical' neo-institutionalisms (Djelic 1999).

Phenomenological neo-institutionalism (DiMaggio and Powell 1983; Scott et al. 1994) defines institutions as sets of cultural rules and norms. The latter have had a tendency, particularly throughout the second part of the twentieth century, to become more and more similar across national boundaries—rationalization describing the overall evolution. In this research tradition, national economies and their constituent parts are defined as emergent social constructions embedded in larger institutional environments understood as sets of cultural rules and norms. Homogenization of institutional environments across national boundaries logically drives worldwide isomorphism in structural arrangements and behavioural scripts, including—but not only—in the economic and business realm. Historical neo-institutionalism, on the other hand, emphasizes the strength and historical significance of cultural and structural rules defined at the national level (Campbell et al. 1991; Dobbin 1994; Fligstein 1990; Hollingsworth and Boyer 1997; Whitley 1999). Historically, the argument goes, different sets of beliefs or structural arrangements have been stabilized and institutionalized at the level of each nation, often through the key role of state actors or political institutions, creating the context for different logics of action and multiple 'rationalities'. Ultimately, national systems of economic organization are shaped by those stable and long-standing rules and structural legacies.

If we are going to focus on the interplay between the transnational and the national—and not on one sphere or the other—it seems that a theoretical cross-breeding between these two variants of neo-institutionalism would indeed make sense. Phenomenological neo-institutionalism is an interesting lens to look at the structuration of a transnational world, its workings and mechanisms. Questions, on the other hand, about the origins of such a structuration process, about its local impact and about the possible associated process of 'translation' or reinterpretation at the national or subnational level, fit much better with the historical variant of neo-institutionalism.

Using such a hybrid theoretical framework, we also insist upon an historical perspective and analysis. This allows us, for both sets of regulation, to delve more into the questions of the origins and to look at processes, in particular when it comes to diffusion. This also allows us to point, beyond institutional constraints, to the role of actors—whether organizations, networks, or individuals—and leads us to ask, finally, about the extent of local adaptation or reinterpretation in each case and about the likelihood of full-scale convergence.

10.3. **Competition: Turning Local Standards into Global Ones**

In our contemporary world, rules of competition appear to transcend national boundaries. Since the mid-twentieth century, around fifty countries have adopted similar sets of principles that set limits to anti-competitive practices and, in particular, regulate cartels and loose agreements. Under the labels 'antitrust' or 'antimonopoly', these principles justify and frame the intervention of national or cross-national agencies in charge of regulating competition. The American Federal Trade Commission (FTC) or the European Commission might reach different conclusions on a given case. Their overall philosophy, though, is not too far apart. Nor is it in contradiction with the general principles that shape the understanding of competition regulation characteristic of the World Trade Organization (WTO).

A foray into history shows that similarity, here, is not a chance happening. Nor has it been driven by a pure logic of efficiency or by the presumed 'natural laws' of the market economy. We point to a direct thread linking the numerous versions of antitrust or antimonopoly standards, policies, and procedures to the 1890 American Sherman Antitrust Act. Without prejudging of the legitimacy, in economic and efficiency terms, of antitrust or antimonopoly standards, we argue that these standards are neither universal nor neutral. What we find is that a particular understanding of competition regulation, which originally emerged in the United States under unique institutional and historical conditions, came to be diffused and transferred during the twentieth century on a nearly global scale.

The transfer took place in two main stages. The first stage started immediately after the end of the Second World War. Competition regulation principles were then exported from the United States into Western European countries as well as into the emerging set of cross-national institutions such as the GATT, the European Coal and Steel Community (ECSC), or the European Economic Community (EEC). The second stage came after 1989 with the opening and radical transformation of former communist countries. The logic behind the transfer was, in both periods, at least as much political and geopolitical as it was economic. Unsurprisingly, the process was not smooth. On the ground, it ran up against pre-existing legacies and it often encountered resistance and obstacles. This accounts in part for local differences in the interpretation and implementation of antitrust or antimonopoly principles.

10.3.1. *Context: the construction of an American antitrust tradition*

In the United States, discussions on a legislation to regulate inter-firm cooperation and competition started in a period of significant economic turbulence. During the years following the Civil War, American firms had to face major disruptions in their environments, to which they reacted by searching for order and control through collusion and cooperation. Loose arrangements or agreements, cartels or pools multiplied at the time, creating significant concern within civil society about their increasing power (Chandler 1990; Fligstein 1990; McCraw 1984). The Populist movement played upon the fear of farmers and small independent business owners, calling for a regulation of competitive practices and a breaking up of the most disruptive aggregates.

While the pressure stemming from this constituency was instrumental in bringing the 'trust' issue onto the agenda of Congress, some Congressmen had their own, more ideological, reasons to push for competition regulation at the federal level (Thorelli 1954). At the end of the nineteenth century, American conservatism was a mixture of classical economics and social Darwinism (Hawkins 1997). Competition, in this ideological framework, was a key value and the sole guarantee of a healthy economy and society. The initial intent of many Congressmen was thus to preserve and impose 'full and free competition' within the federation of American states (Thorelli 1954). The curbing of cartels or trusts, called for by farmers and small business owners, would be a mere side-effect of this more general fight for competition and freedom.

10.3.1.1. *The Sherman Act*

The Sherman Antitrust Act, finally enacted in 1890, fell somewhat short of this ambitious intent. Section I declared illegal 'every contract, combination in the form of trust or otherwise, or conspiracy' but only as long as they were *'in restraint of trade or commerce'* (Thorelli 1954). While inclusion of the 'commerce clause'—as the above excerpt came to be known—and the limits it set to the law did not reflect the original intent of Congressmen, it had not come about by chance. This rewording reflected a number of institutional legacies and constraints weighing on the legislator. In particular, the federal origin of the Sherman Act set limits to its scope and potential reach. The very nature of American political institutions and the existence of two levels of jurisdiction, federal and state, constrained the legislative freedom of Congress. Congress could only work within the boundaries of its competencies—federal-level legislation, interstate or foreign relationships. It could not deal with anti-competitive behaviour taking place within the borders of a given state. One of the first antitrust cases, *US* v. *E. C. Knight* (1895), clearly illustrated and in fact institutionalized the impact of the 'commerce clause' on the American antitrust tradition.

10.3.1.2. US *v.* E. C. Knight *or the impact of the 'commerce clause'*

In 1892, the federal government filed a suit against the 'sugar trust', on grounds of monopoly and attempt to monopolize. Having merged five formerly independent companies, the 'sugar trust' controlled more than 90 per cent of the sugar-refining capacity of the United States. In January 1895, the Supreme Court dismissed the case. Justices had made a distinction between manufacturing and production on the one hand, interstate and foreign commerce on the other. Since all production sites of the sugar trust were located within one state, the Sherman Antitrust Act, the Supreme Court argued, could not apply. Competency lay with state judiciaries.

US v. *E. C. Knight* became the case on which the American antitrust tradition and the particular reading of the Sherman Act then made by the Supreme Court was to be based in many cases to follow. With respect to cartels or loose agreements, which often crossed over state boundaries, the Sherman Act was read as a prohibition law. These forms of collusion became per se 'unreasonable restraints of trade'. On the other hand, tight combinations and mergers that implied legal incorporation within one state could escape prosecution and were thus generally deemed 'reasonable'. Only extreme forms of concentration that created outright monopolies with a clear impact on trade were to be prohibited (Taft 1911). Emerging from early Supreme Court readings, this interpretation was to have significant and unexpected consequences for the American economy.

Following upon the decision in the E. C. Knight case, corporate lawyers were soon encouraging their clients to merge rather than cooperate informally, thus launching the first and most dramatic merger wave in American industrial history (Fligstein 1990; Sklar 1988; Thorelli 1954). The ensuing reconstruction of the American economic landscape along oligopolistic and corporate lines was thus, and ironically, the partially unintended and contingent consequence of a legislation that had originally been enacted under pressure from advocates of small-scale, competitive capitalism (Fligstein 1990; Roy 1997; Thorelli 1954). The American antitrust tradition that was born through this process was quite unique, shaped as it was by peculiar historical legacies and institutional constraints. Somewhat later in the century, its impact would come to be felt in many other countries as well as in the space in between, where cross-national transactions were taking place.

10.3.2. *Transfer and the main actors*

The widespread impact of American antitrust principles was the consequence of a large-scale and cross-national process of transfer. The two main stages of this process had in common the fact that they corresponded in history to periods of American geopolitical strength. In 1945, the USA had achieved unprecedented weight, both geopolitical and economic. In the years that followed, former allies and enemies alike, in the Western sphere, became dependent upon the superpower for survival and revival means. In 1989, communist promises were fully exposed as a sham. The American dream was left relatively uncontested and the USA remained as the only world superpower.

In both periods, power on one side and dependence on the other led to the temptation of homogenization. There was an attempt to lay the foundations of a new economic and political world order in 1945 and an attempt to expand them in 1989. The transformation of economic and social structures was seen as the surest way to anchor weak and dependent countries on the side of 'peace and democracy' (Hoffman 1951; Hogan 1985). In both periods, American models and actors played a significant role.

10.3.2.1. *American missionaries*

In the post-Second World War period, American public agencies in charge of foreign affairs set themselves an ambitious goal. The State Department in Washington, the American Military Government in Germany, or the Economic Cooperation Administration (the agency running the Marshall Plan), saw it as their mission to fight in Europe the 'communist party line', thanks to the 'American production line' (Hoffman 1951). This meant a radical structural transformation of European economies and industries and the redefinition, in particular, of trade patterns on the old continent using the American economic space as the model of reference (Djelic 1998; Hoffman 1951; Hogan 1985; Van der Pijl 1984). A small group of progressive American businessmen, active in Washington since the New Deal, was particularly involved in this project. In their desire to give the rest of the free world 'an opportunity to learn of the principles and advantages of free enterprise', these American missionaries singled out as one of their core priorities the transfer to partner countries of American competition legislation (Djelic 1998; Hoffman 1951; Hogan 1985). They saw the American antitrust tradition as both a key element of the American model and as a potentially powerful tool of its transfer to other countries.

After 1989, American involvement in the transformation of Eastern European countries was less visible, although quite real. Here again, the rationale was that economic prosperity and a democratization of economic structures were the preconditions to political stability and peace. And a democratization of economic structures seemed to imply the transfer of antitrust and antimonopoly policy (Pittman 1996). This time, a key actor on the American side was the Antitrust Division in the US Department of Justice. Russell Pittman, then Chief of the Competition Policy Section of the Antitrust Division was, together with other American experts, closely involved in the drafting of Eastern European antimonopoly acts (Joskow and Tsukanova 1995; Pittman 1996).

10.3.2.2. *European modernizers*

The transfer had the support, at all stages, of small groups within national communities. American missionaries worked together with local actors to push along their ambitious objectives. In Germany, the main local counterpart was Ludwig Erhard, Minister of Economic Affairs and then Chancellor. In the context of European negotiations, the network around the Frenchman Jean Monnet turned out to be key. In Russia, Igor Gaidar was instrumental. Interestingly, these small groups were quite marginal in their own country. Their real influence depended upon the control they had on key positions of institutional power, on their ability to preserve this control over time, and on the support granted to them by foreign and, in particular, American actors.

10.3.3. *Stages of transfer and negotiations*

The first stage of the transfer process, after 1945, had two sides to it. On the one hand, American missionaries worked at the national level, imposing the American model of competition regulation or fostering its voluntary adoption in dependent countries. The case of Germany is presented below as an example of that strategy. On the other hand, Americans initiated or encouraged the setting up of cross-national institutions that would become powerful relays of the American tradition of competition regulation. The ECSC was negotiated in this context. The second stage of transfer followed the fall of the Berlin Wall and is illustrated below by the Russian case.

10.3.3.1. *The case of Germany—from coercion to imitation*
In 1945, Allied forces assimilated the horrors of the Nazi regime with the peculiar structure of German industry. Parallels were drawn, in particular, between political authoritarianism and state-coordinated cartelization of the industry (Martin 1950). When West Germany became, in 1947, a key bulwark in the fight against communism, Western occupying powers thus defined it as their task to bring about not only a democratization of the political regime but also a radical transformation of the German economic and industrial structure. The overwhelming power of the USA in the Western alliance meant that the economic model would be American, and an important feature of that model was the peculiar definition of competition regulation embodied in the antitrust tradition (Berghahn 1986; Djelic 1998; Schwartz 1991).

In 1947, the American Military Government imposed a decartelization and deconcentration law with effect in what would become the Federal Republic of Germany. This law could easily be traced to the American antitrust tradition (Damm 1958; Djelic 1998; Taylor 1979). With respect to restrictive practices, cartels, combines, or trusts, it was a prohibition law, but it said little about size or concentration of production. While intent on transferring to Germany the characteristically

American fight against cartels and restrictive practices, American occupation authorities also imposed on the German industry an oligopolistic structure. The expectation was that American-inspired competition regulation would lead in Germany—as it had done in the USA—to the emergence of oligopolies in most sectors, with firms large enough to allow economies of scale and scope. Americans were of the mind that 'oligopolies, when policed by the vigorous enforcement of antitrust and anticartel laws as in the United States, yield pretty good results' (OMGUS, Bd18).

At the same time, American missionaries were quite aware that radical transformations of that sort would only outlast the period of acute geopolitical dependence if Germans themselves actively appropriated them. In March 1948, American occupation authorities thus asked German agencies to prepare and submit a trade practice law dealing with the problem of agreements and cartels. This law, it was agreed, once accepted by German and Allied authorities, would replace the 1947 legislation. It took ten years for the Germans finally to agree on a bill, and the Federal Law against Restraints of Competition was only enacted in July 1957.

The final version of the German law was, on the whole, quite congruent with American antitrust tradition. Cartels and loose agreements were identified as unreasonable combinations in restraint of trade and were outlawed per se. However, the German legislator provided for a number of exceptions. The Cartel Office (*Bundeskartelamt*), created in 1958 and modelled on the American FTCs, was granted and would come to exert a certain amount of leeway through enforcement of the law and monitoring of the exceptions (Damm 1958).

10.3.3.2. *Towards the definition of cross-national standards: European competition regulation*

While the United States was encouraging or imposing the adoption by individual nations of its antitrust tradition, it was also pressing for initiatives with a cross-national dimension. In Western Europe, the French led the way by proposing in May 1950 a plan for pooling European coal and steel industries. Jean Monnet and the French Planning Council were behind the proposal. To alleviate American fears that this project might lead to the emergence of a European-wide cartel, Monnet insisted that the goal was to create a competitive space to stimulate an increase in production and productivity (Djelic 1998; Monnet 1976). And in fact, a small group of American experts were hard at work in the background, preparing antitrust provisions for the future coal and steel community. Robert Ball, a long-term friend of Jean Monnet, was one of them. But the key figure was Robert Bowie, legal counsel to the High Commission in Germany, who was also closely involved in the drafting of the German anti-cartel act. A former Harvard Law School professor, Robert Bowie was an antitrust specialist. He went to Paris in June 1950 and wrote the provisions that would become articles 60 and 61 of the ECSC treaty (Monnet 1976).

Article 60 dealt with cartels and loose agreements, prohibiting them in principle. However, the European enforcement agency, the High Authority, was granted a certain amount of leeway to authorize, in times of crisis, a number of exceptions. Article 61 of the ECSC treaty dealt with abuses of market power due to concentration. In line with American antitrust tradition, only 'unreasonable' concentrations were prohibited. Concentrations and mergers that could be shown to lead to increased efficiency and productivity without representing a threat to competition could be authorized. Articles 60 and 61 of the ECSC treaty have a particular historical significance because they were transferred to the 1957 Rome Treaty. As Articles 85 and 86, they have thus become the foundation of competition regulation on the Western European market and in today's European Union (Monnet 1976).

10.3.3.3. *Multi-sided negotiations: the case of Russia*
On 22 March 1991, an antimonopoly law was adopted by the Russian parliament. The 'Law on Competition and Limitation of Monopoly Activities in Goods Markets' had been in the making for a little less than a year. A Federal 'Committee on Antimonopoly Policy and Support of New Economic Structures' (GKAP) and eighty local anti-monopoly committees (AMCs) were created on the model of American and European regulatory agencies and put in charge of enforcement. American but also OECD and European experts had been involved in the process. Quite early on, in fact, a debate had emerged as to whether Russia should model its antimonopoly act on the American original or on the European version. In the end, the latter strategy prevailed and a close look at the Russian law shows that it takes after the EEC version of competition legislation rather than directly after the American original (Pittman 1995). Allowing for exceptions, the European version of antitrust seemed less stringent and extreme than the American original. The very idea of competition and competition regulation being so radically foreign, in the

early 1990s, to Russian economic traditions, the preference for a less extreme version made sense. To both foreign advisers and the Russian legislator, it increased the chances that such legislation would be accepted and implemented (Joskow and Tsukanova 1995; Pittman 1996).

In line with both American and European versions of antitrust, the Russian antimonopoly law did not identify market dominance or firm size per se, as a problem. Only an abuse of dominant position could be prosecuted. With respect to cartels and loose agreements, on the other hand, the Russian law differed from both American and European acts. Cartels and loose agreements were not forbidden per se and the Russian law was not a prohibition act. The Russian legislator built upon the European version of antitrust, integrating into the text of the law the possibility for exceptions. Only abusive agreements and cartels were, as a consequence, deemed illegal, and those were defined as cartels and agreements that, 'have or might have as their result a material limitation of competition'. The Russian law, furthermore, allows that 'in exceptional instances', even those abusive agreements or cartels might be deemed 'lawful, if the economic subject proves that his actions facilitated or will facilitate the satiation of goods markets, the improvement of consumer properties of goods, and an increase in their competitiveness, particularly on the foreign market' (GKAP 1991).

10.3.4. *Constraints and limits*

An historical perspective thus points to a common thread—a common 'genetic code'—linking different versions of competition regulation. These different versions can be traced to an American antitrust tradition, which was transferred to other parts of the world during the twentieth century. Beyond common origins, though, local versions of antitrust exhibit a number of important differences. These differences can be explained by the fact that the transfer has been a contested process. They also reflect local institutional constraints that have had an impact, in particular, on implementation.

10.3.4.1. *Legacies, obstacles and resistance*
The project of transferring on a large scale the peculiar American understanding of competition regulation was not, historically, an easy process. It had to face, at each stage, pre-existing legacies, obstacles, and resistance. Whether in Germany, Europe, or Russia, the

most violent reactions initially came from local business communities. In Germany, a powerful and organized opposition slowed down considerably negotiations on a German anticartel act. In fact, to prevent these negotiations from failing altogether, Americans had to keep up pressure for nearly ten years and to provide significant resources, in particular legal counsel. The resistance of business communities to a foreign understanding of competition also created difficulties for ECSC negotiations. This time, American pressure again proved instrumental in preventing the negotiations from falling apart (Damm 1958; Djelic 1998). In the early 1990s, the emergent Russian business community was also the main obstacle to the adoption of American-inspired competition regulation principles.

The consequence of resistance and obstacles was that the transfer has implied partial reinterpretation and local translation. At each stage of the transfer, foreign advisers and local legislators have had to adapt the original tradition to local conditions and constraints. The American Sherman Act was a prohibition law when it came to cartels and loose agreements, outlawing all of them. In its dealings with mergers and tight combinations, it targeted only abuse. It did not prevent concentration per se, but it could be used in cases of abusive or monopolistic market power. The German anticartel law was, in principle, still a prohibition law, but it reflected a difficult drafting process and in the end it was a compromise. Under pressure from the German business community, the legislator had allowed a number of exceptions. Under certain conditions, some cartels were treated as 'reasonable restraints of trade' that could be tolerated and even fostered. Both the European and Russian versions of antitrust have retained the principle of allowing for exceptions and, as a consequence, they have become in practice abuse laws not only in their dealings with mergers or tight combinations but also in their dealings with cartels or loose agreements.

10.3.4.2. *The problem of implementation*
Beyond the text of the law and its evolution at each stage of the transfer, it is also important to consider the problem of implementation. The Sherman Antitrust Act already left a lot of space for interpretation. The role of the Supreme Court and enforcement agencies in shaping the act through its implementation has been quite significant. This space for interpretation through implementation remained at all stages of the transfer process, which turned an American tradition into a 'universal' regulation. The German Cartel Office or the

European High Authority had a certain discretion in their interpretation and use of the various clauses of exceptions allowing the constitution of cartels in times of crisis or in certain core industries (Berghahn 1986; Maxeiner 1986). In the Russian case, definitions and concepts were sufficiently vague that regulatory agencies and judicial courts were bound to have a significant influence with respect to implementation. Circumstances for exemption were, in particular, so broadly defined that implementation became key.

Similarities in the text and in the contents of the law are therefore not enough to point to a universal antimonopoly legislation. Important questions are those of implementation and enforcement. The nature and characteristics of the institutions in charge of interpreting the act and of enforcing it are important variables. The agenda, value structure and set of resources of the groups managing to gain control over these institutions are also naturally important. In the case of Western Europe, the transfer of the American antitrust tradition after the end of the Second World War had come together with a large-scale and institutionalized training and technical assistance programme. The objective had been to familiarize with or even socialize into the antitrust tradition those Europeans who would be in charge of interpreting, implementing, and enforcing the antitrust acts. This particular dimension of the transfer process has not taken place so far, at least to the same extent, in Russia. The lack of a systematic and large-scale technical assistance programme and the absence of long-term and institutionalized links between Western and Russian regulatory agencies are clearly decreasing further the likelihood that the Russian law will be implemented and enforced in the tradition originally defined in the United States.

10.4. CFC Regulation: Negotiating a Global Framework

We now turn to our second case of international regulation, which exemplifies quite a different pattern of emergence and diffusion. In contrast to competition regulation, the regulatory framework for ozone layer protection is not easily traceable to a purely national tradition. Rather, common standards emerged in this case from a process of cross-national negotiation and in response to a global issue.

In 1974, two scientists from the University of California accused CFCs, a set of chemical compounds, of dangerously depleting the stratospheric ozone layer. The ozone layer protects the earth against ultraviolet (UV) rays and its depletion could present important dangers for humans, including greater risks of cancer. Increasing evidence supporting the hypothesis ultimately led, in 1987, to the Montreal International Protocol. The protocol set up an almost global prohibition of CFCs with a dramatic impact for the chemical industry. In this section, we describe and deconstruct the process that has led to such a broad regulation. We ask about key actors and conditions pushing it along. We also look into constraints, in particular at the national level, that set clear limits to a global homogenization of CFC regulation (for an extensive analysis and for methodological information, see Bensedrine 1997).

10.4.1. *The negotiation process and its main stages*

In an immediate response to the 1974 accusations, the USA, Canada, Germany, and Sweden started regulating CFCs, limiting in particular their use in aerosols. Then, in April 1977, the American administration organized a conference with the aim of encouraging all CFC-producing countries to prohibit CFCs in aerosols. At this stage, the American administration seemed to favour national regulations in order to avoid a lengthy and difficult process of international negotiation. In December 1978, representatives from fourteen countries met again, this time in Munich. Americans gave an overview of their recently enacted national legislation prohibiting CFCs in aerosols. By this time, the official American position had evolved significantly and American representatives in fact appeared to encourage a 'unified global approach'. Only a small group of countries aligned themselves on this position. Together with the United States, Canada, Sweden, Norway, Denmark, Holland, and West Germany came to constitute the core of what would later be called 'the Toronto group'. In a 1980 conference hosted by Norway, representatives from these countries called for an immediate reduction in the use of CFCs. In contrast, the EC remained, as an entity, quite opposed to the elaboration of an international framework, although it decided at the time on the partial prohibition of CFCs in aerosols.

The first half of the 1980s was less busy. The deregulatory programme of the Reagan administration combined with the persisting lack of strong evidence regarding ozone layer depletion to slow things down. There was a widespread perception, furthermore, that prohibiting CFCs in aerosols was enough. However, the discovery in

1985 of the ozone hole sparked renewed activity with respect to CFC regulation. Officials from the American Environmental Protection Agency (EPA) again took steps to bring about an international agreement. The American ozone diplomacy became, at that time, more active than ever (Benedick 1991). EPA officials and American diplomats worked together with the United Nations Environment Programme (UNEP) and American agencies such as NASA or the National Oceanic and Atmospheric Agency (NOAA) to organize a series of national and international workshops and scientific meetings on the ozone layer issue. Intensifying their relationships with countries from the Toronto group, American officials and embassies put pressure on those countries such as France or Great Britain that did not push for regulation. Using the US Information Agency network, Americans also launched an extensive media campaign to alert public opinions in Europe and Japan. American officials and scientists were sent all over the world to give speeches, press conferences, and radio and television interviews. Coverage of the issue by national media was thus quite significant. Highest-level officials such as EPA Administrator Lee Thomas, Secretary of State Shultz, or President Reagan himself relayed this campaign through their personal contacts with key foreign decision-makers. At the 1987 Summit of the seven major industrial democracies, President Reagan succeeded in making 'protection of the ozone layer the first priority among environmental issues requiring common action' (Benedick 1991).

The direct consequence of these efforts was the Montreal Protocol. Signed in 1987, the Protocol set a 1999 target for partial CFC prohibition on a global scale. Soon, though, the anticipated reduction in CFC production appeared insufficient, particularly in light of new scientific knowledge. Green pressure groups, together with official representatives of countries from the 'Toronto Group', stepped up pressure by calling for stricter regulation. The result was a revision of the Montreal Protocol in 1990, which now requested total CFC prohibition on a global scale. Another revision in 1992 not only called for an acceleration of the process but also announced a plan to prohibit HCFCs, the first generation of CFC substitutes.

At first sight, such an acceleration and extension of CFC regulation made perfect sense. The nature of the problem—ozone layer depletion—was global and the environmental and human risks associated with it were of great consequences. In reality, though, this evolution was neither easy nor smooth. It took a lot of energy on the part of a rather small group of actors to push along and finally bring about an international prohibition of CFCs.

10.4.2. *Main actors and conditions*

While identification of the main actors is relatively easy, weighing their respective influence seems much more difficult. A few proactive countries, the 'Toronto Group', and their administrations were instrumental in steering the process along. Amongst these countries, the role of the United States was particularly significant. A more detailed analysis reveals, though, that the process was not negotiated only at the level of governmental agencies. The importance of scientists, media, NGOs, and international institutions in pushing the issue through debate as well as direct and indirect political pressure, should not be underestimated. Interestingly, key manufacturers also turned out, at certain points in time, to play an active role.

Scientists provided governments, NGOs, and international institutions with information and evidence on ozone layer depletion. Their research results, though, would not have been so compelling without the large budgets granted by national and international institutions, but also by industry trade associations. International institutions also played an important role by providing a forum where governments could negotiate on a transnational level. National environmental administrations and scientific organizations put significant pressure on governments to take the issue seriously. Their action was strongly reinforced and supplemented by that of environmental NGOs and media supports. In the background, multiple interactions led to the creation of a dense network of individual actors holding key positions of power. This network of actors and institutions triggered, upheld, and accelerated the momentum towards the making of a global regulation. There were multiple motives at play, ranging from environmental protection to the preservation of economic interests or the political will to take the lead on an international issue.

10.4.2.1. *The American lead*

While we have emphasized the multiplicity of actors involved, it is also clear that at different key moments the United States exercised leadership with important consequences. American scientists were the first to propose, in 1974, the ozone layer depletion hypothesis. Immediately, the American media seized upon it, playing a significant part in its early diffusion. As early as November 1974, the powerful

American-based green pressure group, Natural Resources Defence Council (NRDC), reacted by filing petitions with three American government agencies—the Consumer Product Safety Commission (CPSC), the Food and Drug Administration (FDA), and the EPA. The aim, already, was a prohibition of CFCs. In May 1975, it started suing the CPSC because it had not moved on the issue.

American public authorities and governmental agencies were thus the first to experience strong pressure from NGOs and the media. As a consequence, American authorities could not ignore the issue and congressional hearings were repeatedly held on the matter. At the same time, media supports and pressure groups had directly alerted American consumers. As a result, products containing CFCs tended to remain unsold on store shelves. Quite early on, leading American aerosol manufacturers started considering converting their American factories to CFC substitutes. This situation led the USA to enact a national legislation prohibiting CFCs in aerosols as early as 1978. Then, in 1980, the EPA administrator announced her intent to extend CFC regulation to all uses when the Europeans were still discussing a possible recommendation and the Japanese had only just set up a commission to review the situation.

While on the surface things calmed down somewhat during the early 1980s, the issue was in fact still bubbling. The NRDC launched a new judiciary action against the EPA in November 1984. A potential outcome of the litigation was for the EPA to be obliged by the courts to regulate CFCs, no matter what foreign countries were doing. During the proceedings, a new EPA administrator—Lee Thomas —was appointed in January 1985. He immediately announced that ozone depletion was 'a big issue' and he defined a 'timetable to move forward'. The discovery, the same year, of a hole in the ozone layer made the issue even 'bigger' and started off another chain reaction. Americans took the lead once again. The EPA pushed the NRDC and the Alliance for Responsible CFC policy—an ad hoc American trade association—to enter negotiations. Discussions led, in January 1986, to an agreement on a 'Stratospheric Ozone Protection Plan'.

Another important step was made soon after that, when the American firm DuPont, a major producer of CFCs, declared that it would give its support to the prohibition of CFCs if the American government vowed to work towards a global market for substitutes. As soon as enough assurance had been given, DuPont started to encourage other firms to support the process, acting through the seat it held at the board of the Alliance for Responsible CFC Policy. Soon enough, members of the Alliance were converted and the latter came to claim its support for an international regulation. Hence, the American lead in the process of negotiating an international regulation of CFCs can largely be explained by the peculiar nature of American political and legal institutions. Although economic interests and industry support proved important in the end, they were themselves very much the consequence of the institutional context. This context created favourable conditions for NGOs, individuals, or civil society groups to take action against or sue agencies or private companies when they suspected them of not implementing policies that were in their interests.

10.4.2.2. *European support*

Only by the mid-1980s was Europe as an entity ready to accept the idea of an international regulation of CFCs. Conditions had changed dramatically as a consequence of the discovery of the ozone hole but also under the pressure of NGOs, international institutions, foreign governments, and American agencies. Moreover, an international scientific and 'epistemic community' (Haas 1991) had formed in the early 1980s, gaining strong influence amongst key decision-makers in a number of countries. This change in conditions had its first impact in Belgium, leading that country to rally the pro-regulatory camp. This had a particularly significant impact, because Belgium would assume the presidency of the EC during the first half of 1987, which proved to be a key period in the negotiation process. Then came the change of heart of Great Britain. In this case, economic motives played an important part. The official support of the British government for an international regulation of CFCs was only declared after ICI, the biggest national CFC producer, had lifted its opposition. France then remained in an uncomfortable diplomatic position that soon proved to be unsustainable. French support finally opened the way, in 1987, to an internationally binding agreement.

10.4.3. *Constraints and limits*

In spite of strong American involvement and, in time, European support, regulating CFCs was far from an easy task. Protecting the ozone layer would have significant consequences in many industries in all parts of the world. CFCs were used in hundreds of different products (refrigerators, air conditioners, aerosols, fire extinguishers, plastic foams, for example), which were manufactured by thousands of firms all over the world. Furthermore, market prospects for CFCs were still quite significant, since it appeared that they could be used to produce a solvent for the booming electronics and precision mechanics industries.

10.4.3.1. *Obstacles and resistance*

While CFCs had multiple applications, CFC production was concentrated among a small number of economically and politically powerful manufacturers, such as the American DuPont and Allied-Signal, the French Elf-Atochem, the British ICI, and the German Hoechst. These firms provided altogether 75 per cent of the world production, leaving the rest of the market to twenty-two smaller producers operating mainly from the other side of the Iron Curtain, as well as in China and India. The agreement reached in 1987 implied that all producers, on a worldwide level, had to be brought to comply with a set of common norms. This would require transatlantic, East–West and South–North cooperation and means to monitor or even impose compliance.

On top of these difficulties, or because of these difficulties, various countries or groups of countries had in turn coalesced during the negotiation process to slow it down or turn it to their advantage. The two most striking episodes of that sort were the strong initial European opposition and the relative American disengagement during the Reagan administration. Although the EC had decided from the early 1980s on a partial CFC prohibition of aerosols, it remained for another few years quite opposed to the idea of an international regulation. France, Great Britain, and Italy were intent on protecting their national producers and thus rejected the propositions coming from West Germany for a stricter European regulation of CFCs. As late as September 1986, France and Great Britain persisted in opposing the American regulatory project. These countries were able to block the European decision process because, at that time, decisions within the community required unanimity.

Their opposition could not entirely be explained, though, by the existence of domestic producers. After all, Germany and the USA also had many CFC-related activities and they nevertheless were much stricter with respect to CFC regulation. Hence, a particular country's willingness to join or even to lead the international momentum also depended, as it turned out, on the particular political context at any given time. This is clearly illustrated by the case of the USA that radically changed their position in 1981. When President Reagan took office in 1981, the regulatory project of the previous administration was significantly slowed down, if not brought to a halt. The newly appointed head of the EPA immediately asserted that the ozone-depletion theory was 'highly controversial' and could not be accepted as a basis for more governmental action. This viewpoint was echoed in Congress and was strongly supported by the industrial lobby that was then created under the label 'Alliance for Responsible CFC Policy'. At the same time, American public opinion was being convinced that the ozone problem had more or less been solved thanks to the aerosol ban. The international movement for ozone layer protection had temporarily lost, in that period, its strongest supporter.

It would take new scientific evidence in 1985, pointing to a threat much more serious than anybody had envisioned, for attitudes to change. The pressure stemming from the scientific community, public opinion, and NGOs, as well as a new series of judicial actions against governmental agencies, were instrumental in pushing the Americans back into the driving seat.

10.4.3.2. *The problem of implementation*

The 1987 Montreal Protocol and its amended versions defined global standards for the regulation of CFCs. However, in spite of the global nature and reach of this Protocol, significant national and regional differences have remained to this day. These differences have been due to divergent interpretations of an initially loosely defined regulation, to the existence of various statutes under the same regulation for different types of county, to differences between national policy styles, to technological choices, as well as to mere non-compliance problems.

10.4.3.2.1. *An initially loosely defined international regulation.* While

its general direction and objectives were clear, the regulation that emerged from the Montreal Protocol remained rather loose for several years. A number of 'loopholes' were allowed to persist making divergent interpretations possible and indeed, quite likely. A key source of ambiguity was the authorization given to low consuming countries from the developing world to increase their per capita annual CFC use 'in order to meet their basic domestic needs' during a ten-year period. But the concept of 'basic domestic needs' was not precisely defined in the protocol and was therefore open to interpretation. According to some developing country governments, trade barriers should not affect their exports of products containing

CFCs, since export revenues could be considered as a means to satisfy 'basic domestic needs'. According to the US special ambassador, Benedick, negotiators were well aware that these and other issues remained to be solved. However, they had 'made their top priority the setting into motion of an international process' (Benedick, 1991).

10.4.3.2.2. *Various statutes under the same regulation.* The 1990 London amendments to the Montreal Protocol significantly reduced the number of loopholes and the space for interpretation. In particular, parties to the protocol decided that the export of products containing CFCs was inconsistent with the intent of the protocol. Interestingly, though, the discussions that took place in London with an aim to tightening the regulation were not always successful in that respect. A clarification of the Montreal Protocol sometimes led to a differentiation between categories of countries to which different provisions applied. In particular, both Russia and the developing countries remained under a special regime allowing them to increase their CFC production during, respectively, a five and ten year period after these chemicals were prohibited everywhere else. Russia had argued that its five-years plan system imposed an equivalent delay in compliance to the protocol. Developing countries had underlined, among other things, their marginal part in global CFC consumption, as well as their user industries' inability to afford substitutes. Developing countries also obtained the creation of a multilateral fund that would provide them with financial and technical assistance to switch to substitutes. On the one hand, the fund was an instrument of homogenization and it favoured the global extension of the protocol. On the other, it created a disparity among countries, since it increased the cost of the protocol for industrialized countries, while enabling developing countries to join the protocol at a much lower cost than would have been otherwise possible.

Another case of differential treatment under the protocol was illustrated by the special status of the EEC. Originally, the idea was that each member country had to reduce its production and use of CFCs. After harsh negotiations with the United States, the EC finally obtained agreement to be treated as a single consumption unit. Although CFC producers were still constrained by the regulation, this provided European user industries with more operational flexibility. During the Montreal meeting, the Canadian delegation had introduced an 'industrial rationalization' clause that allowed rationalization only between CFC plants of less than 25,000 tons capacity each.

As it turned out, European producers could not take advantage of that clause because the capacity of their plants was above that threshold. In the following years, European negotiators were thus busy lobbying for a change in the rationalization clause. The protocol was finally amended in that direction in 1990 and Europe had from that point on the possibility to increase CFC production in some member countries in counterpart to plant shutdowns in other countries. This way, the EC obtained agreement to be treated as a single production unit while retaining its full voting power—12 votes, at the time.

Hence international heterogeneity did not totally disappear with time. Part of the change was that the source of such heterogeneity switched from divergent interpretations of the protocol, or deficiencies in the protocol, to a relatively increased heterogeneity in the protocol itself. This evolution of the international framework seemed mainly due to the need for gathering as much support as possible from countries that were hitherto unhappy with the terms of the protocol.

10.4.3.2.3. *Differences in national policy styles.* Another source of divergence came from the interplay between the protocol and the national institutions and policy styles through which it was implemented on the ground. The protocol in fact only imposed a series of deadlines for the phasing-out of CFC production and consumption. Each country was left totally free to develop its own policy to reach the targets set by the protocol. At one extreme, Europe mainly relied on what was called a conventional approach, which consisted in voluntary agreements between trade associations and governments. At the other extreme, the United States relied on tax policy and legal penalties for non-compliance.

10.4.3.2.4. *Technological choices.* The concrete implementation of the Montreal Protocol also differed across countries because of different technological choices for the substitution of CFCs. An important difference was related to the focus of some countries on HCFC or HFC substitute technologies, because only the latter was totally ozone friendly (but both had greenhouse effects). Another interesting example was related to the global cosmetic industry. Actually, some national industries have replaced CFCs in deodorant aerosols by other types of propellant that might present safety hazards, whereas, partly because of these concerns, other national industries have completely abandoned the aerosol technology in deodorants.

10.4.3.2.5. *Non-compliance.* Another limit to the institutionalization of an international CFC regulation has come, naturally, from problems of non-compliance. Some countries do not fully comply with the protocol, while even those that try to comply have to struggle with a large black market. In the mid-1990s both environmentalists and company managers strongly denounced CFC smuggling and illegal traffic as a key issue that should be dealt with. According to one company official, CFC smuggling was in 1995 the main black market in Florida, after drug dealing. This seemed mainly due to the lack of enforcement of the protocol in some countries such as Russia, enabling the illegal production of CFCs in those countries and their export to Eastern and Western Europe, to the United States, and elsewhere. So both companies producing substitutes and environmental organizations have pressured governments to step up their enforcement and litigation activities.

10.5. Discussion

We have focused, in this chapter, on transnational regulation as one powerful type of global pressure. Looking in turn at competition regulation and at the regulation of CFCs, we have compared the patterns of emergence, diffusion, and institutionalization of these two sets of norms. Beyond apparently global and universal norms contributing to the worldwide homogenization of economic conditions, we found processes that were both historically contingent and embedded in peculiar sets of institutional constraints. Probing into the origins of both sets of regulations, asking about the actors and mechanisms of their diffusion or implementation, and searching for possible obstacles and resistance, we identified significant differences between our two case studies.

In the case of competition regulation, the beginnings were local. Antitrust emerged in post-Civil War United States, in response to a dramatic increase in the power of business cartels and aggregates. The enactment of the Sherman Act and its early interpretation reflected in part an economic logic. They also revealed, though, a multiplicity of political and social interests and their confrontation within the young federation. After 1945, the American antitrust tradition acquired another dimension. The rules of exchange and competition that regulated trade between American states were turned into universal standards, at least within the Western sphere. This process reflected American geopolitical dominance. It was part of the construction, under American leadership, of an institutional framework for transnational trade. With the fall of the Berlin Wall in the late 1980s, the process of diffusion of an American antitrust tradition entered its second stage. By the mid-1990s, around fifty countries in the world had an antitrust or competition legislation that prohibited cartels and set limits to anti-competitive practices.

In the case of CFC regulation, the pattern of emergence and institutionalization of a worldwide standard was quite different. The process started later, in the early 1970s, and the triggering issue—a large-scale environmental threat—had, by nature, global implications. Regulation in this case was thus from the start negotiated at a cross-national level. The result was a compromise regulation that was then adopted, and in the process also partially adapted, in the countries that signed the protocol. The process and the emerging common standard reflected the multiplicity of actors, the diversity of their interests, and the balance of their resources. As such, it was far from being driven only by an economic logic. It was also an eminently political debate that was constrained by the institutional framework in which it took place.

Our case studies thus illustrate two quite different patterns with respect to the emergence of cross-national regulation. On the one hand, a national model was diffused, at some point in time, to other countries and to supranational communities, becoming in the process a global standard. On the other hand, a set of norms negotiated at a multinational level was then locally adopted—and partially adapted—by individual nations, which signed a common protocol. In the case of antitrust, the emergence, early definition and interpretation, and the diffusion of the regulation owed a lot to the intervention and initiative of public actors, state agencies, and politicians. In the case of CFC regulation, there was a greater diversity of actors and negotiators. The role, in particular, of business groups or representatives, and even more of civil society through the organized scientific community, environmental NGOs, and the media, cannot be underestimated.

While both regulatory frameworks contribute to a partial worldwide homogenization of economic conditions, our double exercise in deconstruction has shown the process of emergence, diffusion, or interpretation of these international regulations to have been historically contingent and highly constrained by unique institutional conditions. Contextualization has made it possible, furthermore, to point to important differences between our two cases of transnational regulation. Beyond those differences, though, we would like to end with what emerged as two important common features. In both stories, we found that the United States played a key role. In the case of competition regulation, they provided the model and fostered its transfer. In the case of CFC regulation, the impact was less direct. Still, the United States led the early process of discussions and negotiations and their varying degree of involvement, throughout the period, drove the ups and downs of international negotiations with a significant impact, ultimately, on the negotiated outcome. Another important conclusion emerging from our two cases is that the making of cross-national regulation says little about its interpretation and implementation on the ground. We show a fair amount of decoupling between global standards and their local implementation. Key filters, in both cases, have been national institutions but also those national communities that opposed and resisted the standards. We found the result to be, with respect to implementation, a hybridization or local translation of global standards. This, naturally, points to the limits of what is called the process of globalization. By the mid-1990s, around fifty countries on six continents had an antitrust or competition legislation that regulated cartels and set limits to anti-competitive practices. By May 1999, 168 countries had ratified the initial agreement of the Montreal Protocol and, for most of them, subsequent amendments. In spite of this apparent widespread diffusion of common regulatory standards, our results lead us to question the ultimate likelihood of a full convergence, on a transnational scale, of institutions, structures, and organizational behaviours.

REFERENCES

Alvarez, J. L. (ed.) (1998), *The Diffusion and Consumption of Business Knowledge*. New York: St. Martin's Press.
Arias, M. E. and Guillén, M. (1998), 'The Transfer of Organizational Techniques across Borders', in J. L. Alvarez (ed.), *The Diffusion and Consumption of Business Knowledge*. New York: St. Martin's Press.
Benedick, R. (1991), *Ozone Diplomacy*. Cambridge, MA: Harvard University Press.
Bensedrine, J. (1997), 'Les Stratégies des entreprises dans les processus institutionnels: le cas des producteurs de CFC et la protection de la couche

d'ozone'. Doctoral Dissertation, ESSEC Graduate School of Business and University of Aix-en-Provence.

Berghahn, V. (1986), *The Americanization of West German Industry*. New York: Cambridge University Press.

Cagin, S. and Dray, P. (1993), *Between Earth and Sky*. New York: Pantheon Books.

Campbell, J., Hollingsworth, R. and Lindberg, L. (eds.) (1991), *Governance of the American Economy*. New York: Cambridge University Press.

Chandler, A. (1990), *Scale and Scope*. Cambridge, MA: Harvard University Press.

Clemens, L. and Cook, J. (1999), 'Politics and Institutionalism: Explaining Durability and Change', *Annual Review of Sociology*, 25: 441–66.

Damm, W. (1958), 'National and International Factors Influencing Cartel Legislation in Germany'. PhD dissertation, University of Chicago.

DiMaggio, P. and Powell, W. (1983), 'The Iron Cage Revisited: Institutional Isomorphism and Collective Rationality in Organizational Fields', *American Sociological Review*, 48: 147–60.

Djelic, M. L. (1998), *Exporting the American Model*. Oxford: Oxford University Press.

—— (1999), 'From a Typology of Neo-institutional Arguments to their Cross-fertilisation'. Unpublished paper.

Dobbin, F. (1994), *Forging Industrial Policy*. New York: Cambridge University Press.

Erhard, L. (1958), *Prosperity through Competition*. New York: Frederick Praeger.

Fligstein, N. (1990), *The Transformation of Corporate Control*. Cambridge, MA: Harvard University Press.

GKAP (1991), 'Law on Competition and Limitation of Monopolistic Activity in Goods Markets'. Adopted by the RSFSR Supreme Soviet, 22 March.

Guillén, M. (1994), *Models of Management*. Chicago, IL: University of Chicago Press.

Haas, P. (1991), 'Policy Responses to Stratospheric Ozone Depletion', *Global Environmental Change*, June: 224–34.

Hawkins, M. (1997), *Social Darwinism in European and American Thought, 1860–1945*. New York: Cambridge University Press.

Hoffman, P. (1951), *Peace can be Won*. New York: Doubleday.

Hogan, M. (1985), 'American Marshall Planners and the Search for a European Neo-Capitalism'. *American Historical Review*, 90(1): 44–72.

Hollingsworth, R. and Boyer, R. (eds.) (1997), *Comparing Capitalisms: The Embeddedness of Institutions*. New York: Cambridge University Press.

Joskow, P. and Tsukanova, N. (1995), Discussions and interviews with Paul Joskow, MIT Professor, and Natasha Tsukanova, Russian Committee on Antimonopoly Policy (GKAP).

Liftin, K. (1994), *Ozone Discourse: Science and Politics in Global Environmental Cooperation*. New York: Columbia University Press.

Martin, J. (1950), *All Honorable Men*. Boston, MA: Little Brown.

Maxeiner, J. (1986), *Policy and Methods in German and American Antitrust Law*. New York: Praeger.

McCraw, T. (1984), *Prophets of Regulation*. Cambridge, MA: Belknap of HUP.

Monnet, J. (1976), *Mémoires*. Paris, France: Fayard.

Ohmae, K. (1995), *The End of the Nation State*. Cambridge, MA: Free Press.

OMGUS Records, Bd18—Bipartite Control Office, Economics Division and Decartelization Branch. Bundesarchiv, Koblenz, Germany.

Pittman, R. (1995), 'Competition Policy in Russia and the United States: The Russian Law and the American Experience'. Unpublished paper.

—— (1996), Discussions with Russell Pittman, Chief of the Competition Policy Section of the Antitrust Division, US Department of Justice.

Rowlands, I. (1995), *The Politics of Global Atmospheric Change*. Manchester, UK: Manchester University Press.

Roy, W. (1997), *Socializing Capital*. Princeton, NJ: Princeton University Press.

Schwartz, T. (1991), *America's Germany*. Cambridge, MA: Harvard University Press.

Scott, R., and Meyer, J. (1994), *Institutional Environments and Organizations*. Newbury Park, CA: Sage.

Sklar, M. (1988), *Corporate Reconstruction of American Capitalism, 1890–1916*. New York: Cambridge University Press.

Taft, W. (1911), 'On the Antitrust Statute', Message of the President of the USA to the House of Congress, 5 December, Washington DC.

Taylor, G. (1979), 'The Rise and Fall of Antitrust in Occupied Germany', *Prologue*, 11.

Thorelli, H. (1954), *The Federal Antitrust Policy: Origination of an American Tradition*. Baltimore, MA: Johns Hopkins University Press.

Van der Pijl, K. (1984), *The Making of an Atlantic Ruling Class*. London: Verso.

Weiss, L. (1988), *Creating Capitalism*. New York: Basil Blackwell.

Whitley, R. (ed.) (1992), *European Business Systems*. London: Sage.

—— (1999), *Divergent Capitalisms*. Oxford: Oxford University Press.

Whitley, R. and Kristensen, P. H. (eds.) (1996), *The Changing European Firm*. London: Routledge.

11

National Trajectories, International Competition, and Transnational Governance in Europe*

DIETER PLEHWE

11.1. Introduction

This chapter examines the interrelationship between regulatory structures and the strategies of firms. As firms internationalize, they seek to shift regulatory structures away from the national level towards an appropriate level of international coordination. By helping to create common standards across national boundaries firms are able to benefit from a level playing field (see Morgan's contribution in Chapter 9), thus increasing potential economies of scale and scope. The process of internationalizing regulatory structures therefore develops at least in part from the efforts of firms to create a framework more suited to the scale of their businesses. However, business 'scale' is not given automatically. It may require firms to reconceptualize how they look at themselves and their businesses. In this process, the potential offered by internationalizing regulation and getting beyond distinctive national markets becomes in itself a force that changes conceptions within firms. This chapter therefore explores the interrelationship between firms and regulatory structures as they interact at the national and international levels.

This objective is achieved through an analysis of developments within the logistics and distribution industry, particularly in the European context. The chapter reveals that the origins of this industry are tied into the development of postal services. Postal services have been dominated until relatively recently by national regulatory regimes which have enforced a state monopoly structure on the sector, based primarily on the notion of the social function of these

A part of the research on which this article is based was supported by a generous grant from the Volkswagen Foundation co-financing a joint research project carried out at the Wissenschaftszentrum, Berlin and the Technical University, Berlin. The project 'Logistics Governance between Europeanization and Globalization' is headed by Prof. Dr Hedwig Rudolph and jointly carried out by the author and Dr Christoph Dörrenbächer and Stefano Vescovi.

services (what is referred to as the universal service obligation, i.e. the requirement to offer a postal system that links all parts of the nation-state at the same price, thus cross-subsidizing rural areas, areas of low population density, or geographically remote locations at the expense of high density, urban centres). In the postwar period, however, there has been an increasing redefinition of these services, which has identified them as crucially part of the circuit of capital—in particular, its distribution element (within the sphere of commercial capital). This recognition has led to an increased focus on both cheapening the cost of distribution (through a variety of measures, including increasing the scale of operations) and seeking to remove barriers that add cost (either directly, e.g. through tariffs, or indirectly by prohibiting firm's abilities to reap economies of scale through maintaining national monopoly systems). This sector reveals very clearly how the strategies of some firms to reduce national barriers are linked to the reconstruction of regulatory orders at new international levels, particularly in this case the level of the European Community (EC). There is a symbiotic relationship between internationalizing firms and internationalizing regulatory structures. This, of course, is not to say that there are not powerful national actors (both firms and regulators) which seek to control this, but the argument here is that the dynamic of the processes unleashed by these simultaneous internationalizing strategies (within firms and within regulatory frameworks) restructures the economic space within which firms can pursue their goals. The result is not convergence of firms and strategies but nor is it simply the reproduction of national characteristics on an international scale. It involves a hybridization process, as the actors themselves are reconstituted within this new economic space, which, paradoxically, they have also been responsible for bringing into being in the first place.

To proceed in this analysis, I will first trace the national constitution of the postal system, creating the space for strictly national varieties of postal markets and organizations. The accompanying international regime of postal exchange framed by the World Postal Union (founded in 1874) was challenged in the 1970s, when shrinking profit margins and increasing competition shifted the focus of rationalization from production to commerce and distribution. This was part of the crisis of Fordism unfolding in the 1970s, when organizational and regulatory innovation in the United States nourished new express service companies dubbed 'integrators' (integrating transport supply chains across transport modes), such as Federal

Express (FedEx) and DHL. These companies eagerly introduced the international attack on protected national postal markets. I will go on to analyse the ensuing political battle over how to redefine postal, general transport, and logistics markets within Europe, relying on an actor-centred institutional approach informed by the neo-Gramscian literature on the international political economy (Murphy 1994). A neo-Gramscian regime approach 'enables analysts to focus on the process of international institutionalization without assuming that interstate co-operation is the result of the exercise of power by a single hegemon or the consensual outcome of inter-state bargaining in the interests of the global community as a whole' (Gale 1998: 253–4). The extension of internationalization to state-related 'infra-structure' services has been cited to support neo-liberal convergence and globalization arguments (Kasper 1988). However, the unfolding of the transnational reorganization of companies and the intensification of transnational governance in Europe's postal, transport, and logistics systems rather support an argument of national and trans-national varieties of capitalism and organizations combining diversity and convergence in new ways. National trajectories are not completely destroyed in the course of Europeanization. Nor is it likely that the transnational transport systems in Europe and North America will become a perfect integrated and seamless whole.

11.2. Twofold Invention: The Historical Contribution of the Postal Organization to National State Formation

An early attempt to understand the social and historical significance of the postal system and its relationship to state formation and inter-nationalization is provided in the work of the German economic historian Werner Sombart. Sombart clarifies the historical contribution of the modern postal organization to societal development by way of emphasizing two distinctive innovations: first, systematic collection and distribution, and, secondly, universal (low) prices for all encompassing services established by nation-states in the nineteenth century. Sombart rightfully regarded the core aspect of the postal system in the function systematically to collect and distribute (letters, products) on a continuous basis for larger groups of people (1969 [1902]: 369). The two innovations are thus related to needs for organizational efficiency and social integration arising from the deepening division

of labour in capitalist societies. The systematic collection and distribution function is today known as logistics in management theory,
whilst the mechanisms of societal inclusion are established under the
national frameworks of 'public interest' and 'universal services'. The
specific combination of organizational efficiency and social integration thus historically depended on the formation of nation-states
(ibid.: 396f.) integrating state and society. This was distinctive from
the mere 'transport' services which characterized earlier eras when
messages were carried over long distances through private means.

Geistbeck (1986 [1895]) adds to Sombart's assessment a third
dimension of the contributions of the postal system. In 1874, the
founding of the World Postal Union by twenty-two nation-states was
strongly promoted by the German postmaster Heinrich von Stephan.
The experience of the German states to negotiate patent regulations
among themselves is widely regarded as a major factor of support for
the rise of public international unions (Murphy 1994: 51). The international regime established in 1874 under the umbrella of the World
Postal Union provided the principal framework to negotiate 'principles, norms, rules, and decision making procedures' (Krasner 1982:
185) specific to the particular issue of exchange between nationally
confined postal systems. It greatly reduced the costly business of
international cooperation (Keohane 1984) and helped to rationalize
the postal system on an international scale—e.g. more than 1,500 different mail charges for one type of letter in the 28 member states
(1878) were reduced to a uniform exchange system shaped by 28
homogeneous national systems (Geistbeck 1986 [1895]: 396).

Thus the invention of systematic collection and distribution (logistics) combined with a universal service redistribution policy on a
national basis provided for a crucial postal infrastructure serving the
national and international communication (letters) and transport
(parcels) needs of modern industrial societies. Within each nation,
postal organizations were protected from private competition in core
postal product markets, though the actual form of these monopolies
differed. While European nation-states integrated postal, telegraph,
and telephony services in PTTs, and frequently added a range of
banking and passenger transport services, the US postal system
developed separately from telephone and telegraphy services with
AT&T remaining a private, though regulated, telephone monopoly
for the major part of the twentieth century.

The extent of the protected monopoly was always limited. Many
private sector transport and forwarding companies emerged as real

or potential competitors to the national postal organizations in the field of less than truckload (LTL) freight akin to postal packages. Austria's Gottfried Schenker first introduced less than wagonload services, thereby transferring the logistics function of systematic collection and distribution to general freight (Matis 1995: 46f.). State ownership, market entry, and price regulations in the various transport sectors, however, served to separate markets politically and thence to preserve the postal monopoly. A national space and society logic dominated commercial aspects. Even a parallel organization as large as UPS, developing into a nation-wide parcel company in the United States in the course of the twentieth century, or the globally operating forwarding company Schenker run by the German railways until privatization in the 1990s, lived by and large in peaceful coexistence with the postal services—until the 1970s. It was believed that the universal service system would simply break down if private commercial interests were allowed to 'cherry-pick' and provide the most profitable services (e.g. bulk mail over short distances in big cities) and leave the costly services in rural areas to a public organization. Until the 1970s, the system therefore basically functioned unchallenged and managed ever growing amounts of national and international mail. Successive rounds of technological and organizational improvement (e.g. in the means of transport, in the development of coding systems—first invented during the Second World War to replace skilled postal labour with good geographical knowledge now needed in the battle field—in the invention and utilization of sorting machines, etc.) were all implemented within this established national and international framework.

11.3. The Introduction of Turbulence: National Origins of Institutional Change

The 1970s arrived with a major challenge to established regimes of accumulation and modes of regulation in advanced industrial societies. The crisis of Fordism (Aglietta 1979) ended several arrangements of (more or less) peaceful coexistence of divergent interests. Shrinking profit margins increased both inter-firm competition and sharpened once again the class conflict between capital and labour. Shrinking state revenues turned the (more or less corporatist) welfare state once again into a battlefield of competing private and public interests. A key, yet under-researched, aspect of the responses to the crisis of Fordism lies in the field of infrastructure services such as the postal and transport system. Some innovative transport companies started up or reinvented themselves within the highly segmented and regulated national framework of the US transport market order (modal, regional, and pricing regulations). The new organizations that originally challenged and later were among the crucial change agents in the transport, logistics, and postal world were of US (FedEx, DHL, UPS) and Australian (TNT) origin. FedEx and DHL, in particular, were the two companies first able to deliver added value to production chains by way of reducing circulation cost.

Instead of the rather slow and inflexible supply of transport services using different organizations along a transport chain, the new companies integrated the whole of the transport chain within their own organization and thereby managed sharply to reduce transshipment stages and transaction costs. In particular, they pioneered new technologies to better integrate handling of freight and freight-related information flows. They introduced marketing to the transport craft and invented the hub and spoke system of transport services widely used in the industry since. These so-called 'integrators' supplied courier, express, and parcel services of superior speed and reliability compared to the older types of supply organizations.

The new express industry challenged both established cooperative business alliances in transport (e.g. brokers/forwarders and airlines) and postal organizations. Premium prices—higher even than prices charged by regulated transport operators—for the services were easily recovered by certain types of customers (banks, insurance companies, trading companies, etc.) due to competitive advantages gained by shorter waiting times, lower losses, and reduced insurance costs. A steadily increasing share of letters and lightweight products were taken away from the older transport chains and absorbed into the integrator businesses.

These efforts encouraged customers to demand new innovations in logistics as part of their effort to improve profitability. Although the share of distribution costs in total costs was as high as 45 per cent in some product markets, before the 1970s it had not been specifically targeted as a business area to be rationalized. 'It would seem, therefore, that the new focus upon efficiency in distribution was a logical outgrowth of the American business environment. That is, one of the last remaining frontiers for significant cost savings in the business firm was the distribution area' (La Londe et al. 1993 [1970]: 7). The 'last frontier' was already recognized in 1962 by Peter Drucker who referred to distribution as the 'dark continent'. He thereby reinforced earlier critiques which had suggested that academicians and practitioners would do better to address the physical distribution side of marketing. James R. Stock summarized this history of thought (and practice), indicating the continuing difficulties in perceiving the whole of the logistics chain (not just distribution) and the strategic aspect of logistics. According to Stock, it was outsiders to the logistics field such as Michael E. Porter who helped more thoroughly to address the centrality of the logistics function to business processes and profitability (Stock 1990: 3–6).

High prices and the poor services of regulated transport and warehousing suppliers became an increasing concern for management. In addition, given shrinking profit margins, the fight between commercial enterprises and industrial producers over the distribution of profit among the different types of capitalist organization along the value chain sharpened. This conflict reinforced the closer look at transport and logistics issues, since both powerful commercial and industrial firms sought to turn rising pressures on their margins over to weaker links in the supply chains. The new management focus on distribution and flow economics emerged in the 1960s and advanced rapidly in the course of the 1970s and 1980s. It was grounded in a sharply increasing amount of academic literature examining issues of distribution management, a development that was later defined as 'logistics', importing yet again a military term into managerial discourse (Bjelicic 1987).

Logistics can be defined as a concept to guide economic *processes* (both at the micro- and macro-level of the economic system) and as a tool of rationalization to optimize specific areas of the labour process focusing initially on transport, reshipment, and warehousing, and including cost reduction for such services (Danckwerts 1991: 39). The increasing impact of logistic costs on profitability was directly linked to increasing international competition in 1970 (La Londe et al. 1993 [1970]: 7)—long before Japanese lean production launched the more public challenge.

Separation of the distribution function was supposed to enable companies to adapt better to faster and more dynamically changing markets with regard both to product cycles and geographical expansion. Four factors were identified as having a determining influence on the development of the distribution function: increasing acceptance of a *systemic* distribution approach; increasing weight of the demand side (buyers market); challenges coming from *multinational* _distribution_; and _increasing state influence_ on distribution policy and practice (La Londe et al. 1993: 9; italics added). By 1980, most internationally operating companies would support the momentum of management specialization by way of _separating_ and _integrating_ the logistics function within the organization. Separation and integration within the firm were a precondition to further intensify specialization; outsourcing of the logistical functions apart from transport gave rise to a new industrial service supply provided by third-party logistics firms (including the express companies and other innovative transport enterprises) in the 1980s and 1990s.

This process of increased specialization within the firm and across the value chain relates to the long-standing contest between finance, industrial, and commercial capital. Defining distribution and logistics as a separate function raises the questions of, first, how it is to be organized (as part of the production firm or part of the commercial firm or as a separate, purchasable service from a specialist firm) and, secondly, how profit is to be generated from this activity (and therefore whose margins are squeezed). The fight over control over logistics operations between producers and traders is thus another example of changing power relations between organizations along the value chain. After the era of merchant capitalism, power centred on the industrial end producer. Toyotist 'lean production' intensified traditional hierarchies by creating first, second, and third tiers of supply companies. A new competitive dynamic has recently been identified under the term 'Wintelism' (Microsoft Windows and Intel). Instead of the traditional end producer, manufacturers of inputs somewhere along the supply chain occupy a more powerful position (Borrus and Zysman 1997).

Large trading companies are increasingly trying to force industrial producers to abandon their own logistics operations (Bretzke 1999; Hector 1998; Plehwe and Bohle 1998: 30–1). Transport firms serving as intermediaries between the two necessarily turn into a target. Market entry and price regulation protecting even small firms had an increasingly uncomfortable place in the arm's length type of contractual relations predominant in the United States (Hollingsworth et al. 1994).

The development of a more integrated approach to logistics became linked in the USA to the effort to develop a more efficient and extensively internationalized field of operations. In particular, the multinational challenges were suggested to be of increasing importance to US companies because the share of international sales was considered too low, with 5 per cent of GDP in the USA compared to 30–40 per cent in Europe. Because of high levels of trade, companies in Europe (including several US-owned firms), therefore, were much more experienced with international distribution. However, US-based companies started to engage in a drive rapidly to increase their international production in ways that would eventually transform the traditional export/import organization. Observers at the time wondered about the future character of supply structures of transport and logistics services:

It might be interesting to speculate on the role of distribution middlemen in the new international environment. Both the evidence to date and the economic logic would seem to indicate that a *new type of capital intensive conglomerate* will emerge during the 1970s to meet the needs of worldwide distribution. The functions of export packaging, shipment consolidation, ship chartering, export–import documentation, stevedoring, storage, customs requirements, and *multi-modal inland distribution* will be offered *by a single firm*. Thus it is suggested that a new form of distribution middleman with intermodal capability and spanning a wide range of intermediate distribution functions will emerge to serve the needs of the multinational distribution manager during the 1970s. (La Londe et al. 1993 [1970]: 11; emphasis added)

It is fascinating to see this forecast coming true, even though it did take a little longer overall than the authors might have anticipated and involved a myriad of reorganization and deregulation battles. Companies such as FedEx and DHL, hybrid transmodal and technologically advanced logistics providers, started up in the early 1970s. UPS and TNT reinvented their business according to the model. However, until deregulation, the integrated services provided were seriously hampered by regulatory constraints. FedEx, for example, had to fly ever growing volumes of express cargo in small aircraft due to market entry restrictions in the air freight sector. Licences were not available for larger aeroplanes, forcing the company to utilize less efficient small planes for which no restrictions applied under the law. Together with transport customers who were unsatisfied with the regulatory structure, the new competitors forged a formidable business lobby for regulatory reform, eventually resulting in a liberalized and integrated transport market order in the United States (Plehwe 2000).

The US Air Cargo Deregulation Act of 1977 was nicknamed the 'FedEx bill' because of the support lobby organized by FedEx CEO, Fred Smith (Hamilton 1990). The law allowed new entrants into the previously closed market and was almost unanimously supported by transport users and suppliers, passing without much public debate, unlike the regulatory reform laws deregulating air passenger, rail, and trucking industries (Derthick and Quirk 1985). The new regulatory structure developed by the Carter and Reagan administrations reinforced arm's length coordination in the transport sector, thereby supporting the rapid expansion of a few large companies at the expense of small and medium-size enterprises and organized labour. Among the winners were the leaders of the courier/express industry. Within a few years, four companies, FedEx, DHL, TNT, and UPS, came to dominate the rapidly growing express market.

Traditional suppliers in the field, the postal organizations and the airline/forwarder alliances almost totally lost out to the express industry. In 1996 the original four big players hold approximately 90 per cent of the market for international express service (*DVZ*, 21 January 1997: 8) and aggressively attacked other market segments— including the still protected national postal market. International express and courier services obviously cannot be provided if regulatory structures in other nations prohibit market entry. If the US companies were to grow abroad, the regulatory reform movement had to be exported to other territories. As demand for the new—initially illegal—service from important customers (banks, insurance companies, etc.: see Wojtek 1987) was growing in other countries and the organizational capability of suppliers was building up, the existing institutional arrangements at the national and international level were threatened. In the late 1970s, UPS systematically started to set up shop in Europe. On the initiative of DHL managers, a new business association was founded to challenge and ultimately fundamentally to change the regulatory structures of Europe's transport and postal markets (Campbell 1994): The 'age of regulatory reform' (Button and Swann 1989) was coming to Europe and 'deregulation' was turned into an international movement (Gayle and Goodrich 1991).

There are numerous accounts focusing on the aspect of intensified national regime competition due to assymetric national strategies of liberalization. However, instead of understanding the European history of privatization and deregulation in this sector as a comparative history of national change, the transnational dimensions of change (transnational reorganization of companies and business associations) and the transnational processes of institutionalization and market-making need to be discussed.

11.4. Competitive Organizations and Supranational Institutionalization: Integrators, New Post Offices, Business Associations, and—the (European) State

UPS as well as the other integrators moved outside of the USA into Europe and Canada during the 1970s (see TURU 1990: 63f.). During the same period, several national competitors of the postal monopolies developed within the trucking and forwarding sector of some European states, forming the nuclei of the later (German and then European) networks of small and medium (and subsidiaries of large) parcel enterprises, such as Deutscher Paketdienst and German Parcel in Germany. These national firms, together with the international express companies, created a strong business force hostile to the postal monopolies in many European countries. Both outsiders and insiders combined forces to put the heat on existing regulatory regimes. The respective national institutional structures (including the post offices as state apparatuses) thence came under siege, due to both internal and external competition of new or redirected private business enterprises.

Until 1984 the private competitors to national PTTs worked in a grey zone of the postal market, as international mail business was still legally reserved for the national monopolies. Most postal authorities, and in particular the French La Poste, undertook considerable efforts to stop the new services (including raids by postal officers with police functions in France, etc.). In 1984, however, German authorities decided on the legality of *express* delivery to Germany by outside firms. The decision was made with regard to the technical question of the monopoly of postal operations. The regulatory body found that Deutsche Post had no proper authority for claiming a monopoly over this type of express business. This legal loophole created a space big enough for the international express companies to come in (for details see Campbell 1994: 133). This legalized an important part of the new services offered by the integrators in one country, thereby securing the first European bridgehead. The courier/express companies took it from there to other countries and involved supranational EC competition authorities (see Djelic and Bensedrine in Chapter 10), which started to side with the private industry firms against national state monopolies as part of the process of moving towards a single European market (Campbell 1994). In this sector, the logic of such a move involved the destruction of 'artificial' barriers to trade created by the national systems of state-owned monopoly of postal services.

The support from EC competition authorities for the private competitors of the national PTTs was even more important, since
European officials enjoy supranational executive powers in the field
of antitrust.

Increasing private pressures on the old international regime were
reinforced by the decision of the Reagan administration to accept uni-
laterally the right of couriers to provide international remail services.
By taking this decision, the largest originating market of international
mail was separated from the established regulatory framework of the
World Postal Union. European (and other) postal authorities, in turn,
started to compete against each other. Despite some postal administrations' eagerness to attract international couriers to their jurisdiction as the main point of entry into Europe for bulk remail, several
postal authorities in the European Postal Union (CEPT) still tried to
work out a collective multinational defence strategy. Postal authorities from the Netherlands, France, Germany, Sweden, and Canada
founded the EMS International Postal Corporation (Campbell 1994:
139). One way to domesticate internationalized market competition
thus relates to collective defence against challengers by way of creation of a 'strategic alliance' of national organizations.

On the initiative of DHL, the private courier companies continuously stepped up their collective strategy in the 1980s and 1990s to
gain access to protected postal markets. The International Express
Carriers Conference (IECC) was originally founded in 1983. Initially
a rather loose association depending heavily on DHL's financial
support, the big four companies strengthened their efforts in 1987,
with TNT and FedEx matching DHL contributions, and UPS becoming a full member in 1988 (ibid.: 125). In 1988, IECC recognized the
increasing importance of the supranational EU level to influence
postal (and other transport) policy. At this time the big four attracted
the smaller national companies from within Europe, which were
having to compete in environments dominated by state monopolies
as allies, thus directly binding EU outsiders and EU insiders with a
common interest together. In Germany, private competitors of the
post office joined the courier/express business association BIEK, led
by the international firms. In the Netherlands, two associations (one
combining 10 international companies, the other organizing 200
SMEs) decided to merge in 1993 (*DVZ*, 14 January 1992).

Some IECC members differed, however, on the character of the
planned European association. DHL wanted to limit the goals of
the European association to traditional express service issues (its

almost exclusive market), whilst the majority agreed on a wider agenda (Campbell 1994: 126). In 1989, therefore, two competing European express associations operated independently. The Association of European Express Carriers (AEEC) was founded by DHL and others, while the other IECC members started the European Express Organization (EEO). Competing strategies notwithstanding, the two associations fought a common battle against the (multi-)national postal monopoly. And on 1 January 2000 the family resolved its internal battles. The two competing associations merged to form the European Express Association.[1] The two partners ordered a consulting report on 'The Importance and Impact of the Express Industry in Europe' (1999) to prepare the merger and to present the express industry as a unified European branch in transport and logistics.

It would be too long for this chapter to trace the national and supranational histories of postal and general transport reform in the EU in detail (see Plehwe 1997). After many rounds of heated discussion based on green and white book proposals of the European Commission to reform the postal market in Europe in the course of the 1990s, considerable national liberalization and European reregulation was finally agreed on 18 December 1996 by the Council of EU ministers. Each step at the European bargaining level involved a considerable amount of input from various national state institutions as well as from private sector actors. Apart from consulting the national postal monopolies, the expertise of the express companies and of their large customers was directly solicited. The increasing importance of the European Parliament after the implementation of the Maastricht reforms attracted a growing lobby army both from postal offices and from the express industry (interview with PostEurope). The outcome of these negotiations was, however, a shift in the balance of power in favour of the private firms and against the state monopolies. The agreement leaves the postal monopolies with a reserved market for standard mail up to 350 grams, but postal affairs have lost their rigid 'state service' character. Even restricted letter services are dealt with as a segment of the larger parcel/postal and express markets, which is in turn seen as a part of the overall

---

[1] At the national level in Germany, however, competition still dominates. While UPS stepped up its lobbying efforts by way of founding a scientific council, Deutsche Post AG and the companies linked to the firm founded a new German association. While Deutsche Post AG speaks out in favour of full liberalization in Europe, as does UPS, the latter company lobbies for unilateral steps towards full liberalization on the national level, whereas the former company conditions full liberalization in Germany on reciprocal steps in all the European markets.

transport market, indicating changing perceptions and regulatory/ organizational practices (Panorama of EU-industry 97, European Parliament 1997).[2]

11.5. Company Trajectories: TNT Post Group and Deutsche Post AG

The breakdown and rearrangement of the old regulatory and institutional structure were a step-by-step process involving various private and state actors reflecting shifting strategies at the national level. A key aspect was the way in which several national post offices began to respond to the competition from internationally organized private couriers and express industries by both internationalizing their own operations and seeking to reduce the national regulatory barriers to this process, whilst others were more conservative and piecemeal in their responses. In this section, I examine the strategies of the Dutch and German postal offices, which took the most dramatic moves towards internationalizing, whilst in the next section, I consider the responses in France and the UK.

A key first step for both the Dutch and the Germans was to deepen the previously established strategic alliance to fend off the US integrators. The national postal organizations from Germany, France, Sweden, the Netherlands, and Canada purchased 50 per cent of the smallest global player: TNT. There were substantial rumours to the effect that the company was in financial trouble (Bolton 1993) and, given the overwhelming strength of the US firms, the formation of the joint venture firm GD Net (headquartered in Amsterdam) in 1991 could be interpreted as an 'anti-American' alliance quite similar to previous European efforts, e.g. in airline production (Airbus). Before this move, the industry was entirely dominated by non-European and, most importantly, US companies. The move towards European

---

[2] At the same time, a wide variety or regulations regarding services that have to be available for every citizen within the EU have been mandated by the European Commission. Many rules and reglementations, including designs for institutional responsibilities at the national and supranational level and for the interchange between public and private organizations, are clearly spelled out by the European Commission. Further steps to reduce the reserved markets and full liberalization eventually had to be decided in 2000, but were still being debated in January 2001 because of the inability of the Council of Europe to reach an agreement on a draft directive reducing weight limits to 150 grams and no future timing on further steps of liberalization. Full liberalization, in any case, depends entirely on finding alternative ways to finance the obligatory universal functions now mandated at the European level (Directive 97/67/EC).

(and Canadian) collective emancipation, however, destroyed the common, multinational public affairs strategy of all postal administrations vis-à-vis the private integrators, and challenged the structure of the private industry alliance, with TNT 'changing sides' (by becoming owned by the former state monopolies). The European Commission approved the joint venture after forcing several amendments on the business agreement, including a two-year limit on exclusive access for the joint venture company to all postal outlets of the five post offices (*FT*, 4 December 1991: 3). Nevertheless, for a five-year period the relations between private integrators and public postal offices remained stable overall, although the joint venture did not succeed in winning market share.

The public/private defence alliance of the five post offices broke down in 1996 when the Dutch post office, KNP, announced the takeover of TNT. In 1995, KNP had become the first national postal operator to be privatized. In 1996, this new private European PTT force decided to move aggressively into foreign markets by way of taking over TNT Express Worldwide as well as German carrier NET Nachtexpress, and Danish DTS Express APS. In 1995, KNP had already bought Dentex BV in the Netherlands and Colandel NV in Belgium (Botelle 1998; *DVZ*, 6 July 1996: 1). Why did the Dutch post office acquire TNT? Apart from the close relationships of KNP and TNT within the GD alliance, given the proximity of the headquarters of GD Net, the history of the Dutch approach to transport industries supports path dependency arguments.

Dutch predominance in European transport affairs can be traced back to the Middle Ages. Only the rise of the British Empire destroyed the Dutch supremacy in ocean trade (Cafruny 1987). Given the role the Dutch harbours played (and continue to play) as main ports in Europe, Dutch interests have held a far greater share of subsequent transport developments than the size of the country or population would suggest. At the same time, the internal economy was always placing Dutch transport industries at a disadvantage against larger neighbours, most obviously Germany. Until the mid-1990s rail services in Germany were used to support the North Sea harbours of Bremen and Hamburg against Rotterdam, until the European Commission levied a fine against Deutsche Bahn (Bukold 1996: 155). Unlike other countries which centred transport policy more on the internal circulation of freight, the Netherlands started to support its international role in distribution and trade early in history (cf. ibid.: 87f.). Quite similar to the early move with regard to post office privatization, the Dutch freight railway NS Cargo (together with British Rail) was the European pioneer in rail privatization in 1995. Here, the government supported the merger of the Dutch railway with Germany's railway Deutsche Bahn AG (Railion), since an independent strategy was not viable in the rail sector. In both the KNP and NS Cargo cases the national infrastructure functions no longer dominated. Instead, the inter- and transnational commerce functions were supported by the nation-state. Quite in line with this national specialization, Dutch representatives (both government and industry) are reported to be extraordinarily active in European transport policy affairs. In 1993, KNP managed to place the company's specialist on international mail, Jan Sertons, at the European Commission to support the liberalization strategy desired. Serton remained on the payroll of KNP during his tenure as a Commission expert (see Ronit 1995 on the involvement of the Dutch government in KLM lobby efforts). Material support by the Dutch nation-state for the privatized KNP was, in any case, strong enough to support the acquisition of TNT, which is likely to secure the former postal office a central position in the wider transport/logistics market. Nevertheless, many cooperators and competitors were completely taken by surprise by the bold action.

The move of KNP triggered a number of defensive and offensive reactions on the part of other actors. The German post office, which in the meantime had been commercialized and renamed Deutsche Post AG, immediately cancelled substantial contracts with TNT's German subsidiary (truckload transport between the major reshipment centres), even making allowance for a prolonged legal battle (*DVZ*, 12 April 1997: 1). Within a year the new competitive strategy of DP AG was worked out under the leadership of CEO, Klaus Zumwinkel. The former McKinsey manager was called in to guide the transformation of the German post office in 1989 by the Christian Democrat/Liberal government coalition firmly committed to privatizing government services—albeit taking a more gradualist approach compared to Anglo-Saxon market radicalism (Benz 1997). Zumwinkel took the post office job after building a management-led organization at the family-run business Quelle, the large catalogue retailer, which happens to be one of the largest customers of the post office. Zumwinkel has used much of the McKinsey wisdom (and personnel) in order to help Europe's largest postal organization eventually to prosper in an internationalized market environment (interview I with DPG, Munzinger Archiv 1999).

Deutsche Post AG's intention to transcend the multinational strategic alliance strategy to develop an integrated cross-border organization became increasingly obvious. Deutsche Post AG moved not only into Dutch territory but also into the major neighbouring markets of France, the UK, and Italy. Starting in 1997, Deutsche Post AG went on an extremely rapid process of expansion both at home and abroad. A \$3.1bn spending spree brought more than 20 companies across Europe, the US and elsewhere with some 100,000 employees under its influence or control. The most important acquisitions included an initial 25 per cent of the international integrator DHL (courier and express services) and 97.4 per cent of Danzas AG (the leading European logistics business from Switzerland). Table 11.1 provides a more detailed overview.

Deutsche Post AG thus did not manage completely to take over another TNT-like company, but it did manage to snap up a share of DHL, the market leader of the international express business. Before the 25 per cent acquisition of DHL by DP AG, the US company was taken over by Lufthansa and Japanese airline and trade interests. Typical of the more cooperative style of coordination (see Whitley, Chapter 1 and 9) in German business, Lufthansa Cargo and Deutsche Post AG are crosslinked by dual membership of top CEOs in the supervisory board. Public media speculation about a prospective cross-investment, if not outright merger, of the two companies is frequently featured, though officially denied. It is quite likely, however, that the two companies will step up efforts fully to control DHL. Deutsche Post AG, in the meantime renamed Deutsche Post World Net, eventually secured the majority share of DHL in 2001. The global express market is certain to remain the bottleneck of the new global transport/logistics market of lighter weight/size goods. The 1999 takeover of Air Express International by Deutsche Post AG (*HB*, 16 November 1999), the largest air freight forwarding company in North America, greatly strengthened the strategic position of the company in North America.

Whether or not the strategy of Deutsche Post AG is viable in the medium and long run is not only of concern for the companies and workers involved with the new postal and logistics giant, but for the general public as well. Sceptical voices have been raised to question a far-fledged business strategy combining very different market segments (weight, size, region, additional services) within a single organization due to costly failures of previous efforts trying to do the same. In particular, the diverse history of companies combined in a

Table 11.1 *Recent takeovers by Deutsche Post AG*

Company	Country	Shares (%)	Price (Million)	Employees	Turnover
Air Express International	USA	100	DM2,100	7,700	US1.52 bn
DHL	USA	51		55,000	US4.5 bn
Securicor Distribution	UK	50	DM620	12,500	
Danzas	Switzerland	97.4	EUR939	16,000	EUR 4.4 bn
Postbank	Germany	100		13,330	
Trans-o-flex	Germany	24.8		2,200	DM695 m
Trans-o-flex	Germany	50.4		3,200	> DM1 bn (Europe)
Ducros Services	France	68		2,200	DM366 m
MIT	Italy	90		1,000	DM176 m
McPaper	Germany	100		885	
Global Mail	US	100		300	USD43 m
IPP	Austria			78	
GP Paketlogistik	Switzerland	'a majority'			
Belgian Parcel	Belgium	100		49	
Merkur GmbH & Co	Germany	51		290	
Servisco	Poland	60		958	
ITG Int'l Spedition	Germany	80		575	DM150 m
Qualipac AG	Switzerland	100			SF21 m
Meadowsfreight	Ireland	100		240	EUR50 m
Nedlloyd (EU Transport)	Netherlands	100	DM1,043	11,500	EUR1.45 bn
ASG AB	Sweden	52.4		5,700	DM2.8 bn
Yellow Stone	US	100			
Siemens Printery	Germany			200	
Netlog	Germany	100		105	
Guipuzcoana	Spain	49		1,700	EUR186 m

Source: FT 26 May 1999: 3; DPG: HV-Information 66/98; *DVZ* 10 July 1999: 2; 21 August 1999: 1; *HB* 16 November 1999: 13; *FT Deutschland* 15 September 2000.

new conglomerate is considered a heavy mortgage (Klaus 1999: 120). This argument carries particular weight in the case of Deutsche Post AG. Due to the very recent expansion, it is too early to assess fully the processes involved, but a number of considerations can be made with regard to the potential viability of the company strategy.

First, previous expansion strategies were far more complicated in the transport sector because of the many restrictions related to market entry and price regulations in the different countries. After liberalization measures implemented across Europe, many active companies too small to cover the whole continent seemed to prefer to drop out of the race, leaving dominant companies with far less resistance against their efforts to achieve full European coverage. After the acquisition of the leading European freight forwarder Danzas AG by Deutsche Post, Dutch Nedlloyd and Swedish ASG were ready to sell out to the erstwhile competitor Danzas. The takeover of ASG amounted almost to a hostile takeover, since Swedish Posten AB tried to prevent the takeover to strengthen the national Swedish organization, ultimately without success (*DVZ*, 14 September 1999: 13). This history was preceded by the takeover of Swedish Bilspedition, another dominant European forwarding enterprise by Germany's Stinnes-Schenker group. Before the takeover of the two Swedish companies, the Swedish market was practically closed to even the larger foreign enterprises.

The Stinnes-Schenker history can also serve to support the viability argument with regard to Deutsche Post AG. Schenker, originally from Austria, was acquired by the German Reichsbahn in 1931. From then on, the company operated its global network as a subsidiary of the other huge state-owned transport organization Deutsche Bahn until privatization at the end of the 1980s and early 1990s. The takeover of Schenker by the Stinnes trading group marked a first wave of replacing state-led transport networks by privately controlled enterprises (see the full history in Plehwe 1994). As happened in the Dutch case, the German government progressively shifted its support from national solutions (combination of German rail interests with the forwarding house) towards favouring the strengthening of international commerce and distribution functions (integration of forwarding house with the largest trading group). The decision to support the expansion of Deutsche Post AG and subsequent privatization is very similar to the previous decision to build up Schenker and privatize the highly successful company. The binding element of the two cases is continued *German control* over internationally operating transport and logistics networks supporting the highly export-oriented German economy. It is quite unlikely that the German government and the German banks (linking industrial producers with production-oriented service companies like Deutsche Post and Stinnes-Schenker) will discontinue support for the two groups. A failure of either of the two companies would ultimately benefit large US or other foreign-controlled companies most and reverse the German history of strong recognition of downstream activities along the value chain within national and international markets.

Finally, the Social Democrat and Green government coalition which replaced the Christian Democrat and Liberal coalition in 1998 further strengthened Deutsche Post AG by selling the Postal Bank back to the transport/logistics company. While the conservative government (like the Dutch government) invested heavily in the modern postal infrastructure to defend the postal system against UPS and Federal Express, the conservatives were inclined to sell the Postal Bank to banking interests. The reversal of this decision is in line with Germany's social partnership history: reintegrating the Post Bank supports the employment stability in a postal organization forced to shed around 100,000 jobs in the 1990s. In both the Dutch and the German cases, government support for large transport and logistics organizations continued, albeit in a modified form. Instead of concentrating on national home markets, however, political decision-makers now lobby for liberalization, thus proactively supporting the internationalization process. Both Deutsche Post AG and TNT Post Group therefore stepped out of the defensive postal alliance of the mid-1990s and now argue for full liberalization and alternative ways to finance universal service obligations. This realignment spells further troubles for competing post offices with originally less national support for transnational reorganization such as French La Poste and the British Post Office.

11.6. La Poste and the Post Office

While the Dutch and German governments were fast to change minds with regard to the future role of postal services within Europe and gained lead time for their respective national organizations in the course of transnational reorganization, other governments came late and were not able to do as much for their state postal monopolies. The reorganization story of major European postal offices ended for the time being with the British post office acquiring the German Parcel (GP) network of small and medium companies and French La Poste acquiring Denkhaus, the major partner of the DPD network of parcel companies, as well as two more family members to eventually obtain full control over this network. Both network operators (originally thought to be a viable SME alternative to large integrated organizations) came under intense pressure when Deutsche Post AG bought national partner firms such as Belgium Parcel from GP and Italian MIT from the DPD network. The DPD network reacted by turning the horizontal franchise system into a vertical franchise system to make hostile bites into the network more difficult. Unanimous decision-making within the network was replaced by majority voting to allow for easier expansion into new business fields such as electronic storage and e-commerce (*HB* 15 January 1998: 38). As evidenced by the La Poste takeover of DPD partner firms, however, the networks of small and medium-size companies lack the long-term viability of large, and more deeply integrated (including transborder operations), companies (see Hertz 1996 for another case study from Sweden). Infrastructure services such as postal, transport, and logistics seem to require centralized control, whether supplied in national or in cross-border operating networks. This argument is strongly supported by the history of the takeover of the German Parcel network by the British Post Office.

The members of the German Parcel family assembled shortly after Germany elected the new coalition government of Social Democrats and Greens. Not surprisingly, the family-run businesses were less than enthusiastic about the prospect of (moderately) rising fuel prices due to the ecological tax reform efforts promised by the incoming government. Frustration was big enough, however, to reverse the general attitude about the future viability of the SME network competing quite successfully with the industry giants up to this point. Though the majority decision to sell out to the British Post Office was triggered by the election results, two other factors were cited by Bischoff (a senior member of the German parcel firm, Bischoff-Spedition) as having a major impact. First, not all the participating firms were willing or able to raise the money needed to invest collectively in technology upgrading to improve information flows. Secondly, the international expansion of the network was severely hampered by the difficulty of finding adequate partner firms matching the capacities of the participating German firms abroad. Again, lack of ability or willingness to take on necessary investments played a major role. At the end, a major partner able to back up a European network was considered better able to serve the interests of the single companies (information based on a conference speech made by Werner Bischoff, Berlin, 30 September 1999).

Both the French and the British case suggest a lack of government support to actively build an internationally operating transport and logistics company out of the national postal system. When major competitors defected from the multinational defence against US intruders, the postal organizations from France and the UK (and the other national postal organizations) had no choice but to rethink their own strategy and eventually also to turn towards transnational reorganization as the only viable alternative. Both France and the UK continue to support a national reserved market to finance universal service obligations—and to gain time for further reorganizations to step up their international presence.

11.7. Conclusion

This chapter has revealed the closely intertwined nature of national and international processes of market-building and the development of firm strategies and structures. Markets are socially embedded within particular contexts. European nation-states developed postal services as part of the construction of a unified territory and population. National state monopolies were the means of maintaining control over these functions. However, the function of the state in these contexts was also affected by the specific history of these societies and this was reflected in how they were implicated in the international economy. The Dutch state was built on the central importance of commercial capital and maritime trade to its development. This involved an attention to the international context of trade generally and the postal and distribution sector in particular. The German state, on the other hand, was committed to supporting German industry through providing an infrastructure that would promote strong exports. This also led to an interest in an international and efficient distribution and postal system. Thus, when, through the pressure of US logistics companies and the actions of small local distribution companies, the barriers to entry created by national state monopolies of postal services were threatened, it was the Dutch and the German post offices which turned most rapidly towards transforming themselves into internationalized companies. The British Post Office found it more difficult to make this transition, trapped as it was within a political and economic context where privatization would mean a loss of state support and therefore probably a lack of capability for achieving takeovers on the scale of the Dutch and German companies. It therefore had to proceed more cautiously and on a smaller scale as did the French La Poste.

In their various ways, the firms took part in the reconstruction of the European market away from a series of segmented national sectors towards a single, liberalized environment. The establishment

of a harmonized supranational regulatory framework for the EC
postal sector is a prime example of new cross-border dimensions of
transnational standardization in state-related infrastructure services.
This movement was part of a broader reconstruction of institutions
(e.g. EC law), markets, firms, and capital itself. The economic space
for the market in distribution services was leveraged to the European
level (with certain increasingly limited exceptions) by the actions of
the firms, as well as national and EU policy-makers. Firms sought
ways to place themselves successfully within this space. Using
nationally distinctive competencies and capabilities, they took different trajectories towards internationalization, whilst reinforcing
the process itself by their own actions. However, this whole trend
remained embedded within the struggle of capital to extract more
profitability by rationalizing the logistics function of commercial
capital in a context where other forms of rationalization (of the work
process) brought increasingly problematic returns. In conclusion, this
chapter has shown how 'organizing internationally' is the outcome
of a complex interplay between markets, regulators, and firms. The
interdependence of these phenomena, however, does not lead to convergence and homogenization. It leads to a process of hybridization
in which international firms reflect their national origins but adapt
those characteristics in new ways.

REFERENCES

Aglietta, M. (1979), *A Theory of Capitalist Regulation: The US Experience.*
London: Verso.
Benz, A. (1997), 'Privatisierung und Regulierung im Post- und Fern-
meldewesen', in Klaus König and Angelika Benz (eds.), *Privatisierung und
Regulierung.* Baden-Baden: NOMOS, 262–346.
Bjelicic, B. (1987), 'Logistik'. *Muttersprache*, 3(4): 153–61.
Bolton, B. (1993), 'Multinationals in Postal Services'. Luxemburg, PTTI-
Mimeo.
Borrus, M. and Zysman, J. (1997), *Wintelism and the Changing Terms of Global
Competition: Prototype of the Future?* Berkeley Roundtable on the Inter-
national Economy, BRIE Working Paper 96b.
Botelle, M. (1998), 'Express Parcels', *Logistics Europe*, 11: 64–8.
Bretzke, W. R. (1999), 'Die Industrie benötigt Anpassungsstrategien', *DVZ*,
11 March: 3.
Bukold, S. (1996), *Kombinierter Verkehr Schien/Straße in Europa.* Frankfurt/
Main: Peter Lang.

Button, K. and Swann, D. (1989), *The Age of Regulatory Reform*. Oxford: Clarendon Press.

Cafruny, A. W. (1987), *Ruling the Waves: The Political Economy of International Shipping*. Berkeley/Los Angeles/London: University of California Press.

Campbell, J. I. (1994), 'Couriers and the European Postal Monopolies', in R.H. Pedler and M. P. C. M. van Schendelen (eds.), *Lobbying the European Community*. Aldershot: Dartmouth, 123–48.

Danckwerts, D. (ed.) (1991), *Logistik und Arbeit im Gütertransportsystem. Rahmenbedingungen, Verlaufsformen und soziale Folgen der Rationalisierung*. Opladen: Westdeutscher Verlag.

Derthick, M. and Quirk, P. J. (1985), *The Politics of Deregulation*. Washington, DC: The Brookings Institution.

Directive 97/67/EC of the European Parliament and of the Council of 15 December 1997 on common rules for the development of the internal market of Community postal services and the improvement of quality of service. *Official Journal* L 015, 21 January 1998: 0014–0025.

DPG (Deutsche Postgewerkschaft) (1998), HV-Information 66/98 (Hauptverwaltungsinformation of Deutsche Postgewerkschaft).

DVZ (Deutsche Verkehrszeitung), several issues.

European Parliament (1997), *Soziale Folgen der Dereglementierung und Liberalisierung im Verkehrssektor der EU*. Luxemburg: European Parliament.

FT (Financial Times), several issues.

Gale, F. (1998), 'Cave "Cave! Hic dragones": a neo-Gramscian Deconstruction and Reconstruction of International Regime Theory', *Review of International Political Economy*, 5(2) (summer): 252–83.

Gayle, D. and Goodrich, J. N. (1991), *Privatization and Deregulation in Global Perspective*. London: Pinter Publishers.

Geistbeck, M. (1986), *Weltverkehr*. Hildesheim: Gerstenberg Verlag (Original: Feiburg 1895).

Hamilton, G. W. (1990). 'Federal Express—L'IBM des messageries exprès', in P. Bowyer (ed.), *I.P.T.T Etudes 60*. Genf: IPTT, 1–37.

HB (Das Handelsblatt), several issues.

Hector, B. (1998), 'Handelsketten wollen neue Wege mit der Spedition', Lagerlogistik (Special Survey of *DVZ*, 21 March 1998): 14–16.

Hertz, S. (1996), 'The Dynamics of International Strategic Allicances. A Study of Freight Transport Companies', *International Studies of Management and Organization*, 26(2): 104–30.

Hollingsworth, J. R., Schmitter, P. C. and Streeck, W. (eds.) (1994), *Governing Capitalist Economies*. New York/Oxford: Oxford University Press.

Kasper, D. M. (1988), *Deregulation and Globalization*. Cambridge: Ballinger Publishing Company.

Keohane, R. O. (1984), *After Hegemony: Cooperation and Discord in the World Political Economy*. Princeton: Princeton University Press

Klaus, P. (1999), 'Logik der Fusionen'. *Logistik Management*, 2: 109–21.

Krasner, S. D. (1982), 'Structural Causes and Regime Consequences: Regimes as Intervening Variables', *International Organization*, 36(3): 185–206.

LaLonde, B. J., Grabner, J. R. and Robeson, J. F. (1993 [1970]), 'Integrated Distribution Systems: A Management Perspective', *International Journal of Physical Distribution & Logistics Management*, 23(5): 4–12.

Matis, H. (1995), *Das Haus Schenker: die Geschichte der internationalen Spedition 1872–1931*. Wien: Ueberreuter.

Murphy, C. N. (1994), *International Organization and Industrial Change*. Cambridge: Polity Press.

Plehwe, D. (1994), *Neue Logistik für deutsche Konzerne*. Duisburg: Sokoop-Verlag.

—— (1997), 'Eurologistik, "Europäische" Verkehrspolitik und die Entwicklung eines transnationalen (Güter-)Transportsystems', *Prokla*, 107: 217–44.

—— (2000), *Deregulierung und transnationale Integration der Transportwirtschaft in Nordamerika*. Münster: Westfälisches Dampfboot.

Plehwe, D. and Bohle, D. (1998), 'Dienstleister in multinationalen Wertschöpfungsnetzwerken Europas: Überlegungen zum Forschungsfeld "Transnationale Organization in Europa"', in D. Plehwe (ed.), *Transformation der Logistik*. Discussion Paper FS I 98–103, Berlin: Social Science Research Center—WZB, 41–71.

Ronit, K. (1995), 'European Actions of Organized Shipping: Global and National Constraints', in J. Greenwood (ed.), *European Casebook on Business Alliances*. Hemel Hempstead: Prentice-Hall, 184–96.

Sombart, W. (1969 [1902]), *Der moderne Kapitalismus* (vol. 2). Berlin: Duncker & Humblot.

Stock, J. R. (1990), 'Logistics Thought and Practice: A Perspective', *International Journal of Physical Distribution & Logistics Management*, 20(1): 3–6.

TURU (1990), 'United Parcel Service Inc.', in P. Bowyer (ed.), *I.P.T.T Etudes 60*. Genf: IPTT, 38–65.

Wojtek, R. (1987), 'Kurier- und Expreßdienste', in Spiegel-Verlag Reihe Märkte im Wandel, *Transportmärkte* (vol. 13). Hamburg: Spiegel-Verlag, 22–41.

Index

StoraEnso 101
Taiwanese firms 63
transport market 286
TRIPs agreement 243
Volkswagen 81
Western alliance and 261
Useem, M. 153, 158–9

van Tulder, R. 27–8, 37–8, 43, 48, 69,
71, 90
VDMA 142
Verainiung der Elektrizitätswerke 142
Veranan, J. 154, 156–7
Verbundchemie principle 78–9
Verbundforschung principle (research
networks) 79
Vernon, R. 178–80
Versailles Treaty 139
VEW (Rheinisch-Westfälische
Electrizitätswerke) 141
vicious circle 165–6, 184, 189
Vickers 136
Villard, Henry 131, 134
virtuous circle 165, 184, 189
'visible hand of management' 20, 200,
203, 215–16, 218
Volkswagen 18, 73, 80, 81–3, 86–7,
89–90
Volvo 247

Wall Street 237
Wall Street Crash 126
WAP (Wireless Application Protocols)
229
Warner, M. 84, 88, 198, 202, 216
Webb Act 146
West, J. 31, 41
West Germany 261, 267
Western Electric 132
Western Europe, American antitrust
tradition 266
Westinghouse 125, 133–4, 136, 146–7
Westney, E. 28, 33–4
Westphalian sovereignty 227
Whitley, R.:
companies' globalization activities 69
economic activity and MNCs 28, 33

effect of foreign owners 167
German TNCs 71–3, 75–6, 78, 83,
90–3, 297
governance systems 97–8, 109
international trade 30
internationalization of capital
markets 153–5
Japanese management 196–8, 216
management of MNCs 16, 18–19
market uncertainty 227
Nordic forest firms 118–19
particularistic environments and 39
regulation 253, 255
subsidiaries of MNCs 192
Wiemar Republic 139
Wilkinson, B. 200, 203
'Wintelism' (Microsoft Windows and
Intel) 288
Wong, J. 200, 209, 217
World Bank 246
World Postal Union (1874) 282, 284,
292
World Trade Organization, *see* WTO
World Wildlife Fund 114
Wortmann, M. 75, 182, 190
Wright, Arthur 132
WTO 30, 241, 243–5, 247, 256

Yamada, J. 202–3
Yaryan, Homer, steam and electrical
plants 132
Yeung, H. W. 45, 51, 63

Zander, I. 14, 59, 190–1, 193
Zeitlin, J. 248, 253
British firm differentiation 34, 36, 50,
55
financial internationalization 13–14
internationalization of capital
markets 169
MNCs 17–18, 20–1, 196
Japanese 200, 202, 209, 211
regulation 253
standards 248
Zentral Verband Electrotechnisher
Industrie 142
Zumwinkel, Klaus 296